FRAGILE MORALITIES AND DANGEROUS SEXUALITIES

This book is dedicated to the memory of my grandparents, Jessie and Robert Highton, and Molly and William Barton, and my dear friends Peggy Townsend and Thelma Williams.

Fragile Moralities and Dangerous Sexualities

Two Centuries of Semi-Penal Institutionalisation for Women

ALANA BARTON

ASHGATE

Published by
Ashgate Publishing Limited
Wey Court East
Union Road
Farnham
Surrey, GU9 7PT
England

Ashgate Publishing Company
110 Cherry Street
Suite 3-1
Burlington
VT 05401-3818
USA

Ashgate website: http://www.ashgate.com

British Library Cataloguing in Publication Data
Barton, Alana
  Fragile moralities and dangerous sexualities : two
  centuries of semi-penal institutionalisation for women
  1. Reformatories for women - Great Britain - History - 19th
  century 2. Reformatories for women - Great Britain - History
  - 20th century 3. Female offenders - Great Britain
  4. Alternatives to imprisonment - Great Britain - History -
  19th century 5. Alternatives to imprisonment - Great Britain
  - History - 20th century
  I. Title
  365.4'3'0941'09034

Library of Congress Cataloging-in-Publication Data
Barton, Alana, 1966-
  Fragile moralities and dangerous sexualities : two centuries of semi-penal
institutionalisation for women / by Alana Barton.
     p. cm.
  Includes bibliographical references and index.
  ISBN 978-0-7546-3829-2
  1. Probation--Great Britain. 2. Female offenders--Great Britain. 3. Sex role--
Great Britain. 4. Corrections--Great Britain. 5. Criminal justice, Administration
of--Great Britain. I. Title.

  HV9278.B578 2004
  365'.43'0941--dc22

                                                                    2004017611

ISBN 978-0-7546-3829-2

Transfered to Digital Printing in 2009

FSC
www.fsc.org

MIX
Paper from
responsible sources
FSC® C013985

Printed in the United Kingdom by Henry Ling Limited,
at the Dorset Press, Dorchester, DT1 1HD

Contents

Acknowledgements

I would like to thank Ashgate Publishing Limited for their endorsement of this book. Thanks are due in particular to the various members of staff who were always available to provide me with help and advice whenever I needed it.

I also owe a huge debt of thanks to the many people who assisted me in conducting the research for the original thesis. I am particularly thankful to the 16 residents and nine members of staff from Vernon Lodge Probation Hostel who so enthusiastically and candidly participated in the interviews. For reasons of confidentiality and anonymity I cannot name people individually but I am very grateful for their time and honesty. I would also like to thank the Vernon Lodge Management Committee for allowing me access to the institution and to the historical records that came to light during the course of the research.

Thank you to George Mair and Joe Sim for supervising the original PhD. I am especially indebted to Joe Sim for his continuing support and guidance. His input has been inspirational and greatly appreciated. Thank you also to my PhD examiners, Gill McIvor and Kate Smith, for their constructive comments and for encouraging me to develop the thesis into a book.

There are numerous friends and colleagues who contributed to this book in many ways. Special thanks are due to Barbara Houghton and Helen Finney. Their technical skills and assistance with proof reading proved invaluable to me in the production of the final camera-ready copy. I am very grateful to Pat Ayers, Frank Boyce and Ray Physick. Working with them on the 'Liverpool project' has been a wonderful experience and has, in no small measure, inspired and motivated me in writing this book. A special acknowledgement is due to Bernie Glover for getting me through 'that year'. Without her friendship it is unlikely the research would ever have been completed. I would like to say a very special thank you to Janet Evans, Karen Corteen, Anette Ballinger, Bev Bethel, Howard Davis, Eileen Berrington, Barbara Houghton, Clare Kinsella, Ann Jemphrey, Julie Read, Julie Keen, Linda Gibson, David Scott, Rebecca Kelly and Helen Elderfield for their advice, encouragement and enthusiasm but mainly for keeping me going with regular doses of good laughs, good music, good films, good books, good food, gardening, guitars, wine, champagne, limousines, Everton and Echo & the Bunnymen.

I want to thank my family for their unconditional support and encouragement in everything I have ever done. So a huge thank you to my parents Marilyn and Larry Barton, to my brother Derry, my sister Jodie and my uncle Roy. Finally, a very special acknowledgement is due to my partner Chris Newby, for his emotional and intellectual support and for giving me the benefit of his love, patience, sense of humour and unique perspective on life. Thank you.

Chapter 1

Introduction

While convention requires women's prisons to *look* like minimum security institutions economic reality decrees that they cannot *be* minimum security... .The result is an atmosphere that in spite of attractive facilities and peaceful surroundings is really very tense and oppressive. The inmate...is reduced to a state of childish dependency. ...The reduction of women to a weak and dependent and helpless status is brought about by more subtle means than by the gun or the high wall (Gibson, 1973, quoted in Carlen, 1983: 21. Emphasis in original).

....this man was requiring his wife to keep a diary of her movements whilst he was serving his sentence. This diary was presented to him during visiting times and if he was not satisfied with her behaviour during his absence she was subjected to a barrage of insults, threats and other public humiliations (Morton, 1994:7).[1]

The image of the 'normal' woman is based around an idealised concept of femininity, which in turn is constructed around dominant discourses of domesticity, respectability, motherhood, sexuality and pathology. For centuries this construct has been utilised to characterise what is appropriate and acceptable female behaviour (Hutter and Williams, 1981). Any deviation from, or violation of, these standards has mobilised a whole set of control strategies, the purpose of which has been to navigate and normalise the deviant female back into her ascribed role. As Smart and Smart (1978) have argued, the social control of women can assume many different guises. It can be formal or informal, public or private, explicitly expressed or subtly implied, and through various combinations of these forms, we see women's lives controlled and their behaviour regulated.

The quotations above refer to two very specific but very distinct forms of social control. The first quotation refers to those practices and regimes that characterise the most formal method of control for women, that which takes place inside custodial institutions. The second concerns a very different, but much more prevalent, method - that being the control of women through 'informal' or 'domestic' processes, such as those that take place within their own homes.

Since the nineteenth century, when it was decided that the association of male and female prisoners was undesirable, particular and specific regimes have been constructed for women in prison, regimes that have primarily been assembled around idealised models of femininity (Zedner, 1991). Women, it was believed, could no longer be housed with male prisoners as they were a particularly 'corruptible' *and* 'corrupting' group who required 'special, closer forms of control and confinement' (Dobash et al, 1986:1).

These 'special' methods of control within women's prisons have been subject to various modifications over the last 100 years or so but to a great extent they have remained centred around two powerful misconceptions regarding the nature of female offending. First, that the causes of women's deviance stem from inherent pathological or biological weaknesses and second, that women offenders have fundamentally deviated from their 'natural' feminine roles (Carlen, 1985). This notion that criminal women have out-stepped the boundaries of 'normal' femininity has provided for the proliferation of custodial regimes based around reformation and domestication (Carlen, 1983; Dobash et al, 1986; Genders and Player, 1987; Zedner, 1991; Faith, 1993). Women who enter the masculine domain of criminal activity require disciplinary procedures that will 'normalise' them to a more appropriate and hence less 'dangerous' position within the social order.

According to Hutter and Williams, 'normal' women are perceived as infantile, irresponsible and in need of protection and supervision.

> The image of the 'normal' woman employed, time and time again, is of a person with something of a childish incapacity to govern herself and in some need of protection - a kind of original sin stemming from Eve's inability to control her desire to seek new knowledge (1981: 12).

For women in prison, this concept of 'childishness' and the need for protection has led to a process of 'infantilisation' (Faith, 1993). Many women prisoners have reported that the custodial regimes they experienced encouraged a dependency culture in which they were denied the rights to make decisions about their lives and which hence reduced them to a child-like status (Carlen, 1983; Rafter, 1983; Faith, 1993; Heidensohn, 1996). As Carlen has stated, for imprisoned women in Scotland ideas around appropriate female roles and behaviour were

> ....incorporated into the prison regime to produce a very fine disciplinary web which denies women both personality and full adult status (1983: 16).

However, it is not only behind the prison walls that women find themselves the objects of scrutiny, surveillance and regulation. On the contrary, as Faith and Davis contend, the term 'deviant' is insufficient to explain and account for the whole range of 'normalised modes of social control' (1987: 171) that have emerged to regulate and control women within their homes, their communities and their everyday lives.

The second quotation at the beginning of this chapter refers to this much more informal, but extremely repressive, method of social control. The woman discussed in the quotation is not formally incarcerated but her behaviour and movements are heavily monitored and governed through a process of manipulation, intimidation and threatened, and actual, abuse.

The family is a major ideological site of social control for women. Heidensohn (1996) argues that this control begins with the socialisation of daughters by mothers. Mothers, she states, may themselves be dominated and restrained by domestic responsibilities but at the same time they collude with these ideologies of 'appropriate' behaviour by attempting to socialise their daughters for the same role in the future. Several authors have likened the family and the home to a regulative institution for women. Dahl and Snare (1978) contend that women are privately and domestically imprisoned within the home and their seclusion and isolation cultivates an intensive web of control by children, husbands and neighbours. According to Christie (1978) the home, like the prison, can be seen as part of an all-encompassing system of regulation, control and surveillance for women. Both, he claimed, are institutions where physical structures and regimes create an environment of 'high visibility' with the potential for part, or total, restriction of movement and behaviour.

Thus, writers have predominantly contextualised the regulation and discipline of women within two distinct sites - the prison and the home. However, there is a third arena of social control and regulation that has, to some degree, been overlooked in much of the existing literature. For over 200 years, a whole range of institutions have existed for women, institutions which were neither 'formal' in the sense of a prison, nor 'informal' in the sense of the home, but which, at the same time, utilised the regulatory methods and disciplinary techniques employed in both the custodial and domestic arenas. The sole purpose of these institutions was to contain, supervise, control and, most importantly, to normalise 'deviant' women (both 'criminal' and 'non criminal') back to an acceptable standard of feminine behaviour. These institutions, which straddled the boundary between 'formal' and 'informal', can be described as 'semi-penal' (Weiner, 1990: 130).

Semi-penal institutions originally developed during the eighteenth and nineteenth centuries in order to accommodate the increasing number of 'exceptional cases' within the prison system (Weiner, 1990: 321). Exceptional cases included juveniles, drunkards, imbeciles, lunatics, vagrants and, of course, women. Consequently a plethora of non-custodial, semi-incarcerative institutions, such as homes, refuges and reformatories were established to cater for such groups.

Throughout the eighteenth and nineteenth centuries women were judged against very complex and specifically constructed ideas of womanhood, morality and respectability. Smart (1992) claims that working class women were categorised within a contradictory set of discourses, being seen as both powerful but at the same time powerless, and as corrupting and dangerous but at the same time easily corrupted and therefore in need of protection. Consequently, young women, like juveniles, were believed to be unsuitable for imprisonment primarily because of the fragility of their morality and their susceptibility to corruption and contamination from others. However, this susceptibility to external influence, the idea that women were in some way 'malleable', made them ideal candidates for reform (Zedner, 1991). If women were so impressionable with regard to negative influence then, it was assumed, they must also be equally receptive to positive influence. The female reformatory movement developed primarily around this belief that the behaviour of (some but not all) women who had 'strayed' or 'fallen' could be reformed due to their 'infantile' characters.

Thus, the perceived infantile nature of women, along with their own incapacity for self governance, made them appropriate beings for reformatory supervision where the practices and discourses that were normally at work within both the prison and the family combined to produce a particular form of regime. Discipline was instilled through religious doctrine and appropriate training (similar to that found within women's prisons), and supervision was provided by a 'matron-mother' figure whose purpose was to provide a good moral role model for the undisciplined inmates, producing a form of the 'mother-daughter' model of social control.

It is a primary contention of this book that semi-penal institutions, with their intensive supervisory regimes and reformist ideals, did not disappear with the demise of the reformatories, refuges and other similar nineteenth century institutions. On the contrary, many of the identifying characteristics of nineteenth century semi-penal institutions could be found in twentieth century establishments such as homes for unmarried mothers, halfway houses and, I will argue, probation hostels for women.

Since the 1914 Criminal Justice Act, the courts have had the power to append additional conditions onto probation orders, most significantly that an offender be required to complete his or her period of probation at a designated address or within a nominated institution (Home Office, 1998). The early 'nominated' institutions were, like the reformatories, largely autonomous of state control and funded and run by voluntary organisations. In addition, with regard to women, their regimes were organised around religious instruction and domestic training. By the end of the 1940s the majority of these institutions came under the central control of the Home Office. However, as far as women were concerned, the regimes and disciplinary techniques changed only superficially. The *Home Office Notes on Homes and Hostels for Young Probationers* (1942) indicates that women were still expected to conform to idealised standards of feminine behaviour and the training schemes established in hostels, which were very close to those provided in custodial institutions (Barry, 1991), were primarily aimed at reforming women and girls into respectable wives and mothers or productive domestic servants.

Both the reformatory and the modern day probation hostel have their roots in the reformist movement of the nineteenth century and, like the reformatory, the probation hostel is neither truly formal or custodial, nor completely informal or 'domestic'. Instead it could be seen to occupy a position somewhere between these two sites on the social control 'continuum'.

There is a distinct lack of literature pertaining to the probation hostel for women. That which does exist (see for example Buckley, 1987; Wincup, 1996) is primarily concerned with conceptualising the probation hostel as a more appropriate environment for women offenders than prison. Consequently, the level of *theoretical* scrutiny that has been applied to studies of custodial regimes for women (Carlen, 1983, 1998; Faith, 1993; Howe, 1994; Smith, 1996; and Bosworth, 1999 to name just a few) has not been employed to analyse the experiences of women within probation hostels.

In addition, although there have been studies which *have* theoretically analysed various semi-penal institutions for women (for example Hunt et al, 1989; Mahood, 1990; Zedner, 1991), these have mainly focussed on specific nineteenth and early twentieth century establishments and have therefore not been concerned with exploring the theoretical issues and discourses that may link these institutions to each other and, more importantly, which may identify historical themes of continuity between institutions of the past and institutions of the present.

The aims of this book therefore are threefold. First, it is my intention to fill a theoretical gap in the feminist literature by analysing the history and consolidation of semi-penal institutionalisation for women, identifying themes of continuity and discontinuity between the nineteenth century reformatory and the twentieth century probation hostel for female offenders. In order to complete both a historical and contemporary analysis, one particular institution will form the basis of my study. Vernon Lodge[2] is currently a bail and probation hostel for women. It is today funded by the Home Office and staffed by Probation Service personnel but it has its origins in the nineteenth century when it was opened, in 1823, as the County Refuge for the Destitute, to accommodate and reform 'deviant' women. Between 1823 and 1948 it was utilised for a variety of purposes. It acted as a refuge for women on release from prison, as a reformatory for recalcitrant or 'wayward' young females, as a home for women released from the court on 'recognizances' (the forerunner to the modern concept of probation) and as an institution for those women deemed to be 'feeble minded'. Finally, in 1948 it became an approved probation hostel for women and continues to fulfil that role today. Through an analysis of original historical data, this book will uncover the experiences of women within this institution throughout the nineteenth and twentieth centuries. It will conclude with an examination of the experiences of women in Vernon Lodge in the 1990s and I will argue that what primarily links the past with the present, in terms of this form of institutionalisation, is the historical constancy of the discourses and practices mobilised to identify, explain and manage 'deviant' women.

This leads to my second aim, which is to analyse the specific strategies through which women within this institution were historically disciplined and controlled and the extent to which these strategies survived through to the end of the twentieth century. The book will explore the ways in which the female inmates have been characterised and categorised according to feminising discourses around domesticity, respectability, motherhood, sexuality and pathology throughout the nineteenth and twentieth centuries. The manifestations of these discourses in terms of the regimes and practices adopted within the institution will also be examined.

Of course, women do not always willingly accept the discipline and methods of control imposed upon them. On the contrary, as many authors have argued, women have historically been able to utilise a range of strategies in order to resist or manage regulatory regimes (see Zedner, 1991; Shaw, 1992; Faith, 1993; Bosworth, 1999). Although much of the literature pertaining to women's resistance has been concerned with women formally incarcerated within custodial institutions, it is the final aim of this book to employ these debates in order to scrutinise the methods through which women managed, or resisted, the disciplinary regimes and discourses they faced within the semi-penal arena.

In order to achieve these aims the book will be organised as follows: Chapter Two will provide a critical examination of the theoretical debates around the punishment and social control of women, the objective being the generation of a feminist theoretical framework within which the experiences of women in the semi-penal institution (past and present) can be analysed. Providing for the fact that there exists a lack of theoretical literature, feminist and critical, relating to the semi-penal institution, and in particular the women-only probation hostel, this chapter will utilise the existing literature around the formal (custodial) and informal (domestic) control of women and will examine the way in which feminising and normalising discourses are utilised to regulate and control 'deviant' females. Finally, the ways in which women (incarcerated or otherwise) are able to take responsibility for their lives, thus asserting a sense of agency or resisting the disciplinary procedures, even when confronted by powerful constraints and confining pressures, will be discussed.

Chapter Three will present a theoretical and chronological examination of the history of 'semi-penal' institutions from the reformatories of the late eighteenth / early nineteenth centuries to the probation hostels for women in the late twentieth century. This history will analyse various nineteenth century institutions such as the Magdalene Homes for prostitutes, the 'rescue' institutions for 'wayward' young women and the reformatories for inebriates, the 'feeble minded' and those women released from prison. In addition, twentieth century institutions such as the halfway houses for 'delinquent' girls, homes for unmarried mothers and probation hostels for women will be examined.

Chapters Four, Five and Six will present my case study. Chapter Four will examine the development of the County Refuge for the Destitute during the nineteenth century, examining the ideological and social conditions that underpinned its creation and the discourses mobilised to categorise and control its female residents. Chapter Five will continue the analysis by examining the development of the institution throughout the twentieth century, through its conversion to a probation hostel in 1948 and its progress in this form up until the 1980s.

Chapter Six brings the case study up to the end of the twentieth century by providing an analysis of the data collected from the period of participant observation and the series of interviews conducted in Vernon Lodge between 1992 and 1994. It is the intention here to draw out some common themes and issues with regard to the 'semi-penal' control of women over two centuries.

Finally Chapter Seven concludes the book by revisiting and drawing together the central themes and arguments of the research. This process will then be utilised in a discussion regarding the significance of the research and the contribution it makes to both historical and contemporary debates around the punishment and disciplining of 'deviant' women. Recent Home Office reports, policy directives and, indeed, the limited academic literature in this area, all highlight the presumption that hostels for women provide an environment that is at once restrictive but also 'curative', uplifting and empowering. It is not the intention of this book to dismiss the probation hostel as redundant or reject the potential role that it can play in reducing the ever-increasing women's prison population. However, this chapter will challenge the taken-for-granted perception that such institutions are inherently beneficial and argue that whilst there is indeed a place for probation hostels in a future system of punishment and justice for women, these institutions must not be simply accepted as salutary, unproblematic environments simply because they are not custodial.

Notes

[1] This quotation refers to the relationship between a male prisoner and his wife.

[2] Vernon Lodge is not the real name of the institution however this name has been given to ensure the anonymity guaranteed with the management of the institution at the time of research.

Chapter 2

Women Behaving Badly: Feminist Theory and the Social Control of Women

One is not born, but rather becomes a woman. No biological, psychological or economic fate determines the figure that the human female presents in society; it is civilisation as a whole that produces this creature, intermediate between male and eunuch, which is described as feminine (DeBeauvoir, 1953:8).

When Pat Carlen (1983) examined the 'moment' and meaning of imprisonment for women in Scotland she found it necessary to move beyond the prison walls and the official discourse of 'punishment' in order to make sense of her data and experiences. She maintained that the real meaning of imprisonment for the women in her study was not to be found within official legal or penal rhetoric, rather it could only be located within the practices, conventions and discourses of the wider aspects of social life and social control. Consequently she contextualised her analysis within women's accepted roles and positions in society, roles which are legitimated and justified through marriage, the family, the 'community', the church, the school, and through the discourses of 'normal' femininity and masculinity. Carlen claimed that this broader perspective was important for two main reasons. First, the women who were most likely to be imprisoned in Scotland were those who, in addition to breaching legal codes, had also transgressed the boundaries of 'domestic' or informal discipline. In other words, the women in Carlen's study were characterised as those who had 'failed' to achieve the ideals of motherhood, domesticity and femininity. Second, women's prisons, Carlen maintained, were concerned, not only with the imposition of formal state punishment, but with the 'normalisation' of women back to the ascribed domestic roles from which they had strayed. She asserted that women's experiences of imprisonment perpetuated the cycle of 'failure' through training regimes aimed at returning them to the home and family with the necessary 'skills' to fulfil the domestic expectations of them as women hence serving to increase their dependence on, and regulation by, the family unit. Thus, Carlen claimed, formal and informal mechanisms of discipline were interwoven within and between the prison and the 'community' in order to produce an all-encompassing and powerful net of social control for women.

The primary concern of this book is not with women's experiences of prison. Rather, the focus is on the way in which women have historically been, and continue to be, controlled and disciplined within the *semi-penal* arena. For over two centuries women have been perceived as suitable candidates for institutionalisation within a range of non-custodial, semi-penal institutions such as refuges, reformatories, homes and hostels, often for reasons other than the committal of a criminal offence. Moreover, these institutions employed a combination of both formal and informal mechanisms of social control, the aim being to regulate and 'normalise' criminal and 'deviant' women back to an acceptable standard of feminine behaviour.

In order to analyse the purpose and practices of these institutions, and to make sense of the experiences of the women who were subjected to their regimes, it is necessary to follow Carlen's example and move beyond the confines of the institution walls. Therefore, in this chapter I will examine feminist debates around the social control of women and the way in which this control can be seen as a continuum from formal to informal techniques and regimes. This examination of formal and informal control will focus specifically on the way in which the concept of 'normal' femininity, constructed around the discourses of domesticity, respectability, motherhood, sexuality and pathology, is utilised to identify who requires regulation and what form that regulation should take.

Of course, this focus on the mechanisms of control and regulation that women are subjected to does not mean to suggest that women are simply passive 'victims'. On the contrary, women possess agency and can, and do, resist the regulatory forces imposed upon them. So this chapter will conclude with an examination of the range of methods and techniques employed by women in order to cope with, or break free from, the disciplinary discourses and regimes that seek to subdue them.

Once established, this feminist theoretical framework will then be utilised in subsequent chapters to underpin the history and development of semi-penal institutions (see Chapter Three) and to contextualise the case study which examines the continuity and change in one particular semi-penal institution between 1823 and 1994 (Chapters Four, Five and Six).

Normality and Deviancy: Two sides of the same coin?

In order to examine the social control of 'deviant' women, one must begin by examining the discourses around 'normal' women, as the construction of what is 'normal' is frequently utilised to define what is 'deviant' (Hutter and Williams, 1981). Furthermore, the mechanisms of control that are mobilised to deal with 'deviant' women symbolise a concept of 'normality' that refers specifically to women, rather than individuals in general.

The concept of 'normal' femininity is a paradoxical construct and in order to understand the term 'femininity', it is first necessary to understand its usage in relation to the term 'masculinity'. Masculinity, according to Connell (1987), is a word that is utilised to differentiate men from other men. The term 'masculine' embodies a particular set of characteristics that describe particular types of men. The term also separates and distinguishes these men from other types of men, for example those who do not enjoy physical contact sports, those who are not interested in sexual conquests, those, in other words, who are not 'masculine'. Although an element of 'masculinity' is perceived to be desirable in men, it is *not* generally expected that *all* men will have 'masculine' qualities. In contrast, however, it *is* assumed that *all* women will, or should, possess feminine qualities and consequently the term 'femininity' is used, not to differentiate women from other women, but rather to differentiate women from men. The result of this is that women are viewed through a whole range of contradictory expectations. As Carlen and Worrall explain,

> Women, then are always-already *not men*. Femininity is constructed on the site vacated by masculinity, and this absence of maleness is manifested in two opposing sets of expectations.... (1987:3. Emphasis in original).

On the one hand femininity is characterised by the ability to be self controlled and responsible. Women's domestic roles demand that they be stable, dependable and rational and in particular their traditional roles as mothers and carers (both at home or in paid employment) demand an exceptionally high level of responsibility and self-governance. However, on the other hand, the concept of normal femininity is also constructed around notions of dependency, irrationality, lack of self-control and the need for protection. Women are frequently portrayed as people with an *incapacity* for self-governance and responsibility and are consequently frequently not accredited with full adult status in society (Smart and Smart, 1978; Hutter and Williams, 1981; Carlen, 1983).[1]

These accepted 'norms' of behaviour have, according to Hutter and Williams (1981), become embedded into our social belief systems and practices and, as a result, have become internalised to such an extent that they are not generally questioned as 'assumptions' but rather they are accepted as 'facts'. Within such a social framework many women (and indeed men) conform to the behaviour expected of them because it is advantageous to do so and thus the legitimacy of these gender 'facts' is perpetuated. Consequently, when women fail to adhere to gender 'facts' or overtly resist such categorisation, their actions are frequently explained within the discourses of pathology and such women are perceived as threatening to social 'normality' and in need of intensive regulation.

This contradiction is carried further when one considers the concept of 'deviance' with regard to women. Generally, it is assumed that 'normal' and 'deviant' are two opposing categories. Often for men this is the case but for women the boundary between these two concepts is not so straightforward.[2] The paradoxical nature of 'normal' femininity means that the difference between what is considered 'normal' and what is considered 'deviant' can be very subtle. In addition it is not a fixed boundary; what is considered 'deviant' behaviour for some women, in some circumstances, may not always be considered as deviant for others in other circumstances. Indeed some types of 'deviant' behaviour can be completely rationalised through the mobilisation of particular discourses.[3]

The following sections of this chapter will discuss this issue further in the context of the different forms of control that women face – formal, informal and semi-penal. The way in which feminising discourses of domesticity, respectability, motherhood, sexuality and pathology are utilised to both determine what is appropriate or 'normal' behaviour for women and in turn to correct or 'normalise' the inappropriate behaviour of women will be examined.

The Formal Regulation of Women

As Pat Carlen (1998) has stated, because of the extent of the informal social controls over women they rarely (in comparison to men) come to the attention of the more formal agencies of control, particularly the criminal justice system. Consequently, when women do enter this arena they are instantly 'out of place' and this incongruity can sometimes lead to more intense and severe sanctions. In comparison to their male counterparts the numbers of females in prison is relatively low, although a large proportion are there for very minor offences and indeed many are there for the first time (Carlen, 1998). More significantly though, is the fact that, as Heidensohn has argued, it is those women who do not conform to 'accepted standards of monogamous, heterosexual stability' (1996:48) who seem to be over-represented within the prison system. In other words, women's prisons generally contain 'deviant women who deviate *as women*' (Heidensohn, 1996:48, emphasis in original) rather than as those who simply deviate from the law.

The contradictory construction of femininity has led to a situation whereby the actions of women offenders can only be rationalised if the women themselves can be 'fitted into' one of three general categories; mad, bad or helpless victim. This categorisation of women has relatively little to do with the offence committed but rather it has to do with the offender's adherence to or deviation from dominant gender role expectations (Ballinger, 1996). As Carlen (1998) argued, these stereotypes of 'appropriate' behaviour can lead to some women (for example those deemed to be sexually deviant, those who have out-stepped the confines of domestic control or those who are destitute) receiving harsh penalties from the court for relatively minor, non-violent offences. In stark contrast to the severe penalties imposed on some women for minor infractions is the often relatively lenient treatment received by other women, often for more serious offences.[4] Sometimes very serious criminal and violent acts committed by women can be justified and rationalised in the courtroom as long as the image and lifestyle of the defendant strictly adheres to the accepted images of femininity and her behaviour in court is in accordance with those images. Worrall provides the example of Kathy, a young woman accused of stabbing her sister to death after an argument. During her trial for manslaughter (reduced from murder on the strength of psychiatric reports) she is described as a 'typical teenager' (1990:49) and is portrayed as a dutiful daughter from a respectable family. In addition her crime is described as 'tragic'. According to Worrall, her status as a 'normal' young woman who fulfils the expectations of femininity results in a sentence of probation with a recommendation for psychiatric treatment. Ironically she did not receive her psychiatric treatment, as it was not deemed necessary by her doctor. Worrall contrasts this with the case of Ivy who stole a jar of coffee from a shop, later claiming she was confused after having recently received electro-convulsive therapy (ECT). Ivy also received a sentence of probation (for three years as opposed to two for Kathy) but, unlike Kathy, continued to receive psychiatric treatment and ECT. Kathy's crime, Worrall asserts, was so incongruous with her and her family's respectable status that justifications had to be found for her actions, as the idea that a 'normal' family could produce a fratricide was unacceptable to conventional sensibilities. Kathy remained within the confines of 'appropriate' femininity even though her offence was one of extreme violence. In addition she was not deemed to be a threat to society because, despite the nature of her offence, she lived at home and was thus still within the control of her family. Ivy on the other hand was already guilty of being a 'gender deviant' as she was divorced (and hence had no male authority to govern her) and her own sexual deviance (her 'unfaithfulness') was highlighted as contributing to the breakdown of her marriage. Kathy and Ivy, it would appear, were sentenced not on the severity of their offences but on their extent to which they were perceived to endorse, or reject, conventional ideals of 'appropriate' feminine behaviour.

Heidensohn (1996) states that women face the criminal justice system on different levels. Obviously they face the 'formal' side of the system (the law, the rules), and then they face the practice (in other words, what happens to them on a day-to-day basis within the system). However, in addition they also face an ideological level that is constructed around the values, belief systems and moral stance of the agents of control. Although men too face these different levels, it has been argued that the impact of ideology is far greater for criminal women and 'delinquent' girls than their male counterparts. Consequently, women are encouraged to behave in a particular way when facing the agents of control. Women who behave 'appropriately' and in accordance with accepted notions of femininity may invoke sympathy and this, in turn, can assist their case in court. Even some feminist probation officers admit to advising female clients to behave in a manner (passive, remorseful, fragile and weak) acceptable and palatable to the court (Kennedy, 1992; Heidensohn, 1996).[5] Likewise, Parker *et al* discuss the way in which girls and boys in the juvenile court are encouraged to behave very differently in order to ensure the best chance of a lenient sentence.

> Girls, in particular, tended to remember their solicitor advised mute passivity....boys say they were encouraged to assert themselves (1981: 111 cited in Heidensohn, 1996:42).

Women and girls who consciously try to resist being categorised in these ways and instead attempt to introduce a more realistic and rational explanation of their behaviour (one which is not constructed within the pathologising mad, bad or victim discourses) can find their accounts silenced or 'muted' (Worrall, 1990:11) by dominant 'knowledges'. Women's accounts can, and will, only be heard if they are expressed through appropriate channels, in other words if they are communicated through the 'dominant modes of expression' (Worrall, 1990:11; see also Ballinger, 1996) which are rooted in feminising discourses around domesticity, respectability, motherhood and sexuality. 'Professional' discourse, according to Worrall (1990), is used to establish, on the woman's behalf, an acceptable and conventional account of the defendant as 'normal' and respectable, an account which the defendant is not deemed able to construct for herself. The purpose of constructing such an account is twofold. First, the utilisation of feminising discourses is meant to explain the woman's offending as not wholly incongruous with her natural female role thus invoking a degree of sympathy from sentencers. As Nagel *et al* explain

> Females whose offence pattern is more consistent with sex role expectations seem to experience less harsh outcomes than females whose offence pattern is less traditional (1980:20, cited in Heidensohn, 1996:44).

The second aim is to compel sentencers to act leniently towards the female defendant because of her role as wife, mother and male 'sex-object'.

> Solicitors place great emphasis on the construction of female law-breakers as family members, in particular as wives and mothers, with responsibilities that render them deserving of both understanding and sympathy (in relation to the motivation for their offence) and of leniency (in relation to their treatment) (Worrall, 1990:86).[6]

Once women are incarcerated they find the same discourses that censured their behaviour, re-mobilised to 'correct' or 'normalise' their behaviour. Bosworth (1999) describes the work undertaken by female inmates at Drake Hall and Winchester prisons, which consisted of industrial sewing, cleaning, gardening and minor repair work. Similarly the education and training courses offered to the women were based around a variety of 'feminine' pursuits.

> It was perhaps in the incidental classes, many of which were run in the evening, that an outmoded idealisation of femininity was most apparent. These classes in both establishments included flower arranging, silk painting, making soft toys, cooking and 'beauty' (Bosworth, 1999: 104).

In addition, Bosworth claims, both prisons were proud of the training provided in their hairdressing salons. It is a key concern of formal penal institutions to promote an ideology that encourages women to gravitate towards their traditional domestic functions and their 'natural' feminine roles (Carlen, 1983; Genders and Player, 1987; Bosworth, 1999).

However, women are not solely regulated and controlled through formal processes such as those employed within the criminal justice system. On the contrary, women have historically found themselves subjected to a whole range of 'informal' disciplinary forces and mechanisms that, through the deployment of dominant, feminising discourses, have attempted to manage and normalise their behaviour.

The Informal Regulation of Women

Sexuality is one of the most significant areas of feminist debate and crucial to any understanding of the social control of women in society (Edwards, 1981; MacKinnon, 1982). Indeed as MacKinnon indicates, the discourses around sexuality and their related controls pervade and impact upon the lives of all women, or to put it another way:

> ....sexuality is to feminism what work is to Marxism (1982: 515).

Edwards (1981) claims that although this issue is so significant for women, and despite the fact that the regulation and control of female sexuality is a characteristic of virtually every social and economic formation, traditional sociological studies regarding the oppression or the social control of women have tended to neglect the subject of sexuality in favour of structural accounts which place the emphasis on the relationship of women to the means of production or the division of labour by sex. However, over the past two decades or so, largely through the influence of post-structuralist accounts of sexuality and social control, the issue has been more widely recognised and has become a focal issue within feminist theory and debate. McNay (1992) asserts that although the work of Foucault was notoriously 'gender-neutral', the weaving of his theories into feminist accounts has at least provided a means through which the sexualised body can be situated at the crux of explanations of women's subordination, something which Marxist accounts fail to do. Feminist theories of sexuality therefore, are not solely concerned with how sexual desires and sexual relationships are shaped and constructed by societal expectations, but rather they are concerned with the way in which, and the extent to which, sexuality relates to women's oppression and control (Richardson, 1993).

According to Burford and Shulman (1992), the sexuality of women has historically been perceived as a threat to male authority. Female sexuality was believed to be a form of power over males and it therefore had to be controlled (see also Humphrey, 1978; Okley, 1978; Richardson, 1993). During the nineteenth century explicit expressions of sexuality or sexual desire were associated with lower class women or prostitutes. Civilised, normal, respectable women, it was believed, did not suffer from such aberrations of femininity (Arthurs and Grimshaw, 1999). Of course, similar desires were not considered abhorrent with regards to nineteenth century men and indeed in contemporary society there still exist explicit double standards of morality for boys and girls, men and women. Sexual promiscuity in males was, and is, condoned and indeed encouraged as an indication of 'normal' masculinity. Promiscuity in females however is condemned and considered at best, unfeminine and immoral, and at worse, pathological behaviour (Smart and Smart, 1978; Harris and Webb, 1987; French, 1992). Consequently the social control of female sexuality operates on a range of different levels (Hanmer and Saunders, 1983; Harris and Webb, 1987; Kelly, 1987; Radford, 1987; Hester, 1992).

One method of controlling these 'dangerous' sexualities has been through the mobilisation of discourses which have served to label and categorise women as 'immoral', thus rendering them with an 'outcast' status. The stark distinction between 'good' women (sexually passive) and 'bad' women (sexually active or aggressive) provides women with the knowledge that in order for them to avoid stigmatisation and in order that they maintain an intact 'reputation' within society, they must adhere to the dominant ideals of femininity.

These ideals prescribe that female sexuality should be aimed specifically and solely at procreation. Sexuality that is not aimed at this goal is deemed to be 'uncontrolled' and problematic. In many cultures the achievement of childbirth is the most significant way in which a woman legitimates her sexuality and thus 'redeems the fallen state of the male-female relationship' (Hirschon, 1978:68). Consequently, motherhood is one of the primary methods of controlling female sexuality. However, although motherhood and child-rearing is regarded as natural for women, it must be conducted within an 'appropriate' context. This 'natural' form of behaviour, and the 'appropriate contexts' in which it is expected to take place, establishes a yardstick through which unnatural or abnormal female behaviour can be measured (Richardson, 1993a). Married women who remain childless are perceived as selfish, whilst lesbian women or single women who have children are perceived as abnormal. So, although many women can and do draw strength and a sense of identity from their roles as mothers (this will be discussed more fully below and again in later chapters), this aspect of 'natural' and 'normal' femininity is heavily utilised in the regulation of women's behaviour.

Once women have children they are expected to remain at home and care for them, and this construction of women as inherently domesticated beings has promoted a range of controls over many aspects of women's lives. Up until the end of the nineteenth century, the 'ideal' of middle class femininity was a weak, passive woman, usually sickly and always in need of care. During the early twentieth century the new ideal became the housewife who was still assumed to be passive, but was now bestowed with much greater responsibilities. As Ehrenreich and English (1979) comment, the twentieth century woman

> ....would be bound to the home just as securely as the invalid *(sic)* had been – not because she was too weak to do anything else, but because she had so much to do there (1979:128).

This new ideal became the model, not just for middle class women, but for *all* women of *all* classes. By the early twentieth century the virtues of the 'home' were espoused by political and religious commentators who identified it as a place of sanctity from external (public) dangers such as alcohol or prostitution, and women's role, as saviours of this domestic sanctuary from external corruption, was established. The construction of discourses around domestication produced rigid boundaries for women between the 'public' and 'private' worlds, leaving them 'appropriately' assigned to the private domestic domain (Imray and Middleton, 1983). Dahl and Snare (1978) assert that women's seclusion in the 'private' world facilitated their surveillance and ensured their close control by husbands, families and neighbours. Women's domestic role left their lives 'open' to scrutiny and surveillance whilst at the same time rendered them relatively invisible and powerless in their private and 'closed' world, a world which should be immune to intervention as far as possible. Domestication can therefore restrict and regulate female behaviour through invisibility as well as through surveillance.

The discourses around domesticity and respectability have led to further, related controls over women's lives in the 'public' world. First, women may be restricted from participating in various leisure activities due to a lack of free time or financial independence. But even those women who are financially independent and have free time to engage in activities outside the home, still find their behaviour regulated through the mobilisation of discourses around 'decency' and 'respectability'. Although, ironically, women are often portrayed and represented as 'leisure objects', their own leisure activities are one of the most heavily regulated and scrutinised aspects of their lives (Green, Hebron and Woodward, 1987).

Traditionally many 'leisure' arenas (such as pubs or night clubs) have been male dominated and women's participation in them has been limited. Women's drinking for example has historically been an area necessary of strict controls (Zedner, 1991). According to Green *et al* (1987), the penalties for women who overstep the accepted limits of 'decency' within these leisure arenas can be severe and range from verbal abuse to the threat of, or actual, male violence.

So we can see the way in which the ideals of appropriate femininity are utilised to explain, discipline and regulate criminal or 'deviant' women by the formal criminal justice agents as well as through more informal mechanisms. However this book is specifically concerned with the punishment, control and discipline of women within the 'semi-penal' arena of social control. An in-depth account of the semi-penal institution is presented in the next chapter, along with a gendered history of such institutions from the early nineteenth century to present day. It is therefore unnecessary to provide any further detail on these issues here. What does require some further discussion here, however, is the position that these institutions occupy on the 'control continuum' and the discourses which ensured that women in particular were seen to be particularly appropriate for this form of social control.

The Punishment of Women in the 'Community'

> The term 'community' is one of the most promiscuous words in contemporary political usage (Worrall, 1997:46).

The third arena of social control, which sits between the 'formal' discipline of the prison and the 'informal' regulation of the domestic sphere, is sometimes described as the 'community'. The community has at various points in history been perceived as an appropriate place for the punishment and control of recalcitrant individuals. Our contemporary understanding of punishment within the community (the modern probation system is the best example and most relevant to this study), combines elements of supervision with the conditional suspension of punishment and emerged in the latter part of the nineteenth century in a climate of changing social attitudes and the development of new theories about the causes of crime (Bochel, 1976; Garland, 1985).

Probation is now a frequently used sentence of the court and, although the work undertaken by the service has in recent years been influenced by the harsh, punishment orientated ideology of the 1990s, it was traditionally considered a welfare-based approach in which the offender was offered (moral as well as practical) advice and support, the aim of which was his or her rehabilitation and reintegration into social life.

Historically probation was seen as an appropriate sentence for women offenders (Leeson, 1914). Police Court Missionaries (the forerunners to probation officers) and magistrates were keen to recommend probation, with its emphasis on care as well as control, as a suitable disposal for impressionable young women. As with juveniles, the idea of punishing and reforming women in the community was perceived to be a more benign, less corruptive and thus more palatable system of control and as such was, and indeed still is, utilised relatively frequently with these 'fragile' offenders.

However, we need to look more carefully at what community actually means in this context. The idea of the community as an inherently positive environment has been severely criticised in recent years. As Lacey and Zedner (1995) point out the appeal of the community is paradoxical. On the one hand we live in a society that commonly believes (and this is often backed up by political rhetoric) that growing crime rates and increasing deviant behaviour amongst the young, are due primarily to the breakdown in 'community values'. On the other hand the concept of community is increasingly held up as the most appropriate arena for curing social disorder, dealing with offenders and preventing crime.

So the community is increasingly seen as a means of both *causing* and *curing* social disorder. In spite of (or perhaps because of) the 'community's' perceived responsibility for causing social problems, it has now become its responsibility to deal with these problems. Lacey and Zedner go on to state that politicians and academics on both the right and left of the political spectrum have (either directly or indirectly) encouraged this movement. The idea of community appeals to those on the political right (and this is evident from legislation and policy changes during the 1980s) not least because of its apparent solution to the fiscal crisis in criminal justice and care services (Frazer and Lacey, 1993). On the other hand the idea of community has also engaged those on the political left because first, it is closely related to a collective, rather than individualistic, approach to the causes of crime and the 'dynamics of penality' (Frazer and Lacey,

1993: 304) and second it raises debates around whether groups which were formerly disempowered (for example offenders within the prison system) might not be more empowered through community-based disposals.

However, many academics have taken issue with those commentators (from both the political left and right) who espouse the notion of community as if it were an accepted and unproblematic concept. These writers have argued that community has been idealised and under-developed as a political and social concept and, as Cohen (1983) and Worrall (1997) have commented, the meaning of community remains vague and inadequately explained. There is also an overwhelming tendency to discuss community as the opposite of custody and this is problematic because this dichotomy sets up a false opposition, suggesting that because custody is a regulative and restrictive environment, the community must be a positive and beneficial arena within which individuals can be contained and controlled. Little or no consideration is given to how the community might also be intrusive, coercive and regulatory. As Cohen (1985) postulated, the very fact that community punishments are perceived to be 'benign' and less intensive than custodial penalties, could lead to the imposition of further, more severe sanctions.

> It is by making the system appear less harsh, that people are encouraged to use it more often. Far from each benevolent intermediate option slowing down the career of delinquency, it facilitates, promotes and accelerates it by making each consecutive decision easier to take (Cohen, 1985:95).

This tendency to draw a stark distinction between custody and community has posed problems for feminist writers. Liberal theory has polarised the discourses around the 'public' and the 'private' (the 'formal' and the 'informal', 'custody' and 'community') when, as Frazer and Lacey (1993) have stated, for women in particular, it is very difficult to identify where the boundaries are drawn. For some women the experience of community can be as restrictive and controlled as an experience of custody.[7]

This lack of a gendered approach to community is one of the major criticisms from feminist writers. Many liberal, Marxist and post-structuralist theorists acknowledge little or no recognition that community might mean very different things for men and women. Frazer and Lacey assert that the notion of community really only exists at the level of rhetoric and it is a rhetoric which appeals to commonly held ideas about the type of ideal society we would like to live in, one where communities exist and support the values of solidarity and reciprocity. This, they maintain, is a romantic notion and even the closest 'communal' unit, the family, frequently fails to live up to these idealised standards. Indeed for women, the family unit frequently embodies the principal features of women's oppression through

> ....the reproduction and reinforcement of coercive heterosexist culture, the sexual division of labour, the objectification of women as property, sexual harassment of women by men (Frazer and Lacey, 1993: 139).

Overall then, the issue of community is a controversial and contentious one and its existence as a benign and benevolent arena has been extensively challenged. However, even these challenges are themselves problematic in that their definition of community is incomplete. In other words, although feminist writers have rightly argued that the community can be a restrictive and oppressive environment for women, they have tended to focus their critique within established boundaries, identifying the community as the opposite of custody. So, discussions of community in the feminist literature rarely move beyond an examination of the home, the neighbourhood and related institutions such as the school, church, or leisure arena. What is missing from this analysis is an acknowledgement that the boundary between community and custody is not always as definite as it might appear. Indeed, as this book will highlight, for countless women over the past 200 years, being reformed or punished in the community did not refer to a form of supervision within the home or neighbourhood, but rather it meant being incarcerated in an institution of some form. Cohen's (1985) argument gets closer to a broader definition in that he acknowledges the blurring of boundaries between the formerly polarised arenas of the prison and the community. Cohen predicted that the increasing use of community penalties, from the 1970s onwards, represented a magnification and expansion of existing mechanisms of social control. He asserted that the expansion of this programme would lead first to the entrapment of individuals who would not otherwise have been 'at risk', thus causing an increase in the overall number of individuals caught up in the formal control system (a process he termed 'widening the net'). Second, he argued that the emphasis on more intensive supervision would lead to an increase in the *amount* of intervention that individuals would be subjected to (or a 'thinning of the mesh'). Third, Cohen stated that the proliferation of non-custodial penalties would lead to an obscuring of the boundaries between 'custody' and 'community' ('blurring') and finally that the social control mechanisms normally restricted to the prison (methods of surveillance and discipline) would permeate into the informal networks of society and would thus not provide an alternative to the penal system but rather an amplification of it ('penetration'). This is a sophisticated and useful explanation, however from a historical and gendered perspective, Cohen's analysis is problematic. As far as women were concerned the 'disciplinary project' Cohen talked of (the widening of the net, the thinning of the mesh, the blurring of custodial and communal boundaries and the penetration of social control into the community) did not begin in the 1970s as he suggests, but rather had already been in progress for over 200 years. Thus institutions such as reformatories, homes, halfway houses and hostels may be regarded as the ultimate consequence of the 'blurring' between penal and non-penal environments. Subsequent chapters of this book will challenge the accepted definitions of community by analysing the way in which a whole range of semi-penal institutions have historically functioned to 'play down' the punishment and disciplining of women by disguising these processes within the discourses of care, protection, empowerment and, indeed, 'community'.

This chapter has so far examined the formal and informal disciplining of women. However, it should not be assumed that just because women are regulated according to 'patriarchal' assumptions, they are regulated solely by men. On the contrary women have historically played a significant role in the social control of other women and, indeed, of themselves. Nor should it be assumed that women are persistently subjugated. Women are, of course, agentic subjects in their own right and can, and do, resist the forces of oppression.

Many of the feminist theories utilised in the preceding discussions are drawn from the early feminist literature around social control. These debates remain useful in that they allow feminists to articulate an understanding of the extent to which, and the plethora of ways in which, women's lives are regulated in patriarchal society. However, in recent years post-structuralist feminists have challenged these explanations, complaining that they are too 'universal'. This concept of power as centralised and 'total', as McNay (1992) argues, does not adequately unpack the sophisticated, complex and subtle nature of power relations. The remaining sections of this chapter will take up some of these debates, examining first the role that women have played in the regulation and disciplining of other women. This discussion will be followed by a consideration of the production of the 'docile' or 'disciplined' female body. Finally the ways in which women can draw on their individual experiences and 'race-class-gender' identities in order to manage or resist disciplinary forces, both 'formal' and 'informal', will be addressed.

Sisters Doing it for Themselves: Women controlling women

Women as controllers of other women

Historically, women have been expected to, and have often been willing to, participate in the regulation of their sisters. Women's role in the control of other women can be found in many areas of social life. First, it is apparent in the home where women have traditionally been responsible for the socialisation of their children, encouraging them to accept their gender roles (Oakley, 1980; Heidensohn, 1996). Second, women are frequently employed in welfare-based institutions (such as nursing homes or hospitals) where their 'natural' caring abilities and desires can be put to good use in the care, protection *and* control of their female patients. Finally, women's presence in the judicial system and penal institutions has been necessary to provide a form of 'feminine' discipline appropriate for 'deviant' females and, historically at least, to provide an acceptable and realistic role model to which 'deviant' women could aspire (see Rafter, 1983; Lindfield, 1992).

From the early years of the nineteenth century, women were heavily involved in philanthropic projects or social work practices which were aimed at both relieving and reforming the lives of the poor (see Ehrenreich and English, 1979; Lewis, 1992). Although these activities were frequently rooted in religious zeal and a desire to 'do good' the reality was that they often served to increase surveillance over working class women's lives.[8] For the many middle class women involved in such projects, their work could be viewed as a method of resistance to the constraints placed upon their own lives with regard to employment or activities outside of the home. However for the most part, female workers were useful in these philanthropic roles as the social control of (predominantly working class) women could be better legitimated if facilitated by other (predominantly middle class or 'respectable' working class) women. These 'respectable' women not only provided material and moral relief and support for their 'failing' clients but in addition they provided an important role model to which the women under their care and surveillance were encouraged to live up to (Simey, 1951; Lewis, 1992).

In the early reformatory movement women were often employed as matrons and, in addition to the day to day running of the institutions, were charged with the setting of a good example to the wayward residents. These female managers, however, were themselves managed by male dominated committees or organisations and informed and instructed by male 'experts'. Such women could provide mediation between the male professionals and the female clients by interpreting and translating the 'knowledge' of the male experts into 'common sense' ideas that could then be assumed by the 'deficient' women. Worrall (1990) states that it is still the case today. Although dominant discourses, which serve to regulate the behaviour of women, are legitimised by male professionals the power is frequently delegated to female, semi-professionals (for example nurses, prison officers or magistrates). Worrall maintains that female control agents, such as magistrates, are themselves constructed within various discourses that both associate them with and distance them from the women defendants who stand before them.[9] The fact that women magistrates are in fact *women* means they can provide a 'special and authoritative understanding' (Worrall, 1990:66) of 'deviant' females in court, but the fact that women magistrates are *magistrates* instantly removes them from the world of female defendants and this then allows them the objectivity to pass sentence.

It is imperative, Worrall argues, that women magistrates remain ideologically isolated from female defendants because any over-identification with these women, and their oppression, might lead them to challenge the dominance of their male colleagues. Women who enter the judicial arena must accept and adhere to the practices set by their male counterparts because although around 50 per cent of magistrates are female, as Worrall states, 'real' magistrates (like 'real' criminals) are believed to be male and thus their objective, dispassionate and sexist values must be taken as the 'real' standard of judgement. These sets of 'common-sense' values can be particularly alienating to female defendants because

> ....*common* sense does not allow for different material circumstances (Worrall, 1990: 70. Emphasis in original).

Overall once women magistrates become involved in the male dominated judicial arena, they are compelled to distance themselves from their own experiences as women and thus reject any understanding of gender inequalities within society.

Whereas magistrates are expected to separate their professional activities from their experiences as women, female prison or probation officers, it has been argued, are encouraged to utilise their femininity in their professional roles. Faith (1993) comments that women prison officers often attempt to provide a 'mother-figure' for the women and girls in their charge. Similar to the early reformatory matrons, female prison officers are defined as women who, on behalf of a patriarchal judicial system, can provide suitable role models for acceptable behaviour aimed at keeping deviant females in their place (Kramarae and Treichler, 1985, cited in Faith, 1993:161). Female guards, it has historically been (and indeed still is) assumed are better equipped than men to inform and train women in the domestic and maternal duties expected of them by society. Their very presence in institutions is more effective in the 'normalisation' process than any amount of male instruction.

Likewise, female probation officers (and indeed male probation officers) have been required to develop some form of relationship with their clients in order for supervision (their controlling function) to be effective. During the early years of the probation service women officers were expected to supervise women offenders. Between the mid 1930s and the mid 1960s the idea that women could provide the best role model for other women was embodied in legislation that actually prevented men from supervising women and girls (Parsloe, 1972). Parsloe explains how female officers were expected to provide a form of 'motherly' supervision over both male and female clients. For their female clients this would provide the much needed role-model of 'appropriate' behaviour and for their male clients the 'motherly' approach would provide support with no sexual threat or challenge.

Thus we can see the ways in which women have been, and still are, utilised in the control and regulation of other women. However, what should not be overlooked is the extent to which women conform to conventional, patriarchal discourses and in doing so act as self-regulating subjects.

Women as self-regulatory bodies

The issue of self-discipline relates closely to Foucault's analysis (although he did not address the issue of gender directly in his work) and consequently many feminist writers have elaborated on Foucault's theories, either subtly or explicitly, when examining the social control of women (see for example Okley, 1978; Weedon, 1987; Diamond and Quimby, 1988; Worrall, 1990; Sawicki, 1991; McNay, 1992; Faith, 1994; Howe, 1994; Naffine, 1997; Worrall, 1997).

Okley (1978) argues that it is expected that the behaviour of girls, who from infancy are reared to be passive and submissive, will be rooted in internalised notions of self-control and self-negation. Her study of a girls' boarding school highlights many instances of the promotion of self-regulation. She asserts that girls in public schools, unlike boys in similar institutions, were not afforded the right to make decisions for themselves. Boys, she claims, were allocated many rights, including some fairly dictatorial powers such as the right to inflict corporal punishment on other boys, the right to establish rules and the utilisation of junior boys as servants (fags). As a result

[Boys] thus acquire near-adult authority before they leave school (Okley, 1978: 124).

Okley concludes that as a consequence of not having the opportunity to make personal decisions for themselves, the girls in her study had to learn to exercise a great deal of self-discipline. This self-discipline was often tested by the very triviality of many of the rules and regulations imposed within the institution, for example those that restricted movement (not being allowed to leave the premises without permission) or communication (only being allowed to talk to other students at specific times). She asserts that the idea was for this self-discipline to extend beyond the simple compliance with school rules into the broader realms of sexual behaviour.

Bartky (1988) elaborates on these debates. Basing her work largely on Foucault's theory of 'docile bodies' she examines the mechanisms through which disciplined bodies are subjected to a fragmentation and a partitioning of time, space and movement. However, whereas Foucault based his (ungendered) account of docile bodies within the more formal social control institutions such as the school or the prison, Bartky expands on this concept and claims that the production of 'docile' female bodies occurs, not within a single institution, but rather on a continuum from informal to formal mechanisms. In addition, Bartky argues, these mechanisms of discipline have become embedded into social culture through the proliferation of 'benign' structures such as dietary, exercise and make-up regimes, medical discourses and popularised media images, to such an extent that they have been absorbed by women themselves. Consequently, she states, women have become self-regulating bodies who are frequently content and/or compelled to conform to these notions of personal self-discipline. Furthermore, women are not just self-regulating but self-policing too in the sense that they can punish themselves if they fail to adhere or live up to the standards which are set for them and which they set for themselves.

The lack of formal public sanctions does not mean that a woman who is unable or unwilling to submit herself to the appropriate body discipline will face no sanctions at all. On the contrary, she faces a very severe sanction indeed in a world dominated by men: the refusal of male patronage....women punish themselves too for the failure to conform. The growing literature on women's body size is filled with wrenching confessions of shame from the overweight... The depth of these women's shame is a measure of the extent to which all women have internalised patriarchal standards of bodily acceptability (Bartky, 1988: 76).

Grimshaw (1999) agrees, stating that women are not just self-regulating with regard to their behaviour, but also with regard to their lifestyle, looks and body shape. Women, she contends, have become pre-occupied with rigid dietary regimes and exercise routines in order that they can be seen to have an 'appropriate' lifestyle and, more importantly, an 'appropriate' body shape. So what is commonly accepted in society as 'free choice' (for example, losing weight, exercising, making up) is in reality a process of normalisation.

> ....despite the frequent popular presentation of body change and shaping as a matter of mere individual choice and will....the body that women want is a highly normalized one (Grimshaw, 1999: 93).

Women, she argues, are trapped within a process of self-surveillance, perpetuated by the powerful visual images of an idealised female body. This 'fetishisation' of the idealised female shape, and the desire of many women to conform to it, can lead to extreme behaviours and responses from women, for example eating disorders (Bordo, 1988; Hopwood, 1995), breast implants (Bordo, 1993) or other forms of surgical intervention (Davis, 1997) which, in turn, can lead to poor health, disfigurement and sometimes death.

So we must ask why women are so compelled or so willing to undertake such extreme measures and indeed, why women want to, and do, conform to such idealised images. This question is a complex and in many ways a contentious one. Care needs to be taken to avoid labelling women as totally 'docile' and passive, or ignorant of the discourses which pervade and regulate their lives. In addition, it should be remembered that women frequently *do not* conform to self-regulatory regimes, indeed they often resist them. However, before the issue of resistance can be tackled, the question of willingness to conform and self-policing should be addressed.

Okley (1978) argued that boarding school girls actively participated in their own regulation because they were consciously aware that those who conformed received less attention from authority than those who did not, so in this case, conformity and self-regulation were utilised as a means of avoiding or resisting further, more intense, external intervention and supervision. Ardener (1978) however, takes a different view, stating that women's conformity can be a sign of self-policing for the purposes of achieving a (socially acceptable) goal. She contends that women often have a vested interest in their own regulation as it might serve to convey status. For example, the only real status that a working class woman in the nineteenth century could realistically achieve was that of a *respectable* working class woman and thus the route to this status was through self-regulation, control and conformity to acceptable standards of decency and femininity. In contemporary society, the 'goal' might be to reach the status of wife and mother, either as a symbol of personal achievement or as a route out of poverty or other material problems (Marshment, 1993), thus women may readily submit to self-regulatory regimes in order to attract (and keep) a partner.

Bordo (1993) on the other hand, maintains that women often conform, particularly with regard to body image, not because they want to get married and have children, but because they believe this to be a route to independence and liberation. She highlights this with examples of female celebrities who are generally portrayed and perceived as being strong, liberated and decontrolled (for example Cher or Madonna). However, Bordo claims that in reality, although these women are financially independent and assertive, they have still adhered to, and indeed perpetuate, conventional images of femininity and have normalised themselves either through training regimes or through cosmetic surgery.

> ....in Foucauldian terminology, Cher has gradually 'normalised' herself. Her normalised image (the only 'reality' which counts) now acts as a standard against which other women will measure, judge, discipline and 'correct' themselves' (Bordo, 1993: 197).

According to Grimshaw (1999) the 'fetishisation' of the body has led women to accept that control of their bodies is indicative of control their lives, and hence this makes rigid beauty regimes and exercise regimes more acceptable and desirable (see also Brook, 1999). In addition, physical appearance has often been held as indicative of the state of a woman's mental health and women (particularly within institutions) have frequently been compelled to 'look good' as this can be perceived as an expression of their mental stability. Of course this debate could be taken somewhat further and it could be argued that many women conform to acceptable notions of beauty, dress and appearance as this can *contribute* to their mental well-being and mental health in that 'looking good' is a source of pleasure, and possibly power, for women (Frost, 1999). Many women may be self-regulating and accept conventional images of femininity, partly because a patriarchal ideology has achieved a general hegemony within society and thus these images become 'taken for granted', but also because women acknowledge that conforming to such images may have particular (short term) advantages and benefits for them such as an increase in confidence and self esteem, the feeling of acceptance and the avoidance of stigmatisation and the 'outcast' status associated with alternative looks or lifestyles (Marshment, 1993).

So we can see how feminists have generated an understanding of why women conform to standards of femininity and, more importantly, why they internalise these discourses to such a degree that they become self-regulating and self-policing.

Grimshaw (1993) comments that in a great deal of Foucault's writing the (male) 'self' is created by discourse. What many feminists within this tradition have done is attempt to analyse how women's experiences can also be constructed within discourses and power relationships. So they have shifted the emphasis from the male self to the female self, however the emphasis is still on the self as the *effect* of discourse. This is problematic for some feminist scholars as it leaves little room for a consideration of the ways in which women might reject such discourses and insufficient recognition of the methods of resistance they might employ to assert their identity and thus, to some degree, free themselves from these forms of regulation. Foucault stated that power is 'capillary' in that it does not necessarily originate from one particular source and nor is it necessarily in the possession of one specific group or individual. So, as discussed above, subjects are not just regulated by 'others' with power, but can be participatory in their own regulation. But as Grimshaw (1993) and Howe (1994) ask, if women are so self-regulating and their subordination so self-imposed, how is it that some women manage to break out of these constraints? If regulation, control and the 'norms' of femininity are not always *imposed* upon women from external sources, how can, and do, they resist them? Much of the early feminist-Foucauldian literature around 'women of discourse', normalisation and self-regulation failed to deal adequately with these questions and the issues of resistance and agency were insufficiently discussed.[10]

Foucault stated that power and resistance co-existed, or 'where there is power there is resistance' (1980:95), and many feminist writers have consequently utilised this concept in their work. However, as Deveaux maintains, although Foucault's work in this area is useful as it provides feminists with the opportunity to move beyond simplistic explanations of gender relations (with women as objects of subordination and victimisation within a 'top-down', male dominated power relationship) towards a more complete understanding of the existence of 'multiple power relations' (Deveaux, 1994: 231) in which the possibility of resistance over domination is highlighted, it nonetheless still fails to provide a sufficient concept of agency.

> [Foucault's] lack of a rounded theory of subjectivity or agency conflicts with a fundamental aim of the feminist project to rediscover and re-evaluate the experiences of women (McNay, 1991, quoted in Deveaux, 1994: 232).

One of the major problems with Foucault's theory for feminism is the fact that Foucault's concept of power is generalised from his analysis of the power relationships and practices within institutions. This is insufficient because, as McNay argues,

> ....the discipline of the feminine body is hard to locate in so far as it is 'uninstitutionally bound' (1992: 33).

In other words, women are not only subjected to formal external disciplinary regimes, as are all individuals, but are subjected to informal mechanisms of control as well as 'internalised' forms of regulation. Therefore, going back to Grimshaw and Howe's question, resistance to external constraints is a more straightforward concept to consider and explain than resistance to those discourses that have become internalised. Daly and Maher (1998) acknowledge this problem and raise the difficulties in trying to construct a feminist framework which connects both the issues around 'women of discourse' and those pertaining to the lives of 'real women'; women whose bodies and lives cannot be simply described as the *effects of discourse* but rather women whose identity is constructed through their socio-economic and cultural experiences, women who have agency over their own lives, women who resist.

Subjectivity, Resistance and Agency

Henning (1999) states that because of the historical link between femininity and vulnerability, the concept of femininity has traditionally been linked with passivity whereas masculinity has been associated with agency. She argues that during the last century, and for the early part of this century, because men were expected to hold power (in both their private and public lives), women were not seriously considered as social agents, even during those times when they constituted a real political threat (for example during the suffragette movement). However for as long as there have been power relationships, a whole range of resistance strategies (including political, legal, academic and personal strategies) have existed for women. Women can and do resist the formal and informal restraints imposed upon them and the expectations of them in everyday life, through a variety of methods which range from explicit confrontations with authority (Mandaraka-Sheppard, 1986), to the rejection of convention and the adoption of alternative lifestyles and appearances (see Kidd, 1999), to the *embracing* of conventional aspects of femininity (for example motherhood or 'appropriate' physical appearance) which women then utilise to their 'own ends' as a source of power and self-esteem (Marshment, 1993; Faith, 1994; Frost, 1999; Bosworth, 1999).

Before a discussion of these strategies of resistance can take place, however, it is necessary to highlight that the concept of resistance can be a contentious one for feminists. According to Cooper (1995) and Brown (1995) the notion of resistance can be misused by scholars and researchers. Cooper is concerned with what actually constitutes resistance whilst Brown asserts that an over-emphasis on women's ability to resist can potentially legitimate oppression by allowing middle class writers to 'feel good' about marginalised and relatively powerless groups thus providing little motivation to challenge established oppressions or practices. However, as Bosworth (1999) argues, an emphasis on resistance does not have to mean that women's actual oppression is ignored. Indeed as Carlen (1994) points out, it is impossible to discuss women in prison for example without recognising that the majority are, and have been, 'victims' of a whole range of socio-economic, racial and gender based oppressions.

According to Bosworth, an examination of resistance demands an 'appreciation of difference' (1999: 128) and an acknowledgement that women are not a unified group with unified experiences. Rather, as Bryson (1999) explains, women can be divided, as well as united, through their experiences of being women. Women experience *informal* forms of social controls that differ according to their class and ethnicity. Those who enter the formal arenas of social control (eg. the prison) or the semi-penal arenas (eg. the reformatory or the probation hostel) do so therefore with a conceptual framework which has been forged by their class, race and gender experiences. It is thus unsurprising that these women are then compelled to negotiate and evaluate their confinement in relation to their lived experiences. As Bosworth states, such women utilise their race-class-gender identities to navigate the 'pains of imprisonment' (1999: 127) through either a rejection of, or an endorsement of, dominant regimes. Of course the ability to resist in this way is not restricted to imprisonment, or indeed to any form of institutionalisation. Women (as discussed above) may adopt conventional feminine images in their everyday lives (through marriage, beauty regimes, diets, exercise and so on) as a means of breaking out of poverty, improving self esteem or simply to avoid being marginalised even further.

Given that this book is specifically concerned with institutionalised women the discussion that follows will draw primarily from the literature around institutional resistance. As the overwhelming majority of literature in this area is concerned with those women who are institutionalised within formal custodial institutions, it is this literature that will be primarily utilised in the following sections. However, it is my intention to use this literature in order to construct a theoretical framework that can then be utilised to examine the specific experiences and methods of resistance of women within semi-penal institutions.

Confrontation as resistance

Historically, women in prison have not been involved in collective protest to the same extent as incarcerated men (Madaraka-Sheppard, 1986). However, as Shaw (1992) argues, this does not mean that women should be considered as conformers or perpetual victims who simply submit to the forces of oppression. First, it is likely that many incidents of resistance may have gone unrecorded through the history of women's imprisonment as institutionalised women did not often have a voice with which to articulate their protests (see Dobash *et al*, 1986; Lindfield, 1992; Howe, 1994). Any historical records are likely to have been written by men and women in authority and thus may omit true accounts of institutional resistance, or disregard their significance.[11] Instead, Shaw states, we should acknowledge women's desire and ability to take control over their own lives, even when they are forcibly confined. Indeed, resistance in some form (whether subtle or explicit) has always been a more common response to female confinement than compliance (Faith, 1993; Mandaraka-Sheppard, 1986). Zedner (1991), in her discussion of female imprisonment during the nineteenth century, declares that women were generally considered to be *more* disruptive and *less* likely to yield to prison discipline than their male counterparts. Women were believed to be powerful and corrupting and therefore more likely to resist through 'riotous behaviour' (Zedner, 1991:184). Even in contemporary prisons, women are often felt to pose a greater threat to authority than men. Staff who have worked in both male and female prisons report that women are 'more emotional' (Faith, 1993: 165) and therefore are more difficult to manage when in prison.

Although these comments are rooted in dominant discourses around femininity (women as unstable, irrational and governed by their emotions) there may be some element of truth in these statements. It may be the case that women are more likely to reveal their feelings regarding particular issues on a more frequent (but *individual*) basis than men, instead of reacting occasionally but collectively, and it is this concept of 'individuality' that is crucial to an understanding of women's resistance within prison.

Most women in prison belong to the lower socio-economic sections of society and a disproportionate number are black (Carlen, 1998). As noted above, women negotiate imprisonment within the framework of their individual socio-economic and cultural experiences (in addition to their experiences of religion, sexuality and ethnicity). Bosworth's (1999) study highlighted that women in prison constantly utilised aspects of their cultural identity to declare their individuality and their independence from penal regimes. For example women would often refuse to eat ordinary prison meals, insisting instead on Halal or Kosher meat, vegetarian dishes, or no food at all during religious days of fasting. In addition, they would sometimes refuse to engage in the passive feminine behaviour that was encouraged within the prison, complaining about the excessively feminised education and training regimes. Black women frequently complained that, despite the high proportion of women from ethnic minorities within the prison system, regimes did not recognise their specific needs and demands. Even the 'feminised' forms of training available such as hairdressing, did not cater for Afro-Caribbean hair and thus effectively excluded black women's participation whilst still expecting their co-operation.

For the women in Bosworth's study, non-compliance usually took the form of minor verbal challenges to the staff and confrontation rarely went beyond these forms of behaviour. However, that is not to suggest that women are never involved in major, collective forms of resistance. Ferrari-Bravo and Arcidiancono (1989) discuss the case of a juvenile detention centre in Italy in which an attempt was made to integrate girls into, what had previously been, an all boys' institution. A collective revolt took place in the institution shortly after it opened involving eight girls and 30 boys. After the incident a 16 year old girl was identified as the 'ringleader' and was subsequently described by the authors as

> ....a very marked personality, with characteristics of extreme reactivity and aggressiveness (Ferrari-Bravo and Arcidiancono, 1989:151).

They go on to discuss how the actions of this girl became legendary within the institution, being perceived as a figure for which there was no male equivalent in the prison. It would appear that her explicit resistance was so incongruous with her female status that her behaviour was perceived as much more threatening than that of her male companions.

The perception of women who resist disciplinary regimes is rooted in the contradictory ideas of femininity. On the one hand women are expected to be irrational and emotional and consequently, as stated above, incarcerated women have historically been perceived as *more* likely to resist and protest (albeit in individual ways). On the other hand, but at the same time, 'normal' women are expected to be passive and compliant and these ideals are encouraged and reinforced through institutional regimes. Therefore when women resist these regimes their actions are perceived as dangerous and warranting further controls. So because of the danger that these women potentially pose, they are often punished for 'indiscipline' more regularly than male prisoners (Faith, 1993).

As Faith (1993) argues, women in prison are more likely to be perceived as being unruly and undisciplined because they are more likely to be *accused* of prison indiscipline than men. Minor infractions which would be overlooked in men's prisons are often punishable in women's because, first, women's aggression conflicts with common-sense assumptions about femininity and second, men's aggression is so 'in character' with the ideals of masculinity that it goes virtually unnoticed. Consequently, Faith claims, women can find themselves disciplined for trivial 'offences' such as using bad language, possessing minor contraband (such as lemonade) and for sitting in other prisoners' cells.

Perhaps because of the extent to which women are surveyed in prison and disciplined for very minor rule infringements, women's resistance does not always take the form of explicit challenges to authority. On the contrary, women's resistance can be subtle and can consist of an *endorsement* rather than a *rejection* of the discourses and practices that aim to control them.

Endorsement as resistance

> Resistance may....be a choreographed demonstration of co-operation (Faith, 1994: 39).

The construction of the female identity is crucial to an understanding of women's resistance to control. Often both institutional and 'common sense' notions of female identity conflict with women's own personal ideas of identity and, as Bosworth (1999) argues, the very concept of 'identity' is not in fact static, but rather it is a notion which is subject to constant negotiation. As a result women may choose to utilise the methods of control imposed upon them to articulate their resistance and to reduce the 'pains' of their imprisonment.

> Femininity plays a crucial, albeit paradoxical, role in [women's] resistance: while it represents the goal and form of their imprisonment, it is also the means by which they achieve their own ends (Bosworth, 1999: 7).

Bosworth takes up Marshment's (1993) discussion of the way in which women often accept and subscribe to conventional images of femininity, stating that women often do not reject the feminine roles encouraged by institutional regimes and social convention, but rather they knowingly adopt and adhere to them in order to develop a sense of agency and identity.

So, for example, the women in Bosworth's study did not always challenge the goals encouraged by the prison because they did not necessarily perceive the ideals of femininity to be a negative aspect of their lives. Instead, many of them interpreted the ideals of femininity as positive attributes and in doing so they re-negotiated and redefined the meaning of femininity through their experiences of race, class and sexuality and utilised this as a source of resistance rather than a source of disempowerment. As Baudrillard points out, sometimes

....the best answer to an adversary manoeuvre is not to retreat, but to go along with it, turning it to one's own advantage....(1987:65).

So although one primary objective of prison regimes is to produce an acceptable 'feminine identity', one homogenous, uniform identity does not emerge. Rather,

....women are able to construct competing feminine identities, through which they resist some of the disempowering effects of imprisonment (Bosworth, 1999: 107).

Bosworth describes how women would use the bodily aspects of femininity to win various disputes. For example, the women in one prison entered into a dispute with prison management over the replacement of ordinary toilet paper with the medicated, non-absorbent kind and at first used techniques such as direct action (stealing paper from staff toilets and demonstrations) as a means of protest. These means failed and so they employed a strategy which, at first, appeared to endorse aspects of feminine weakness, but was actually utilised as a form of unity and strength. The women informed the governor that this new paper was not suitable for women who were menstruating or women with medical conditions like thrush and consequently the original paper was returned.

The women also employed a similar strategy to complain about the over-starchy food provided in prison. They mobilised the discourses pertaining to feminine attractiveness, complaining that for women a lack of vitamins, minerals and iron led to poor hair, nails and skin. This, of course, was not simply a cynical manipulation of these discourses aimed at winning the dispute. On the contrary, as Marshment (1993) argues, women frequently use discourses of femininity in everyday life, not just to get their own way, but to genuinely improve their physical appearance thus enhancing their levels of confidence and general mental well being. It is likely therefore that the women in prison were sincere in their desire for a better diet as this would improve their physical appearance which in turn could be used as a source of strength and provide an area over which the women could have some control.

One of the most significant aspects of 'idealised femininity' endorsed by the women in Bosworth's study was the traditional ideal of motherhood. Although some women in prison may not generally be perceived as conventionally 'ideal' mothers (drug users, alcoholics, habitual offenders, women in lesbian relationships inside or outside of prison and women accused of violence, abuse or neglect for example) Bosworth highlights how many of the women she interviewed treasured their role as mothers and indeed they used this role in a positive way. First, the status of being a mother was utilised to bring meaning to the lives of the women in that they could strive towards the goal of reuniting their families after their release. Second, being perceived as a caring and 'good' mother would improve the women's self-esteem and sense of identity.

So it can be seen that women are able to endorse potentially oppressive, dominant discourses and utilise the common sense assumptions made about them to their own advantage. However, as Bosworth warns, this strategy is only possible for some women at some times and care should be taken so as not to 'glamorise' the position of incarcerated mothers or accept that, because of their abilities to resist, the situation for them in prison is unproblematic. For some women in Bosworth's study the ability to draw strength from their maternal identity was severely restricted, not least for geographical reasons. Institutionalised women are, after all, physically separated from their families and the pain of this separation, and the practical difficulties it can cause, can often over-ride any positive sense of self a woman may draw from her role as mother. The situation for women in probation hostels can sometimes be more difficult than for those in prison because, although in a hostel women are not physically prevented from leaving the institution during the daytime, due to the exceptionally small numbers of such institutions women often find themselves hundreds of miles away from home and thus visits may be less frequent than they would expect if in custody.

In addition to the problem of potentially over-glamorising or under-estimating the difficulties faced by women in prison, the identification of the endorsement of dominant discourses (such as those around motherhood for example) as a means of resistance is itself a contentious issue. As Cooper (1995) asks, what is it about such behaviour that identifies it as resistance? Who acknowledges these acts as a means of resistance? Is the woman herself conscious of her resistance and does the dominant institution have to recognise it as resistance for an act to be such? Incarcerated women endorsing idealised images of motherhood could be seen as simple acquiescence to, and more significantly as a 'success' for, the feminising regimes of the institutional regime. It will be argued in Chapter Six that although on occasions the endorsement of dominant discourses by institutionalised women can actually promote the very regime they seek to resist, such behaviour can still be regarded as resistance as it allocates women with a measure of resilience to, and a means of withstanding, the often crushing forces of control they are subjected to.

So to conclude, I have argued that women have historically been subjected to a whole range of regulating, pathologising discourses based around idealised notions of femininity, domesticity, respectability, motherhood and sexuality. In addition, these discourses have been, and still are, utilised in the regulation and control of women, both formally and informally. However, I have also shown that women do not always willingly accept these regulatory discourses nor do they always submit to the forces of social control. Rather they are able to utilise a range of strategies that allow them the opportunities to resist the oppressive regimes enforced upon them.

What this chapter has established is a theoretical framework regarding the continuum of control methods used to deal with 'deviant' women and the various strategies used by women to resist or reject that control. This framework of analysis can now be applied to an examination of the semi-penal institutionalisation of women over the past 200 years.

Notes

[1]   See also Harris and Webb (1987) for a discussion of how historically the formal methods of both punishment and welfare for women have been bound up with the methods of punishment and welfare for children.

[2]   It should also be acknowledged that, due to the nature of conventional definitions of and attitudes towards the concept of masculinity, defining what is 'deviant' and what is simply an extension of 'normal' male behaviour can also be difficult.

[3]   See also Smart and Smart 1978; Hutter and Williams, 1981; Carlen, 1983; Carlen and Worrall, 1987; French, 1992; Ballinger, 1996, for discussions of the way in which women's extreme or even violent behaviour can be rationalised and understood as long as it is explained through acceptable modes of expression.

[4]   The term 'lenient' is of course highly debatable. Often sentences that are commonly assumed to be 'lenient' (eg. those that include psychiatric or medical intervention or other forms of 'treatment') are indeterminate and thus can be more intensive, regulatory and oppressive than a determinate custodial sentence. It should also be acknowledged here that the discussion which follows does not mean to infer that that all women who commit minor offences are treated more severely than those who commit more serious offences. The intention is to indicate the often excessive extent to which extra-legal factors contribute to the judicial decision making process with regard to women defendants. The comparison between the treatment of minor offenders and more serious offenders is simply to highlight this issue more dramatically.

[5]   Also for further discussion on the extent to which demeanour and behaviour in court can influence the way in which women defendants are perceived and dealt with, see Ballinger's (1996) account of the trials of Ruth Ellis and Marie Fahmy.

[6]   Many women offenders, of course, do not benefit from this ideal of women as domesticated, respectable wives and mothers. This is apparent by the fact that the female prison population has increased dramatically in recent years.

[7]   The second quotation at the beginning of Chapter One highlights this point significantly.

[8]   It should be acknowledged here that although regulation and reform was high on the agenda of many philanthropic groups, from a feminist perspective one should not simply dismiss the, often pioneering, efforts of many charitable workers such as Eleanor Rathbone and Josephine Butler.

[9]   See also Evers' (1981) account of the way in which female nurses maintain a sense of social distance from their patients in order to adequately perform their controlling tasks.

[10]   For extensive discussion of the utilisation of Foucauldian theory and the development of resistance as a concept in feminist theory, see Weedon, 1987; Faith, 1994; Cooper, 1995.

[11]   For a further discussion of women's invisibility in historical records as a methodological issue see Barton (2001).

Chapter 3

'Wayward Girls and Wicked Women'[1]: The History and Development of the Semi-Penal Institution

The unruly woman is the undisciplined woman. She is a renegade from the disciplinary practices which would mould her as a gendered being. She is the defiant woman who rejects authority which would subjugate her and render her docile. She is the offensive woman who acts in her own interests. She is the unmanageable woman who claims her own body, the whore, the wanton woman, the wild woman out of control. She is the woman who cannot be silenced. She is a rebel. She is trouble (Faith, 1993:1).

As discussed in the previous chapter, women are deemed to be 'deviant' or 'unruly' for many different reasons. Consequently, they are subjected to a whole range of strategies, applied within both formal and informal arenas of social control, all of which are designed to regulate, discipline and reform these recalcitrant women back to an appropriate standard of feminine behaviour. It is the purpose of this chapter to critically examine the history and development of one particular arena of social control, an arena which combined both formal and informal strategies of discipline and regulation, an arena which Weiner (1990) described as semi-penal. Weiner uses the term semi-penal to define those institutions created during the nineteenth century for the purpose of containing, controlling and reforming 'deviant' individuals (particularly women and juveniles). The focus of this book is specifically the use of semi-penal institutions for women and Weiner's definition will therefore be utilised in this context. I will, however, argue that such institutions originated in the eighteenth century, somewhat earlier than Weiner suggests. In addition, I propose that such institutions continued to exist, in one form or another, throughout the twentieth century, much later than he claims.[2]

In this chapter I will examine the genesis and development of these institutions, analysing the methods and discourses employed to regulate and reform their female residents. A specific focus will be on the way in which these institutions united the formal control strategies of the prison with the more informal methods of social and domestic control found within the family and the home.

Semi-penal institutions in the eighteenth and nineteenth centuries existed under a variety of names (for example asylums, refuges, reformatories and homes), names which in many ways conjure up images of care, sanctuary and welfare and thus detract from their other, more regulative and punitive purposes. These institutions catered for a variety of different 'types' of women, all of who were perceived to be in some way dangerous or unruly, all of who had broken away from the boundaries of appropriate female behaviour. Such women included convicted offenders, prostitutes, inebriates, the 'feeble minded' and others who, it was believed, required a form of *preventative* regulation and guidance to stop them from straying into a life of crime of vice. However, the concept of semi-penal institutionalisation did not disappear with the demise of the reformatory movement. As I will illustrate, semi-penal institutions continued to exist for women into and throughout the twentieth century in the form of halfway houses, homes for unmarried mothers and, most recently, probation hostels.

Fragile Moralities: The Characteristics of the Semi-Penal Institution

The first, and one of the most significant, characteristics of the institutions created to reform deviant women was that they were essentially outside of state control (as, indeed, were prisons for much of the nineteenth century), set up by private organisations or charitable agencies and run by self elected management committees. In some instances the state did play a role in the creation or supervision of these institutions. The Inebriates Act (1898), for example, provided for the creation of certified and state reformatories to supplement the voluntary institutions already in existence (Zedner 1991) and for some years there had existed government-appointed HM Inspectors of Reformatories (Rimmer, 1986). However, for the most part, the various semi-penal institutions (whether they be for 'fallen', criminal, wayward or 'feeble minded' women) were private organisations, housed in privately owned buildings, run and managed by non-statutory bodies (for example the Temperance Society or one of the various Gentlemen's and Ladies Charitable Organisations) and therefore almost completely beyond the reach of state regulation.

Second, as they were not officially custodial and were thus very separate from the formal judicial system, most admissions were classed as voluntary. So women were not (at least in some of the early institutions) *sentenced* to a period of residence in refuges or reformatories, instead their consent was required before they could be admitted. Indeed, most institutions would only accept women who were desirous of being reformed and therefore *keen* to be admitted (Mahood, 1990). Given that these institutions were usually funded by charitable donations, some level of effectiveness and success had to be achieved. It was therefore necessary to ensure that only those women likely to conform and reform be admitted and this was accomplished through strict gatekeeping procedures.

Also as Finnegan (1979) states, women had to be consenting, compliant and co-operative in order for these establishments to function effectively, as being non-statutory they had no power to confine women against their will. However, as Dobash *et al* (1986) point out, women were frequently pressured into giving their consent to a period of residence through a network of influence which included family, friends, reformers, charity workers, police, court officials, clergy and prison staff. Also, often women would agree to be admitted to these institutions, and consequently conform to their regimes, because the alternatives (or potential alternatives) presented to them were so appalling (Rimmer, 1986). Young women labelled as 'immoral', for example, might be willing to submit to a period of semi-penal confinement as they would be made well aware that if they were to become pregnant they stood a fair chance of being forcibly admitted, as were many unmarried mothers, to a 'lunatic' asylum as long term inmates. Likewise, 'wayward' girls in danger of falling foul of the law would be regularly reminded about the severe conditions in local prisons, Bridewells and Borough Gaols.

Not all admissions were voluntary however, as specific pieces of legislation meant some women could be sent by the courts to particular institutions. For example, the Inebriates Act (1898) allowed for women to be committed by the courts to a specified period in an inebriate reformatory (Zedner, 1991). Also, after the passing of the Probation of Offenders Act of 1907, young women could be referred by the courts to a refuge or reformatory as a condition of their probation order. These institutions, although slightly different to the traditional 'voluntary' reformatories, will still be discussed and analysed here as semi-penal as they were portrayed as non-custodial institutions or 'alternatives' to prison and they still employed regimes based more around reformation than punishment. Consequently, these institutions occupied an important place within the ever-expanding network of non-custodial, semi-penal control of women.

Third, although these institutions were not fully custodial or penal in the formal sense, they were not truly 'community-based' either. In fact, for the most part, once a woman had entered a reformatory, refuge or home, contact with her former 'community' was limited, if not prohibited completely. The aim of these institutions was to provide women with a positive and appropriate role model, and therefore other external influences were kept to a minimum. If a woman had deviated from the norm within her own 'community' then any continued influence from that community was not considered conducive to her reformation. Contact with 'respectable' family members could be maintained (if deemed appropriate) through letters and visits, although these were usually infrequent and heavily monitored (Rimmer, 1986). Women would be allowed occasional contact with the outside world, usually in the form of organised day trips, church visits or for the purposes of employment, although, as will be discussed more fully in this and the next chapter, it was more common for religious worship and instruction, and even paid work, to be conducted on the premises. The female residents of these institutions may not have been formally incarcerated but their liberty was certainly heavily restricted. They were required to conform to a disciplinary and regulatory regime and their behaviour and movements were supervised and monitored. Many of the practices employed within the prison could be observed within these non-custodial environments.

This leads to the fourth defining characteristic. The semi-penal institution combined those formal regulatory practices, normally restricted to the prison, with a more informal, 'benign' form of discipline reminiscent of that employed within the domestic sphere. The reformation of women, it was believed, could be best achieved through a disciplinary process modelled around that which existed within the family. Rules were enforced by those in charge, usually either an unmarried female matron or a married couple. These individuals would act as appropriate role model figures for the impressionable inmates, providing the sort of maternal/parental discipline that was considered to have been missing from the women's home lives. Respectable working class women were the ideal choice to oversee these institutions, and they, in turn, were governed by a (usually male and middle class) management committee. These women were not only positive role models but they were also 'matron-mother' figures (Rafter, 1983) who could enforce discipline and encourage conformity under the guise of maternal 'protection', similar in many ways to the socialising of daughters by mothers within the family, or what Walkowitz (1982) describes as the 'hierarchical female network'.

The fifth feature which distinguished these institutions as semi-penal, was the fact that they did not deal solely with women who had committed criminal offences. Fitting in securely with eighteenth and nineteenth century notions of unacceptable female behaviour, the reformers targeted a whole range of women who had failed to adhere to, or achieve, required standards of behaviour. Consequently, non-criminal women (for example those considered to be immoral, wayward or 'at risk') were problematised as in need of reform and could be institutionalised in order for this process to take place. As Weiner (1990) asserts semi-penal institutions were considered to be for the purposes of 'protecting' women by offering an alternative to, or impeding the progress towards, imprisonment. However, in reality they served to extend those disciplinary measures normally confined to the prison to cases of 'less-than-full criminality' (Weiner, 1990: 130).

Although the reformist movement claimed that its intention was to 'protect' and rescue women from the brutality of prison and the criminal justice system, the ascendancy and consolidation of the semi-penal project had the effect of expanding what was already a fairly encompassing system of social control and regulation for working class women. Dobash *et al* conclude that

> These refuges, reformatories and shelters were not necessarily penal, but what they established was a wide, interlocking carceral network, based on the assumption that females needed a firm paternalistic hand to guide their development (1986: 72).

The concept of reform (like the twentieth century concept of rehabilitation) is rooted in the notion that the individual requiring such treatment is suffering from some fundamental weakness or deficiency and this can only be remedied through external help (Faith, 1993; Worrall, 1997), hence the concept of supervision. I will argue in the following chapters that the supervisory processes employed within semi-penal institutions (based around the notion of 'parental' discipline) resulted in, what Faith (1993) and Carlen (1983) have termed, the 'infantilisation' of the female residents. Women have always been perceived as immature and puerile (Hutter and Williams, 1981) and nowhere has this been more strongly reflected than in the regimes created to discipline and reform 'deviant' women. As Rafter (1983) observed, women within such institutions were frequently reduced to the status of dependent children and denied the rights that non-incarcerated females, or even incarcerated males, took for granted. [3]

So, from the late eighteenth century women's lives and behaviour became increasingly open to scrutiny and many different 'types' of women were defined by social commentators and targeted by reformers and charity workers as in need of discipline and reform. I will now provide an examination of the specific semi-penal institutions that were created from the late eighteenth century through to the early twentieth century for the purposes of controlling and reforming unruly women. Five groups of women have been identified for the purpose of this analysis; prostitutes, criminals, the 'wayward', inebriates and the 'feeble minded', and the particular institutions created to cater for each of these groups will be examined in turn. It should be acknowledged here though that such differentiation is problematic for two reasons. First, some women cannot be confined to one 'category'. Prostitutes, for example, were often labelled as alcoholics (and vice-versa) and, due to the nature of the law, criminals as well. Second, some semi-penal institutions catered for more than one 'type' of woman. Often, in order to remain financially viable, the nature of these institutions changed over time and they often targeted different types of women at different periods in their history. Nonetheless, in order to provide some form of chronological examination, and in order to highlight the wide range of institutions created to increase the social control of women, this categorisation will be employed as an organising principle on which to build the analysis.

Semi-Penal Institutions of the Eighteenth and Nineteenth Centuries

Institutions for 'immoral' women

Of all the women who have been targeted by social and religious commentators or charitable and philanthropic groups and reformers, prostitutes have historically been the focus of particular scrutiny. Prostitutes, more than any other 'type' of women, were considered to be morally corrupting and responsible for the spread of vice amongst the respectable poor. They were perceived to be a considerable threat to the notions of the traditional patriarchal family by posing an unwanted temptation to husbands and sons (Mahood, 1990). Immorality was, and it could be argued still is, believed to be the worst form of deviance in women.

Because of the perceived fragility of female morality and the growing associations between sexual activity and moral decay, moral reformers towards the end of the eighteenth and beginning of the nineteenth century, were becoming increasingly critical of the effectiveness of custodial institutions with regards to their appropriateness for female inmates. There was growing concern that impressionable young women, particularly those charged with offences relating to sexual misconduct, required a separate environment in which they could be reformed and disciplined to adhere to appropriate standards of behaviour (Mahood, 1990). This would not be achieved in an institution where they could mix freely with other, more 'hardened' and corrupting offenders.

Consequently, prostitutes were the first group of women to become subjected to semi-penal institutionalisation (See Mahood, 1990; Lindfield, 1992; Dobash *et al*, 1986). Towards the end of the eighteenth century new non-statutory, non-custodial female penitentiaries were established where women could be 'voluntarily' admitted (although often for indefinite periods) and receive moral education along with industrial and / or domestic training. These institutions existed under a variety of names but were most commonly known as Magdalene Homes or Asylums.

The sexual 'deviance' of women was at first dealt with through the formation of the Lock Hospitals. There existed both statutory and voluntary Lock Hospitals and although they were not semi-penal institutions in the same sense as the Magdalene Homes, because their primary role was the provision of medical treatment for women with syphilis and other venereal diseases (Lindfield, 1992), they are worth some mention here as they constituted part of a wider network of sexual and moral regulation for women during the eighteenth and nineteenth centuries. Significantly, the term 'lock' originated from the word 'loke' which was a house for lepers. Mahood (1990) states that the Lock Hospitals gained their name because the first one opened in Southwark, London on the site of a medieval leper house however, as Walkowitz (1980) comments, there is another significance to the adoption of this name, as prostitutes were considered to be the 'social lepers' of the eighteenth and nineteenth centuries. She states that during this period

> ....syphilis replaced leprosy as the symbol of social contagion and disease (Walkowitz, 1980: 59).

As Mahood (1990) points out the Lock Hospitals were heavily criticised by religious fundamentalists who felt that such institutions would fail in their attempts to 'cure' women as they only focused on medical remedies for the body. What was required to complement this was some provision to restore and rehabilitate the mind and soul, an establishment that could provide moral reform and would thus prevent women returning to 'immoral' practices on their discharge from hospital. It was therefore decided that some further provision in the form of a home or penitentiary where the moral character of the woman could be rescued and reformed be provided, and the Magdalene Homes were the result.

The voluntary Magdalene Homes were usually private, charitable institutions and like many of the other types of semi-penal institution, were aimed at rescuing young women who were not yet too 'hardened' to be reclaimed and reformed.

Women were expected to be grateful for the opportunity afforded them by the Magdalene institutions and anxious to repent of their past sins. As stated above, the success of these voluntary institutions depended heavily upon the co-operation of their female inmates and so admittance could be refused to those women who did not appear susceptible to reforming influence or sincere in their wish to improve their lives. Hence for the most part the main pre-requisites for admission were a demonstration of remorse for previous conduct and a sincere intention to reform to the middle class standards of femininity endorsed by the institutions (Finnegan, 1979; Mahood, 1990). For example, in 1809 a Magdalene Home (known as the Female Penitentiary) was established in Liverpool, its purpose being

> ....to afford an asylum to females who, having deviated from the paths of virtue, are *desirous of being restored*, by religious instruction and the formation of moral and industrious habits, to a respectable station in society (Smithers, 1825: 279. Emphasis added).

This transformation from immorality to respectability was to be achieved through a strict regime of industrial and / or domestic training and moral and religious education, a disciplinary routine consisting of work, prayer and penitence (Walkowitz, 1980). In her study of the nineteenth century Albion Reformatory in New York, Rafter explains that this institution used moral and domestic training in order to increase the social control of young working class women in two distinct, but 'mutually reinforcing' (1983: 291) ways. First, she claims, Albion provided vocational control over its inmates by training them to become wives, mothers or domestic servants. Second, it provided sexual control over the women by training them to conform to middle class notions of chastity, respectability and femininity, all the time reinforcing the virtues of marriage and fidelity.[4] Although Rafter is discussing a reformatory in the late nineteenth century, and one which dealt with all types of 'young misdemeanants' (1983: 289) not just prostitutes, her analysis can be applied to the early nineteenth century Magdalene Homes. The combination of domestic and moral training was aimed at making women productive (as wives, mothers, servants or legitimate workers) and non-threatening (chaste, respectable, married). Women were expected to become self-sufficient, dependable, wholesome and harmless. As the governors of the London Female Penitentiary for prostitutes commented, the aim of the institution was

> ....to destroy the habits of idleness and vice and to substitute those of honest and profitable industry, thus benefiting society whilst the individual is restored (in Dobash *et al*, 1986: 73).

Institutions for 'guilty' women

Given the high standards of behaviour that were set for women during the nineteenth century, it is not surprising that those women who had transgressed legal, as well as moral, boundaries were considered more deviant and more morally corrupting than their male counterparts. As Dobash *et al* (1986) comment, male offenders who had served a prison sentence were either released unconditionally or released on licence, but either way they were allowed to return directly to their communities. However, for women, the completion of a prison sentence did not necessarily qualify them for social re-integration. Instead, some women were subjected to an 'intermediate period of confinement' (Dobash *et al*, 1986: 72) after their official prison sentence had ended.

Weiner (1990) cites two major institutions that were built for the reception of women leaving prison, these being the Fulham Refuge in England and the Golden Bridge Reformatory in Dublin, Ireland. Women entered these institutions as a condition of their early release from gaol and once there they would be discharged only when 'judged reformed' (Weiner, 1990: 140). The female superintendent of the Golden Bridge Reformatory (cited in Dobash *et al*, 1986: 75) justified the utility of these institutions, arguing that women offenders required longer periods of detention than their male counterparts because they were more difficult to reform than men. This statement does appear to conflict with the dominant ideas of the day which proclaimed that women were *more* impressionable and hence *more* reformable than men. However, offending behaviour was not as incongruous with nineteenth century notions of masculinity as it was with the dominant ideas around femininity. Therefore, unlike male offenders, for whom a single punitive sentence was sufficient, female offenders were perceived to be in need of something more than punishment for their offences, they required a further process of moral rehabilitation before they were fully reformed.

The superintendent goes on to argue that after release from prison men would usually undertake outside employment, whereas women would be occupied within the domestic sphere (either in their own homes or as a domestic servant in the homes of other people). Consequently, given the high level of responsibility required to run their own, or other people's homes, a longer period of 'training and testing' was required (Dobash *et al*, 1986: 75). Finally, she asserted that female offenders were inherently inadequate and deficient, and so before they could be reformed and retrained, they first required a period where they could be 'untrained' and thus 'unlearn' their bad behaviour.

So, these institutions, with their reformist regimes, were developed to 'supplement and in part replace the work of jails and prisons' (Weiner, 1990: 131). Their regimes and routines were similar to those in the Magdalene Homes, and many other types of semi-penal institutions throughout the nineteenth century. Although sent from prison, women would only be admitted if first, they had a genuine 'desire to reform' and second, if there was some likelihood of reformation being achieved. As with the Magdalene Homes, many women would be deemed unsuitable for admission to these refuges if they were believed to be 'hardened' criminals and therefore beyond hope of reformation.

The regimes of these institutions were primarily based on training and moral reform. Women were isolated from the world outside and provided with a positive role model, usually in the form of a 'matron-mother' figure. However, these 'post-prison' refuges differed from other types of semi-penal institution in one significant way in that they had an extra element of threat due to the fact that they could return women to prison at any time. Although these refuges were technically 'voluntary' institutions, their operation did not depend completely upon the co-operation of their inmates in quite the same way as Magdalene Homes or other types of 'pre-prison' institution. Women were under real pressure to behave and conform or face a return to custody.

Institutions for 'wayward' women

In contrast to those women who were sent to reformatories *after* they had served a sentence in prison, many young women and girls were institutionalised without ever having committed a criminal offence at all. One of the most common types of establishment within this network of control was that which aimed to 'rescue' females *in danger of becoming* criminal or immoral. As stated previously, during the nineteenth century, women were considered 'childlike' and immature, and their good behaviour required constant reinforcement and supervision. Their fragile characters could be easily corrupted through contact with undesirable associates and so prison was deemed particularly unsuitable for their delicate moral states. Subjecting women to a system of reform after they had been in prison was not thought to be appropriate for many women as by then the damage may have already been done. Instead what was required for some girls and women was a period of reform aimed at *preventing* their certain degeneration into a life of crime or sin.

This preventative work could not be achieved whilst women were allowed to continue their normal daily lives and their association with undesirable acquaintances and so the creation of rescue homes and reformatories became popular philanthropic projects (Lindfield, 1992). As stated previously, women during the nineteenth century were perceived to be both 'corruptible' and 'corrupting', 'in danger' and 'dangerous' at the same time. Consequently, 'wayward' girls and women were not admitted to these homes for purely philanthropic reasons, instead corrective training was required in order to reduce the threat that these working class women (and 'immoral' working class women in particular) posed to middle class sensibilities. This is highlighted in the emotive language used to describe the young female residents of the Mount Vernon Green and Toxteth Park Girls' Reformatories in Liverpool.

> The girls are taken from a class which is familiar with criminal practice and immoral living. The life, from day to day, under the discipline of the [institutions]….gives evidence of what lies beneath the surface, and of the strong passions more or less kept under control. During the past year there have been outbreaks of evil tendency and inclinations reverting to acts of theft, lying, disobedience, rudeness and impropriety... .To raise such a class from the depth of depravity and utter neglect in which they have been sunk is indeed a work of Christian charity and mercy; but it is one of labour and difficulty, and only a certain amount of success can be anticipated (Major Inglis, HM Inspector of Reformatories, 1880, quoted in Rimmer, 1986: 45).

The purpose of these institutions was to offer the moral training and conditions for reform that impressionable young women would not find in their communities and homes. Indeed, women were most commonly committed to these institutions by their own husbands or families if they were believed to be 'out of control'.

Once a woman entered such an institution her period of residence would depend primarily on her assessed character and she would not be released until judged reformed. In reality though, these rescue homes did not have the coercive powers of the reformatories for women released from prison and so could not officially hold women and girls against their will. Indeed, more than any other type of semi-penal institution, these homes relied considerably upon the co-operation of their inmates for their effective operation. In addition, they relied on the industry of their inmates for their financial survival. For the most part these institutions were funded by charitable donations but many had to find other ways of supplementing their income. Dobash *et al* (1986) cite the Dean Bank refuge in Scotland. This institution took in washing and ironing for local families, charging a nominal sum. By doing this it could not only provide productive domestic training for its inmates but it could also pay for the running of the institution. This form of 'training' however was hard, laborious and often dangerous. Rimmer describes the hazardous conditions faced by the young inmates of the School for Delinquent Girls at Ford.

> Work in the laundry was like slavery, with limited and defective equipment in appalling conditions... .All the water....had to be heated, and this operation resulted in horrendous accidents, scalds and burns... .In December 1873 a piece of soap slipped down the back of the copper and whilst trying to retrieve it [one of the inmates] stood upon the pieces of loose wood which covered the boiler. The wood cracked and the screaming girl plunged into the boiling water, scalding her legs.... [she] died the next day from shock... .The floor of the laundry was constantly awash and there were many instances of girls and staff slipping and breaking limbs. Harsh soap peeled the skin from chilblained hands and the dark, foul atmosphere and searing fumes took their toll on constitutionally weakened lungs and rheumaticky limbs (1986: 53).

Like the Magdalene Homes and the 'post-prison' reformatories, the regimes of these institutions were based around 'family-style' discipline. As Lindfield (1992) comments, they provided a form of regulation, for working class girls and women, that their middle class and 'respectable' working class sisters received at home. This was mainly achieved through constructive training, however in contrast to the industrial or manufacturing work undertaken in some reformatories and many prisons, in the rescue institutions women were trained primarily in household and domestic skills. As well as laundry work (washing and ironing) women were trained to sew, weave, knit (often mending and making their own clothes), cook and clean (see Dobash *et al*, 1986; Rimmer, 1986). These institutions were effectively schools for servants (Dobash *et al*, 1986). Of course the inmates were also subjected to a process of moral training. If they were to enter middle class homes as domestic servants they would need to meet the required standards of decency and respectability. The desired result of the reform process in these institutions therefore was the same as that within the Magdalene Homes, in that the young inmates would become not only non-threatening to the middle class but a productive source of labour for them too.

The institutions I have discussed so far existed throughout the nineteenth century, with some continuing into the early twentieth century. The institutions which catered for the two other groups of women highlighted at the beginning of this chapter (inebriates and the 'feeble-minded') did not emerge until the late nineteenth century and, in comparison to the other types of semi-penal institution, were relatively short lived. They are discussed below.

Institutions for 'drunken' women

From the early part of the nineteenth century, alcohol was considered to be a severe social problem. It is not surprising then that a strong association should have been made by the 'respectable classes' between poverty, escalating crime and excessive drinking. Contemporary observers tendered a plethora of 'cause and effect' opinions to account for this phenomenon and to many, the conditions experienced by the poor were seen to be a direct result of their excessive consumption of alcohol. Consequently, bars and pubs were seen to be the breeding ground for evil and criminality.

> The tavern throughout the centuries has been the ante-chamber to the workhouse, the chapel of ease to the asylum, the recruiting station for the hospital, the rendezvous of the gambler, the gathering ground for the jail (Burns, 1904, quoted in Loweson and Myerscough, 1977: 67).

These assumptions were believed to be especially true where women were concerned. Women were considered to be more susceptible to the corrupting effects of alcohol than men and, because of their accepted status as family makers, they were condemned more fiercely. Shimmin refers to the female clientele of the nineteenth century dancing halls as being 'in their transition state from virtue to vice' (1856: 53). He goes on to observe that

> A girl may come here innocent and chaste, but after spending an evening in such company she cannot leave without contamination. From this point the descent is rapid, easily made; the return is doubtful, and seldom, if ever, effected (1856: 53)

Family life and social stability were perceived to be severely threatened by female alcoholism. As Zedner (1991) explains, fears that society was degenerating through hereditary drunkenness led to an increasing focus on women as the agents responsible for these problems. Female alcoholics were considered to be dangerous individuals responsible for the destitution and suffering of their children. A commentary in the *Liverpool Review* recounts the popular feeling of the period.

> No form of domestic misery is more hopeless and few more frequent than that caused by the intemperance of a mother (1899: 11).

In addition, women were often held accountable for the corruption and moral deterioration of their husbands.

> Sometimes husbands, far from selfishly squandering the family income, came home to find that their wife had drunk away the furniture....even where....male selfishness did exist, there were good reasons for it (Harrison, 1971: 69).

Furthermore, they were even sometimes believed to be responsible for the downfall of whole communities.

> One drunken woman in a street will set all the women in it drinking. A woman is so often talking with her neighbours; if she drinks they will go with her (Booth, 1970, quoted in Hunt, Mellor and Turner, 1989: 249).

As Zedner explains, it is in fact very difficult to get a true picture of the actual, rather than perceived, extent of female alcoholism during this period in history. However, she does state that during the nineteenth century the largest category of summary convictions for both sexes was for drunkenness and it accounted for a greater proportion of female convictions than for male convictions. Nonetheless, such statistics do need to be approached with caution, as they do not necessarily indicate a widespread problem of female intemperance. Rather, it is likely that women were more prone to arrest than men when inebriated because drunkenness represented such an aberration from 'appropriate' feminine behaviour. Drunkenness amongst men, on the other hand, was likely to give validity to nineteenth century notions of masculinity. Thus, as Harrison (1971) notes, statistics showing rising numbers of arrests were probably not a reflection of increasing alcohol consumption and related crime. Instead what they were more likely to reflect, especially towards the end of the nineteenth century, was a growing fear of, and intolerance towards, drinking and drunkenness, especially amongst women.

Whatever the extent of female inebriety, female drinking and drunkenness were certainly considered to be growing social problems, problems that required urgent remedy and this remedy came in the form of the 1898 Inebriates Act. The Act focused on two main groups, these being habitual drunkards and those who had committed serious criminal offences whilst inebriated (Zedner, 1991) and it allowed for individuals to be committed to an inebriate reformatory for a period of up to three years, in order that they might overcome their addiction and hence reform their lives. According to Zedner, many magistrates believed that the Act was more appropriate to women than men, and consequently they were more willing to detain women in these institutions. The Medical Officer of Millbank Prison encapsulated these common sense assumptions when he stated that some women, including those convicted of drunkenness, required

....not only preventive, but protective detention in some kind of institution other than a prison for a much longer period than any term of penal sentence their offences would justify (Quinton quoted in Sim, 1990: 137).

A Departmental Committee established after the 1898 Act, determined that the inebriate institutions would aim to reform, not punish, inmates and therefore they should not be used for punitive purposes (Zedner, 1991). This was not always adhered to and there are examples of harsh punishments being enforced on recalcitrant women within these institutions. Reports indicate that women at the Farmfield Inebriate Reformatory in Surrey could be confined in cells for periods of up to six days for offences ranging from violence to bad language or attempting to escape (Hunt *et al*, 1989: 263). This method of control stands in sharp contrast to the 'family-style' discipline that was also employed within the institution. The staff, for example, were known as 'sisters', implying a regime based on empathy and support. However, regardless of the implication, the fact that the women within the inebriate reformatories had been *committed* there meant that the regime was in a sense more penal than in any other type of semi-penal institution.

The aim of the inebriate reformatories was to effect long term changes in the behaviour and lives of their inmates and, as with the institutions already discussed, this was to be achieved through regular hard work and religious and moral training. Hunt *et al* (1989) discuss the regime at the Farmfield institution, where women worked for eight hours per day on a variety of tasks including laundry work, general domestic chores or farmwork (the institution having its own farm and dairy). Even recreation time was filled with domestic tasks such as sewing and making clothes. In addition to domestic and moral training, a degree of importance was placed on the physical appearance of the women inmates. The emphasis on encouraging the women to take an interest in their hair and clothing, according to Zedner, served several functions. First, it outwardly portrayed an improvement in physical and moral health. Second, an improvement in outward appearance was seen to encourage a degree of self-esteem and self-respect and, third, possibly the most significant purpose was that

> Such superficial alterations to appearance were clearly seen as reflective of a more profound feminization of character (Zedner, 1991: 242).

Once women had served their sentence they were released. Some women were released on licence a short time before their sentence officially ended. This allowed the institution to maintain some element of control over the women once they re-entered the community and any woman found to be inebriated whilst on this conditional release would be immediately returned to the reformatory to complete the remainder of her sentence (Zedner, 1991). The inebriate reformatory differed from the other types of semi-penal institution due to this element of continued supervision after release. Farmfield employed a 'travelling sister' to monitor and report on the progress of women once they re-entered the community. Records from the institution appear to indicate only a limited amount of success with accounts of women returning to drinking as soon as they returned home (Hunt *et al*, 1989).

However, it was not solely lack of success that led to the demise of the inebriate reformatory movement. Understandings of, and explanations for, inebriety had begun to change. Whereas at the start of the experiment it was believed that drunkards could be *morally* cured and reformed, by the end of the experiment this moral discourse had been largely supplanted by a 'pseudo-psychiatric discourse' (Zedner, 1991: 260) and those drinkers who had once been considered morally depraved were now believed to be mentally inadequate. By the early years of the twentieth century, feeble-mindedness was considered a *cause* rather than a *consequence* of inebriety and these explanations were utilised particularly when explaining women's behaviour. During the nineteenth century women had already been perceived as neurotic and over-emotional (Showalter, 1981, 1987) and so these new psychiatric discourses were quickly accepted as unproblematic when discussing deviant or drunken women.

The medicalisation of drunkenness meant that the inebriate reformatories no longer had a legitimate role in society. As inebriates were now considered to be feeble-minded rather than morally corrupt there was little, or no, hope of their reformation and the reformatories thus became redundant. However, the 'discovery' of feeble mindedness as an explanation for behaviour did not spell the end of semi-penal incarceration for women. Instead, as the discussion below will highlight, 'mad' women became subjected to the forms of control and regulation that had previously been employed with 'bad' women.

Institutions for 'mad' women

The end of the nineteenth century was a time of increasing social concern and fear of intemperance, moral degeneration and the prevalence of petty crime. In accordance with these growing concerns, criminology at the beginning of the twentieth century was dominated by attempts to identify the causal factors of criminal behaviour and increasing credibility was given to emerging positivistic theories. Consequently, criminal behaviour became individualised and pathologised and the positivistic paradigm gave credence to an increasing amount of psychological and social intervention by scientific 'experts'. Deterministic theories legitimated methods of sentencing that focused on the criminal rather than the crime (May, 1991; Harris, 1995).

Poverty, intemperance and crime, which had previously been blamed on the lack of morality amongst the poor, were, by this time, beginning to be seen as the result of mental inadequacy. The eugenics movement proclaimed that these social deficiencies would be 'bred' into future generations by the mentally defective poor if left unchecked and accordingly 'feeble-mindedness' became viewed as a dangerous social condition.

'Deviant' working class women became particular targets for the attention of the eugenics movement. By the early twentieth century, sexual promiscuity was considered to be evidence of mental inadequacy[5] and it was argued that if these socially inept, promiscuous women were allowed to retain their liberty, they would procreate freely and cause the degeneration of the race (Zedner, 1991). It was imperative therefore, to contain, control and, hopefully 'cure' these women and to achieve this, special reformatories were developed. These new specialist, non-custodial institutions claimed to have supplanted the notion of moral reformation and instead focused on the medical treatment of inmates.

Showalter (1981) has commented that women constituted a high proportion of inmates within all types of public and private institutions for the 'mentally defective', including reformatories, 'lunatic' asylums, homes and hospitals. She suggests that women were certified as insane or feeble-minded much more readily than men and often for very trivial reasons such as perceived promiscuity or dominant, assertive behaviour.

The Mental Deficiency Act of 1913 required local authorities to establish committees that would provide community and institutional 'care' and support for the various categories of mental defectives as defined by the Act. These included the feeble-minded, idiots, imbeciles and moral imbeciles. This classification of madness served to expand the concept of mentally inadequate to a whole range of individuals including the poor, inebriates, offenders, pregnant or promiscuous girls and single mothers, considerably widening the regulatory net for women (Ussher, 1991; Zedner, 1991).

Zedner comments that although the 1913 Act emerged from the new scientific theories which explained deviant behaviour as a consequence of pathological, rather than moral, deficiencies, where women were concerned the two discourses were never entirely separate. As I will argue in subsequent chapters, for institutionalised women, the notion of moral reform was never entirely abandoned. Instead, the new psycho-medical theories and discourses served mainly to justify, legitimate and reinforce the ever-present moral expectations of women.

The first half of the twentieth century saw the demise of institutions for the 'feeble-minded' as well as institutions such as the Magdalene Homes for immoral women, the refuges for 'wayward' girls, and the reformatories for inebriates. However, many of the fundamental concepts which underpinned the reformatory movement persisted and were apparent in the rise of other semi-penal institutions during the twentieth century.

The following section of this chapter will identify three types of twentieth century institution as semi-penal: homes for unmarried mothers, halfway houses for delinquent girls and finally, and most pertinent to this study, probation hostels for women.

Semi-Penal Institutions of the Twentieth Century

Institutions for unmarried mothers

> ....on the whole, morality as regards women has nothing to do with ethics; it means sexual morality and nothing but sexual morality.... .This means it is far easier for a

woman to lead a blameless life than it is for a man. All she has to do is avoid sexual intercourse like the plague (Carter, 1986: x).

One of the major themes which has emerged from this chapter so far is the threat that those women who have outstepped their traditional domestic and maternal roles have been seen to pose. Women's sexuality and sexual behaviour have historically been considered dangerous and contaminating unless controlled within the confines of marriage and domesticity. Consequently, women who indulged in sexual activity outside of those confines were in need of urgent regulation.

Spensky states that until very recently unmarried mothers were considered to be the 'delinquents of gender relations' (1992: 101). During the nineteenth century women who bore illegitimate children often found themselves in the workhouse or, worse still, in mental hospitals or asylums where, as Rimmer comments, their outcast status meant they were often treated quite differently and more severely than the other inmates.

'Lunatics and Idiots allowed visitors' read the notice posted on the wall. Unmarried mothers were not permitted visitors (1986: 48).

Ideas about women's immorality appeared to alter little between the mid nineteenth and the mid twentieth century. Although women's deviant behaviour became medicalised and pathologised, the discourses of morality never disappeared entirely and were often used in conjunction with the new scientific discourses in the treatment of delinquent women. The first institutions set up specifically to deal with unmarried mothers were opened in the 1860s by the Female Mission (Spensky, 1992). Here women would stay with their children for periods of one to two years. As with the early reformatories, they were expected to repent of their sinful behaviour.

Pregnant and immoral girls were frequently banished to a penitentiary to spend many hours on their knees in devout prayer asking the Lord to forgive the error of their ways (Rimmer, 1986:49).

In addition to the emphasis on penance, women would be trained for employment, most commonly domestic service. Spensky argues that although the main objective underlying the development of these institutions was to reduce the numbers of pregnant girls and unmarried mothers entering the workhouse, this was not their only aim. She states that these homes were utilised as a way of regulating female sexuality and, as Rafter (1983) also comments, as a way of altering the whole way of life of the inmate, transforming them into domesticated, productive workers.

Once an inmate had completed her period of training she would be found employment in order to pay for her child's upkeep. Although the child would be placed with foster parents, contact with the biological mother was strongly encouraged although the primary goal was always to ensure the women did not go on to have more illegitimate children. Homes for unmarried mothers, according to Spensky, remained based around these ideals and regimes until the Second World War, after which time their purpose and philosophies changed dramatically. By the 1950s, unmarried mothers were no longer considered to be solely sinful or foolish, rather they were identified as pathological. However, even during the mid twentieth century, psycho-medical theories were not the sole influence on institutional regimes for women. Rather they worked in conjunction with, and gave some scientific credibility and legitimacy to, the established ideas around respectability and morality. Consequently, as Spensky notes, after the Second World War the institutions for unmarried mothers functioned not to transform the deviant woman into a good mother capable of financially supporting her child, as had been the case previously, but rather to 'correct' or 'legitimate' the situation in a wholly different way. Women entered the homes prior to the birth of their child, after which time they could remain together for only a few weeks. The baby would then be adopted. This process served to reinforce the notions of respectability and the 'normal' family in three ways. First, the 'illegitimate' child would become 'legitimate' by being adopted by a married couple. Second, the married couple would in turn become a proper, well-adjusted family by the addition of a child and thus a childless, but otherwise 'normal', married woman would be provided with the means to fulfil her 'natural' role in life. Finally, the unmarried mother would be 'legitimated' by the removal of the child, thus proving she was not excessively pathologically disturbed for wanting to keep the baby and, indeed, for all intents and purposes, not pathological at all as no one need ever know she had had a child.

In many ways the treatment of unmarried mothers during the twentieth century was depressingly reminiscent of the treatment of prostitutes during the eighteenth and nineteenth centuries. In fact, the term Magdalene Home or Magdalene Laundry was by this time used for those institutions catering for unmarried mothers or sexually promiscuous girls. The dominance and persistence of discourses around sexuality and morality for women in both centuries meant that both unmarried mothers and prostitutes were exposed to intense scrutiny and regulation. Both groups were allocated an outcast status and both were subjected to a combination of moral, social, psychological and medical intervention. This, however, is not the only example of continuity between the semi-penal institutionalisation of women in the nineteenth and twentieth centuries. Just as reformatories had been developed for women released from prison in the nineteenth century, so the halfway house movement was utilised to receive and reform girls and young women on release from custody during the twentieth century.

Institutions for delinquent girls

> The ethos of the halfway houses....have a peculiarly indefinable quality; they are neither like a traditional....institution nor a 'home' (Apte, 1968: 58).

As discussed previously, it was not uncommon for women during the nineteenth century to be admitted to a semi-penal institution, on release from prison, before they could return to their communities. Some 100 years later, during the 1960s, several projects were set up to assist girls and young women on release from custody (Elder, 1972).[6] They aimed to provide an element of support and care, in the form of 'halfway' accommodation, for girls who had been released from borstal but who were 'without intact homes' and the objective was to assist these girls towards independent living (Elder, 1972: 357).[7] The literature on the way in which halfway houses were utilised for women and girls is generally scarce however, in a discussion of one particular institution, 'Avalon House', Elder (1972) maintains that these homes were not intended to be punitive or disciplinary, but instead were based around the concepts of care and rehabilitation. However, on reading Elder's report, it quickly becomes clear that in Avalon House this 'rehabilitation' did not take the form of practical assistance but rather was orientated around notions of moral and psychological reform.

The staff at Avalon, described by Elder as caring but 'firm', came primarily from psychiatric and nursing backgrounds. Before any girl could be admitted she would be seen by a psychiatrist (Elder) and tested by a psychologist. This process of analysis was used as a method of screening in order to exclude cases of

> ....firmly established homosexuality....drug involvement, mental deficiency and pregnancy (Elder, 1972: 359).

The dominant discourse within which women and girls were classified at Avalon was rooted in the notions of pathology and all of the residents were categorised as having some form of 'character disorder'. In his report the young residents are frequently discussed within medical terms, many being described as 'depressive' or 'compulsive'. Anne, for example, had given birth prematurely to her first baby who had consequently died at three days old. She became pregnant for a second time but decided to have an abortion. Only a few weeks later she discovered she was pregnant again and decided to keep this child. Anne was an unmarried woman whose 'men friends were always tenuous partners' (1972: 367) and she did not want to marry the father of her child. She was consequently described as having a 'compulsion towards pregnancy' (1972: 367) and her sexual behaviour and her maternal status were considered abnormal.

The control of women's sexuality was of primary importance. Staff wanted to avoid pregnancies amongst the residents at all costs and so birth control was offered, although as Elder states, this 'advice' was often strongly resisted by the women and girls.

> ....birth control was considered taboo and usually offensive, and above all the notion of routine vaginal examination was held in utmost fear (1972: 358).

In spite of the fact that Elder's report cites only a small number of women who did become pregnant, *all* of the residents were continually offered birth control and 'routine vaginal examinations', the assumption being that *all* of the women and girls were inherently promiscuous.

One of the main reasons why pregnant residents were unwanted at Avalon was that, in line with the nineteenth century notions of women as both corruptive and corruptible, the staff believed that pregnant women had a negative effect on the other residents. Pregnancy, it was believed, led to a pathological state of 'physical regression' in some women, the symptoms of which were shying away from work and taking no interest in personal appearance. These symptoms, it was believed, would 'spread' to other women.

> Staff discouraged this as far as was humanely possible but the strength of the regressive need was so strong that it overcame all their efforts. The effect of the pregnant girls' regressive needs was to evoke parallel regressions in the non-pregnant ones (1972: 367).

In keeping with the overriding medical model of the institution, and strangely reminiscent of the feminising goals of the inebriate reformatories, a resident's outward physical appearance was taken to be indicative of the condition of her internal mental health. Elder discusses Kelly, who was one of the first residents to arrive. Her newborn baby had recently died and her fiancé was still serving a prison sentence. Consequently, on her arrival

> She looked depressed and apathetic. She slumped around with little regard for her sloppy, ill-clad appearance (1972: 360).

Over a period of months, through a process of 'minimal' staff intervention, Kelly is described as nursing herself back to health. Her new found physical and mental well-being were apparent through her change in appearance.

> When three months had elapsed she was transformed. Her hair and face were full of life, her clothes were carefully chosen, she was pretty and had purpose (1972: 361).

Avalon House was eventually judged to be a failure and was subsequently closed, as were many similar institutions. Elder lays the responsibility for the failure of these institutions on the inherent deficiencies of the residents themselves proclaiming that their psychological abnormalities became more obvious, and hence more difficult to control, in the 'socially normal' world of Avalon. He concludes that

> ....the anti-social acts which bring [the women] to court are one facet of broad personality difficulty or incompetence. That being so, it is possible that early 'taking off' from Avalon was precipitated by it being 'too good'. If Avalon indeed offered optimal opportunity for working towards 'normal' social living, then the obviousness of personality distortion was maximised (1972: 371).

Although Elder's report only focuses on one particular institution, it is useful as a method of demonstrating how many of the discourses around women and their 'deviant' behaviour changed little over a period of almost 200 years. It also highlights how the discourses of pathology and morality were frequently used interchangeably and were indeed believed to be mutually supportive in institutional regimes for girls and women.

All of the institutions discussed so far can quite easily be identified as semi-penal in the sense that they fit the five criteria outlined at the beginning of this chapter. Most of the institutions were created and run by private, charitable organisations and even those which functioned in accordance with some formal intervention from the state (such as the inebriate reformatories or the halfway houses for delinquent girls) still managed to retain some degree of autonomy and independence. Most of the institutions relied on voluntary admissions and many did not deal solely with women who had committed criminal offences. The most significant factors which link the institutions discussed above however are that they *all* managed to merge and combine the formal methods of control normally found within custodial institutions (restrictions on liberty, punishments for misbehaviour and enforced labour or training) with the more informal practices normally found within the home ('maternal/parental' style discipline, domestic training, 'communal' living arrangements, reduction of residents to a 'childlike' status). In addition, *all* of the institutions utilised this combination of practices not solely to punish their female residents but rather to ensure their normalisation and reformation.

However, the halfway house is not the final semi-penal institution identified by this study. The dominant feminising discourses that underpinned the regimes at the range of institutions identified throughout this chapter were still found to be evident in probation hostels for women at the end of the twentieth century.

The Probation Hostel for Women as a Semi-Penal Institution

> ....[the hostels'] precise functions are as difficult to pin down as are those of the family, which serves a similar type of general purpose for its young, dependent, members (Otto and Orford, 1978: 27).

It is difficult to provide a completely gendered history of the probation hostel as so little has been written specifically about it. Much of the literature pertaining to hostels throughout the twentieth century focuses on their use for male offenders. Yet the history of the hostel is very closely linked with the reformatory movement which, as shown in this chapter, was a particularly 'gendered' phenomenon. Some of the first individuals to be admitted to non-custodial, semi-penal institutions as part of probation orders were in fact women.

The system of probation supervision developed primarily through the missionary work of religious groups, in particular the Church of England

Temperance Society. Between the mid to late nineteenth century concern was growing about the extent to which the work of the church was being hampered by drunkenness, and levels of drink related offences appeared to confirm this. Consequently, in 1862 the Church of England Temperance Society (CETS) was formed, its original purpose being to carry out practical temperance work throughout England and its primary focus being the rescue of individual inebriates who required reclamation from a life of insobriety and sin (McWilliams, 1983). On the instigation of Frederick Rainer the church began to attach its temperance missionaries to the police courts in order to 'reclaim' those drunkards who agreed to sign the 'pledge'.

Garland describes organisations like the CETS as 'private agents of moralisation' (1985: 44), arguing that they constituted part of a co-ordinated network of agencies which was primarily concerned with regulating and controlling the lives of the poor. Indeed, after discharging offenders under the Summary Jurisdiction[8] and various other Acts, magistrates would often call upon a missionary to exercise supervision over the released offender (Bochel, 1976). By the time the Probation of First Offenders Act of 1887 was passed, missionaries were responsible for conducting social inquiries about offenders. These allowed the courts to determine more easily those offenders for whom probation might be appropriate (Brownlee, 1998).

The last few decades of the nineteenth century were characterised by the growing science of criminology. Pseudo-scientific explanations for deviant behaviour had begun to dominate contemporary thinking, and discourses around criminal activity had begun to shift away from notions of sin and inherent wickedness towards pathological explanations for deviancy. However, it is important to acknowledge that groups such as the CETS missionaries, probably the most significant and important independent charitable agents working with offenders at that time, still relied heavily on the notion of salvation through religious doctrine whilst at the same time adhering to the reformative and individualised ideals of the new criminological programme. The Howard Association for example lobbied and campaigned for the same supervisory programmes that were being demanded by advocates of the 'new criminology' (Garland, 1985). In other words, both were calling for increasing use of non-custodial supervision and reformative programmes. However, the Howard Association (and this is also true of the CETS missionaries) were at the same time rejecting the crucial convictions of criminological science and continuing to adhere to evangelical and religious doctrine.

Police court missionaries and magistrates were particularly keen to recommend probation as a suitable disposal for young women who were too impressionable for prison but who still required some form of intensive supervision nonetheless. As Leeson (1914) comments, magistrates were frequently reluctant to prosecute girls and young women for fear that a conviction would mean their committal to an industrial school or prison. Here, it was believed, vulnerable females would be exposed to further contamination and degradation and would quickly become 'irredeemable'.

The result was that female offenders were often hopeless even before their first arrest. The probation system [had] the special advantage in these cases in that it [was] not repugnant to public feeling (Leeson, 1914: 149).

In other words, in the pre-probation years, female offenders were often perceived to be beyond help and hope because of their assumed corruptibility and a general reluctance to prosecute them. This meant further degeneration was likely because no 'help' was made available to them. Probation supervision was therefore held up to be particularly appropriate because is constituted a disposal that combined a humane approach (palatable to the agents of justice) with a method of reform that tackled their deviant behaviour.

> When it becomes generally known that prosecution of girl offenders is likely to result in friendly supervision and help, rather than commitment to an industrial school or other such institution, it is probable that the early offences will no longer go uncorrected (Leeson, 1914: 149).

By the early twentieth century probation had been generally accepted as an appropriate disposal for women. Supervising wives and mothers in their communities would avoid breaking down the family unit, as this, it was argued, caused more harm than good (Bochel, 1976). However, it was asserted in the 1907 Probation of Offenders Act that, although the individual was not being sent to prison, it was often not desirable that she or he be left to return to the precise conditions within which she or he originally offended.

At the beginning of the twentieth century, the police court missionaries set up temporary homes where boys on probation could be housed and receive supervision as an alternative to both prison and their own homes (Andrews, 1979). According to Sinclair (1971) boys would be placed in these homes as an emergency measure, residing for usually no more than a few weeks before being sent to more permanent living-in jobs. For girls and women the situation was to develop somewhat differently. Magistrates, although reluctant to send women to prison, still considered institutionalisation a more appropriate option than mere supervision within the community. However, unlike boys on probation, girls and young women were not sent to institutions as an emergency measure until employment could be found, rather they were sent with the aim of a longer term process of reformation. So with the aid of the missionaries, females were often found places within one of the established semi-penal institutions (such as the reformatories or refuges) where they would still receive their non-custodial supervision but where they would also receive a more intense form of reformation. The regimes for the female probationers within these institutions were the same as for the other female inmates. Records for the County Refuge for the Destitute indicate that the women on probation did the same jobs (usually laundry work), were exposed to the same methods of moral reform (usually religious instruction), participated in the same activities and were subject to the same rules and regulations as the non-probationers.

So for the early years of the twentieth century the institutions to which probationers were sent were run by private, voluntary organisations such as the Church of England Temperance Society or the affiliated police court missionaries and were consequently not under any central control (Barry, 1991). Furthermore the process of referral was extremely informal and intermittent. The situation became more formalised after the implementation of the 1914 Criminal Justice Administration Act, which introduced the first residential probation orders, but the probation service still continued to utilise the homes and refuges run by voluntary and charitable organisations. Barry (1991) points out that the new residential orders, which integrated the welfare-based techniques of probation supervision with the elements of confinement and constraint fundamental to any form of institutionalisation, established the paradoxical and contradictory nature of probation hostels (in other words the combination of formal and informal, or punitive and welfare based regimes) which remained a contentious issue throughout the twentieth century.

In 1927 the Report of the Departmental Committee on the Treatment of Young Offenders noted that a period of residency in a home or hostel, coupled with a probation order, was not just a means of reforming individuals, or an alternative to unsuitable home circumstances, but was actually a real opportunity to divert offenders from custody. It therefore recommended that these institutions be formally inspected and approved and that a central body be responsible for their financial support.

The Home Office accepted the Committee's recommendations and agreed to set up a scheme to formally approve hostels and then make a financial contribution towards their upkeep. A report issued the following year encouraged the use of conditions of residence but outlawed the use of training programmes in hostels (Sinclair, 1971; Barry, 1991). For those young offenders who were deemed to lack discipline, alternative accommodation was provided in the form of Probation *Homes*. Homes differed from hostels as they employed regimes which were specifically designed around training. The object of a Home was to prepare a probationer for employment.

> One or two kinds of training might be selected for boys such as small holding, market gardening, gardening and greenhouse work; woodwork, carpentry and joinery; electrical and motor engineering; bakery; building construction, bricklaying; painting, plastering, domestic jobbing. For girls there are all the branches of domestic work, laundry, secretarial work, greenhouse work, market-gardening and the like (Home Office, 1942: 2).

By the 1930s and 1940s the emphasis within hostels was on 'family' style discipline, similar to that employed in the semi-penal institutions for women during the nineteenth century. The Home Office's *Notes on Homes and Hostels for Young Probationers* states that institutions should be 'small so that a homely atmosphere may prevail and institutionalisation be avoided' (1942: 2). The recommendation for a recreation area within hostels clearly highlights the differences in the way in which male and female probationers were perceived.

> ....there should be small rooms where boys can carry on hobbies or where girls, when they return from work can wash, iron and mend their personal clothing, do dressmaking or carry on any other small activities. For boys in particular there should be a playground and if possible a large indoor room where high spirits can find an outlet (1942: 2).

This statement raises two issues. First, the way in which the young female probationers were expected to behave stands in sharp contrast to the expectations of their male counterparts. Boys, it would appear, were expected to be boisterous, high spirited, and in need of space and entertaining activities. Girls, on the other hand, were expected to be respectable and domesticated and apparently without need of further mental stimulation or physical exercise. Domestic chores for girls and women were meant to fulfil both their training and their recreational needs. Second, this therefore implies a much more repressive and regulative regime for females. In their semi-penal world, life was all work and no play.

> In a Hostel, the probationers who go out to work cannot be expected to do much domestic work, though girls naturally do more than boys (Home Office, 1942: 2).

The 1948 Criminal Justice Act gave the Home Office the power to inspect, approve and fund probation hostels. This Act also reversed the 1927 Committee's ban on training and required that hostels (as well as homes) provide some useful training scheme for residents. The training schemes ultimately created were very close to those in prisons and other penal establishments (Barry, 1991). The Act also ensured that hostel wardens were no longer able to use their discretion and reject referrals that they would previously have considered 'unsuitable'. This practice, which had been used a great deal in the past with regard to women, was aimed at keeping particular cases (specifically those deemed unlikely to be a 'success') out of institutions. Whilst hostels, homes and refuges were dependant on charitable donations, this selection procedure could be easily justified, however once funding became formalised and centralised, the court had greater control over admissions. Nonetheless, the *Approved Probation Hostel and Home Rules* (Home Office, 1949) still advocated fairly strict guidelines for probation officers, court officials and hostel wardens with regard to the selection of suitable residents. As Monger (1972) states, this meant that many of those probationers deemed 'suitable' might not have been the ones in most need of help and support.

> ....hostel residents were expected to be, if not paragons of virtue, at least more solidly equipped with social virtues than many probationers. They were to be healthy, amenable to discipline, reliable employees, and with difficulties which it was reasonable to expect could be dealt with in six months, in most cases. If all

these conditions were satisfied, it might be wondered, was a period in a hostel really necessary (Monger, 1972: 170).

By the 1950s and 1960s the emphasis within hostels was on a 'complete' rehabilitation of the individual. The Morrison Committee (1962) re-affirmed the benefits of combining training, treatment and reform, recommending the importance of work, physical activities *and* social and relationship skills. They stated that hostels should provide

> ....training, with mature adult support and control, in regular habits of work, in the useful employment of leisure, in personal hygiene and, above all, in living acceptably with contemporaries and older people (Morrison Committee, quoted in Sinclair, 1971: 13).

It was still believed that the best way to provide emotional support and practical skills within hostels was through the 'quasi-family' environment. These institutions were still usually supervised by couples who combined the roles of warden and matron with those of husband and wife (Sinclair, 1975) and still attempted to combine the methods of control from both the formal penal sphere (training, regular work, routine) with those more informal methods from the 'community' or family (parental discipline, provision of socialisation skills, control of leisure pursuits, domestication of females).

Sinclair (1975) argues that much of the literature on institutions has been based around the influential work of Goffman (1961) which identified the 'total institution' and the family as two opposing and polarised environments. Consequently, according to Sinclair, insufficient sociological attention has been given to the relationship between the role of families and the role of these institutions. Sinclair examined the extent to which hostels operated like families and the extent to which the influence of warden and matron was analogous to that of parents. He found that those institutions with the highest rate of success were those where the regimes were 'paternalistic' (1975: 130). In other words, those institutions where the male warden was the dominant role model and where his matron-wife complied with his ideals and practices. Sinclair cites a probation officer who describes one such successful scenario.

> The matron fitted in with the paternalistic pattern. She was a very charming person not unduly dominated by her husband. He was very much the master in his own household and I think she played along with this. I think the boys saw her as a mother figure although she was not sloppy (1975: 131).

Another officer explains why some hostels had a *low* success rate. Much of the blame for failure appeared to be centred on the over-assertive or dominant role of the matron.

> In two regimes, the warden and matron had problems with their marriage which in turn probably affected their behaviour. In one, the matron withdrew almost

completely from the hostel and....only came into it to shout at the boys for not cleaning the dishes. In the other....the matron became provocative towards the boys and obsessional about the house. In other regimes, the matron usurped her husband's disciplinary role and was bitterly resented for it (1975: 131).

Otto and Orford (1978) make much of the intentional similarities between the hostel and the 'normal' family home. The home they state is

....small and informal, and there is no hierarchy, at least amongst the adult members. There is much contact with the outside world and the expectation is that members will interact much, will show a great deal of friendly and supportive behaviour towards one another, and will feel that others care about them and that they can rely upon them (1978: 1).

They assert that this is the impression that most people hold about the realities of family life and it is also the image that most people believe constitutes the best set of circumstances under which to live a free, responsible and respectable life. Of course, as Dahl and Snare (1978) argue, this idealistic vision of the family home does not necessarily accord with reality for women as wives, mothers or daughters. Otto and Orford go on to examine the 'family-related' functions that hostels attempt to fulfil. First, they claim that hostels (whether they be for alcoholics, young delinquents, offenders, or any other group requiring 'behavioural correction' (1978: 28)) endeavour to provide a process of 'socialisation' for their residents. In addition, they state, hostels aim to provide residents with appropriate skills and resources necessary to live productive and independent lives in society and they claim that this function is particularly useful for those individuals who have no family support.

Although the studies discussed above are mainly based on research conducted in hostels for boys and men, their conclusions have important implications for women and gender relations. First, the very lack of studies of women in hostels has hidden the experiences of these women from public scrutiny, placing them even further away from the reach of formal accountability. Second, as Sinclair's study highlights, it was assumed that the socialisation of deviant youth could best be achieved through a 'quasi-family' environment in which the female matron was submissive to her warden-husband. Any independence of thought or action on the matron's part was deemed to be detrimental to the success of the institution. These ideals of male dominance and female acquiescence were presented as 'normal' models of social and family life and played a significant role in the socialisation of both male and female residents. Third, Sinclair argues that the most successful institutions were those that showed evidence of 'interdependance' between staff and residents (1975: 133). Parsons and Bales (1955) state that although parents influence their children, they cannot play their role adequately without the children's co-operation. Therefore the effective running of a hostel depended not only on the matron and warden accepting their submissive and dominant parental roles, but also on the residents accepting their roles as submissive and co-operative 'children'.[9] Thus, the process of 'infantilisation' is justified for the successful reformation of deviant women.

By the end of the 1960s the definitive objectives of hostels were becoming considerably blurred and varied. The *Approved Probation Hostel and Home Rules* (1949) had allowed each individual warden and hostel committee a significant amount of freedom with regard to the management and function of their institutions. As a result, hostel regimes varied considerably from one institution to the next. Some institutions acted mainly as accommodation units, some provided therapeutic conditions under which psychological problems could be dealt with, some focused on vocational and/or social training and some aimed to provide full and complete rehabilitation. In addition, some (as the Wooton Report recommended) were used simply to '*contain*....immature and inadequate offenders' (quoted in Barry, 1991: 20, emphasis added).

By the 1970s concern was growing about the imprisonment of women with children and the greater use of community penalties for mothers was advocated. A report from the Howard League (1979) highlights how the call for decarceration for particular women was not a purely humanitarian movement. Rather it was to preserve the sanctity of the family unit (at a time of growing unemployment and social discontent) and to ensure that women did not stray too far from their ascribed roles.

> We believe that it is particularly important to the health of society that women, especially mothers, should be dealt with in a way that does not make matters worse for the next generation, their children....the choice of sanctions....should above all do the family no harm... .For those who need to acquire social, housekeeping or mothering skills, probation with attendance at a day or evening centre, or with support from a specially trained home help, could be suitable (Howard League, 1979: 3).

A study by Sheppard (1979) found that the decision to recommend individuals for a condition of residence did not depend on factors such as the risk of a custodial sentence or the nature of the offence, but rather on the personal characteristics of the offender, as interpreted by the probation officer. Sheppard states that those recommended for hostel places were those likely to be 'seen to be in need of the 'structured environment'' and naturally 'such an offender is more likely to be young and female' (1979: 21).

However, although it can be seen that women were still deemed to be inherently *unsuitable* for prison and inherently *suitable* for this form of semi-penal institutionalisation, by the 1980s female only probation hostels were consistently failing to meet minimum levels of occupancy. One reason for this paradoxical situation could have been the restrictive gatekeeping procedures that these institutions employed. As Carlen (1990) comments many women-only hostels were fairly exclusive and refused to accept particular groups of women, for example drug users, alcoholics, those with psychiatric and mental health problems, women with children, or women convicted of violence or arson. Although decisions not to accept such women would most likely be made on the basis of safety considerations, it could be argued that, as with the nineteenth century reformatories, some women are deemed to be just *too* problematic or *too* dangerous to be successfully rehabilitated.

During the 1980s a combination of factors, including the problems with under-occupancy, the need to provide accommodation for individuals on bail and the need to deal 'appropriately' with the more serious offenders, led to significant policy developments with regard to hostel accommodation. Bifurcation meant a tougher response to offenders convicted of sexual or violent crimes (through longer prison sentences) and a less severe approach to those convicted of non-violent offences. These non-violent offenders, it was believed, should be diverted from custody and dealt with through suitable community based penalties. The Government's Green Paper *'Punishment, Custody and the Community'* (Home Office, 1988) and the subsequent White Paper *'Crime, Justice and Protecting the Public'* (Home Office, 1990) spelled out the proposals for diverting these offenders and introduced recommendations for new, tougher non-custodial penalties. The Green Paper suggested that the new penalties should combine elements of punishment and deprivation of liberty with strategies to reduce offending behaviour, and advocated the use of home curfews and conditions of residence in suitable hostels as restrictive methods. Contrary to what many probation officers articulated at the time, these ideas of restriction of liberty, regulation and control were not in any way new to probation hostels. As this chapter has shown these elements have always played a significant role in probation hostel history. However, as Barry states, what was new was the concept of utilising these regulatory and controlling elements '...without the justification of welfare objectives inherent in the traditional concept of the probation order' (1991: 21). Rather than combining the concepts of 'care' and 'control' the new proposals meant the notions of rehabilitation and welfare were to be diminished *in favour* of punitive ideals. This new restrictive approach was intended to provide sentencers with more credible community based sentences.

> It is believed that the courts are attracted to, and have an expectation of, a more intensive level of probation supervision with a stronger element of control via the condition of residence and the curfew (Devaney, 1986, quoted in Barry, 1991: 5).

However, although by the late 1980s and early 1990s hostel managers had acknowledged that their institutions provided a method through which offenders could be punished within the community, according to Barry none of the 21 hostels in his study had adopted, or had any intention of adopting, the 'government inspired correctional concepts....highlighted in the Green paper' (1991: 6). Some were considerably more liberal than others. An information sheet for Norfolk Park hostel states that in 1989 their purpose was

> ....to *advise, assist and befriend* residents with an emphasis on residents setting their own aims and objectives (Barry, 1991: 6. Emphasis added).

Likewise a hostel in London was reported to have adopted '....a non-authoritarian regime where privacy and the individuality of the resident is respected and valued' (Barry, 1991: 7) and yet another combined

> ....a community based residential facility with a liberal regime within the constraints of the order....residents are allowed maximum individual freedom whilst at the same time learning to co-operate with each other in work and play (1991: 7).

However, some hostels in Barry's study had taken a more restrictive and punitive approach, with one claiming to offer 'a way in which the offender can be *punished* in the community' (1991: 6, emphasis added) and another stating that 'Courts and the Probation Service can be assured Elm Bank is not a soft option' (1991: 6). Although Barry's study does not make any explicit reference to hostels for women it does highlight two important factors. First, as had historically been the case, many probation hostels appeared to be resisting national changes in probation practice thus remaining, essentially, on the periphery of state control. Second, they tended to vary significantly in their aims and objectives, a lack of standardisation that was essentially a reflection of the individual ideals of managers and staff.

Barry argues that this level of diversity, individuality and independence within the hostel system meant hostels were left exposed to accusations of inconsistency. As the HM Inspectorate of Probation stated

> There was a tendency for approved probation and bail hostels to form an adjunct to mainstream probation service activity rather than being fully integrated into its work (1993: 13).

However, hostel managers were still concerned that any method of national standardisation would lead to more restrictive and punitive regimes and leave little or no room for liberal, welfare based social work. On the surface it would be easy to justify this resistance to the introduction of a punitive system of control in favour of retaining more welfare orientated hostel regimes, but it should not be forgotten that with regard to women, the independence that hostels, and similar institutions, have historically had over admissions and regimes, meant that many female residents were subjected to a whole range of dubious 'treatments', training methods and moral expectations, which were, to a great extent, administered outside the realms of state regulation and accountability.

Anne Worrall claimed that by the 1990s much of the work carried out with individuals on probation was based on the idea of 'confronting offending behaviour' (1997: 101). As such, programmes were no longer intended to reform the whole personality or character of the probationer, but rather to focus on those 'particular pieces of unacceptable behaviour' (1997: 101) and attempt to change them. So, according to Worrall, at the end of the twentieth century reformation (whether 'complete' or 'partial') was still on the probation agenda. She goes on to identify two sites within which this form of 'help' took place, namely the probation day centre, providing 'programmes of normalising instruction to compulsorily attending groups of offenders' (1997: 101) and the probation hostel, an institution which had become 'less a roof over one's head and more of a *house of correction* in its own right' (1997: 107. Emphasis added).

The Criminal Justice Act (1991) introduced minimum National Standards for community penalties, including the management and administration of probation hostels, and these came into effect in October 1992. These National Standards stated that hostels should be 'offering an enhanced level of supervision within a structured and supportive environment' (HM Inspectorate of Probation, 1993: 13). As Davies (1996) contended, the purpose of hostels would be to assist offenders to lead a responsible and law abiding lifestyle, and to help them to find work and suitable accommodation on departure. However, by 1993, when the Inspectorate report was compiled, it was found that many hostels were still 'struggling to find a regime suited to the new rationale'(HM Inspectorate of Probation 1993:13) and a diversity of programmes and management systems was still evident.

These last two issues, those raised by Worrall and the HM Inspectorate of Probation, signify a suitable point at which to end this chapter. Worrall's comments about the 'corrective' nature of probation hostels and the fact that reform is still perceived to be a function of the probation service appear to bring the debates in this chapter full circle, confirming to some extent the position of probation hostels as semi-penal institutions. It is not really important that Worrall is not specifically talking about women's hostels as that case will be taken up in great depth in the case study presented over the next three chapters. Also the comments made in the Inspectorate report about the diversity of hostel practices and regimes also confirms this chapter's contention that probation hostels can be considered semi-penal in that they are able to adapt, or even resist, formal state regulation in a way that conventional probation programmes cannot and as such they manage (however tenuously) to remain on the periphery of full state control.

Finally, as the research conducted for this book was undertaken between 1992 and 1994, it seems inappropriate to continue this examination of the developments in women's hostels beyond this date. The analysis of the data collected is presented in Chapters Four, Five and Six and will pick up on the points raised in this and the preceding chapters. The way in which one particular reformatory/hostel has managed, over a period of nearly 200 years, to remain largely autonomous of full state control will be discussed. Additionally, the way in which the dominant feminising discourses of domesticity, respectability, motherhood, sexuality and pathology, in conjunction with the ideals of normalisation and reform, have influenced and determined the treatment of women within that institution will be critically analysed. The analysis begins in the following chapter with an examination of the genesis of the institution and its early years as a reformatory throughout the nineteenth century.

Notes

1   The title of this chapter was inspired by the title of an anthology of feminist stories (Carter, ed, 1986).

2   See also Bosworth's (2000) article in which she challenges male definitions of historical time-periods as they apply to women.

3   See Rafter, 1983; Faith, 1993; Heidensohn, 1996; Carlen, 1983 for discussions of this issue in both a historical and contemporary context.

4   Rafter states that this was achieved not only through a process of instruction and education but also through other methods of negative reinforcement such as parole revocation for any lapses of behaviour whilst on conditional release, or the threat of transfer to a custodial institution for the 'feeble-minded' where women could be held for indefinite periods.

5   The discussions which preceded the Mental Deficiency Act of 1913 went as far as proposing a new category of 'sexually feeble-minded' which referred specifically to sexually 'immoral' women. See Zedner (1991a).

6   See also Timms (1968) for a discussion of two other projects which, although they did not provide institutional 'care' for girls on release from borstal, did attempt some post-custodial support in the form of assisted lodging schemes and day centres.

7   In addition, some of these institutions accepted referrals from probation officers for girls on probation orders

8   The Summary Jurisdiction Act of 1879 served to increase the range of offences with which the magistrates' court could deal as well as providing a statutory basis for the suspension of punishment. Offenders could have a prison sentence suspended on their recognisance of good behaviour and their agreement to supervision in the community. This Act had the effect of involving the missionaries for the first time in official supervision of offenders.

9   For further research on the relationship between home circumstances and delinquency see Davies (1969); for further research on the relationship between family life, hostels and delinquency see Davies and Sinclair (1971).

Chapter 4

Domestic Discipline: Semi-Penal Institutionalisation in the Nineteenth Century

Vernon Lodge is a women's probation and bail hostel in England, funded by the Home Office but owned and co-managed by the Church of England Council for Social Aid (CECSA). It is an institution with an extensive history. It is one of the oldest Diocesan charities in the area, older than the Diocese itself, and its origins can be traced back to the early nineteenth century and the influence of penal reformer Elizabeth Fry. It is my intention in this and the following chapter to utilise original historical data found during two years of research within the hostel in order to examine the genesis and evolution of Vernon Lodge from a nineteenth century refuge for destitute women to a twentieth century bail and probation hostel. This chapter will focus specifically on the origins of this institution and its development throughout the nineteenth century whilst the following chapters will bring the debates up to date by charting the history throughout the twentieth century. It is the intention of these chapters to provide a critical analysis of the way in which women were regulated and disciplined within this institution during the nineteenth and twentieth centuries and, in doing so, begin to uncover those themes of continuity which link its previous existence with its present one.

The analysis will include an examination of the way in which women coped with or resisted the regimes and discourses that sought to discipline and normalise them. It is worth noting, however, that this was not an easy task. All of the original historical data gathered for this research were in the form of documents written by 'experts' or professionals who claimed to 'know' these women of history. No documentation was found which recorded the experiences or motives of the women themselves. Consequently although several incidents of recalcitrant behaviour were recorded within the official documentation, these were always contextualised within the discourses of morality or pathology, labelling the women concerned as inherently morally or mentally deficient. Without the women's own explanations of their behaviour, the motives behind their actions can only be assumed. Nonetheless, as Cain (1993) has argued, the ultimate form of knowledge subjugation is the ignorance, or refusal to accept, that experiences are still valid even if there exists no discourse within which to articulate them. She highlights the case of sexual harassment as an example stating that women experienced such incidents long before a name was given to the issue. Thus, the fact that women's unruly or rebellious behaviour was not defined as acts of resistance may be because such a discourse was unavailable to the women or was suppressed by other, dominant (moral / pseudo-scientific) discourses. Therefore, in order to remain faithful to the feminist methodological and theoretical approach that influenced this research, and in order to 'liberate' these women of history from the feminising discourses that have historically bound them, incidents of confrontation, insurgency and insubordination will be analysed within feminist debates around women's agency and resistance.

The Early Years: Origins, organisation and paternalistic discipline

Elizabeth Fry had family connections in the north of England. She is reported to have called upon her relatives sometime around 1820, possibly around the same time as her venture to Kirkdale gaol.[1] Details of her relatives are sketchy but examination of the Fry family tree indicates that they were most likely Mrs. Ann Waterhouse, her husband Nicholas and their 13 children (Smith, 1878). The Waterhouses were Merchant Cotton Brokers and were wealthy, well connected and 'locally distinguished for their public spirit and good deeds' (*The Welldoer*, 1909: 2). It is not surprising then that they were enthusiastic and excited to hear about their cousin's unprecedented philanthropic work. Like many other middle class Quaker families of their day they were keen to become involved (or at least be seen to partake) in charitable enterprises and so as a result of Fry's visit they became determined to undertake some 'rescue work' of their own. The Waterhouses bought a property and, in 1823, opened it as the County Refuge for the Destitute.

The Refuge was a charitable organisation, supervised by a Matron and managed by a Ladies' Committee and a Gentlemen's Committee. Early documentation indicates that although the Ladies' Committee was primarily responsible for the day-to-day management of the Refuge, major decisions (for example those regarding staff appointments, resident admissions and financial matters) were made by (or at least could not be made without the approval of) the Gentlemen's Committee.[2] There are no records to suggest that permission or approval for any decisions taken at the institution was sought by any higher authority than the self-appointed Gentlemen's Committee and thus, during the first century of its existence at least, the Refuge operated well beyond the reach of formal state control.

During its early years of operation, women were received at the Refuge directly from prison, being recommended by the Prison Chaplain or the Ladies' Prison Association.[3] The original aim of the Refuge was to help women who had been imprisoned for theft or debt. However this did not mean that *any* female thief or debtor would be admitted. The Refuge had particularly strict gatekeeping policies that were strongly enforced in order to ensure only particular 'types' of women were admitted. An Annual Report from the following century describes the Refuge of 1823 as being utilised for the reception of

> ....discharged female prisoners and others of whose desire to reform their life (*sic*) there appears to be a reasonable hope (Vernon Lodge Annual Report, 1963).

This statement indicates two important criteria that were used as a form of gatekeeping at the newly opened Refuge. First, all admissions were required to show a 'desire to reform' their lives, an acknowledgement of, and sense of remorse for, their previous behaviour. As discussed previously, this wish to reform was often an essential criterion for admission to the various semi-penal institutions for women. Women would therefore only be considered for entry to the County Refuge, if they voluntarily renounced their past 'sins' and showed a genuine desire to amend their ways. Given their non-formal status, semi-penal institutions such as the Refuge technically had no power to confine women against their will (although women were often subjected to a great deal of pressure from both the reformers and their families and thus the boundary between consent and coercion would become somewhat blurred). Consequently this meant that women were essentially 'voluntary' admissions and as such only those who seemed likely and willing to submit to the reforming regimes were accepted.

Second, there had to be some early indication, or 'reasonable hope', that reform was possible. The assessment of 'reasonable hope of reform' was of course subjective and prone to moral judgements, and it was therefore uncommon for women with long criminal histories or known prostitutes to be admitted. These women were generally believed to be morally corrupt, capable of corrupting others and beyond hope of reform. Only on those occasions when such women were represented as helpless and hapless casualties of circumstance would admission be granted.

Once women were admitted to the Refuge they were subjected to a regime based primarily around moral reform and religious instruction. This was supported by a schedule of strict and arduous domestic work. This work, unlike the more formalised 'training' introduced during the twentieth century, was not necessarily a means of reform in its own right, but rather served to compliment and reinforce the process of moral salvation. Hard work was seen as a means of atonement for previous sinful and deviant behaviour. In addition, hard labour was essential as idleness was equated with sin, and thus industry was perceived as a means of preventing further moral degeneration. Indolence was considered to be a significant cause of women's deviant behaviour.

> Ladies, hard work is important to the Refuge for several reasons, not least because it occupies the women's day. As we are all aware the devil frequently finds mischief for idle hands (Letter from the Matron to the Ladies' Committee 19 June 1835).

The first set of rules and the early Matron's report books indicate that life was extremely structured for women within the institution. They had to rise at 6 am in the summer and 7 am in the winter, make their beds and clean their rooms before attending 'family worship'. After breakfast they were expected to work until eight o'clock in the evening with an hour's break for dinner and exercise and a half hour break for supper. The work itself consisted of knitting, spinning, making shoes, laundry work and general housekeeping duties. Occasionally the women were offered some education in basic literacy skills but this was rare and considerably more emphasis was placed on domestic work in order that they might be reformed to be obedient and diligent wives, mothers or servants.[4]

Although the domestic work at the Refuge was hard and laborious, it was represented by the Ladies' and Gentlemen's Committees as a benevolent, 'homely' form of discipline that, under normal circumstances, the women would have received from their families. However this training was not quite as 'benign' as the Committees proclaimed. First, the domestic discipline was supported and maintained by a much more formal, custodial style of control. Whilst at the Refuge women were allowed no visitors and were only allowed to leave the premises with special permission from the Matron and even then, they often had to be accompanied by a chaperone. In addition they were intensely supervised and a detailed daily record of their activities and behaviour was kept in the form of Matron's Reports. Second, the domestic training itself was not imposed on the residents solely to facilitate their reformation. Mahood's (1990) analysis of the Magdalene Homes highlights how, because of their charitable status, the women in the Homes were required to work, not only because they might be morally and domestically reformed, but also because they could help raise money to keep the institutions financially viable. The women at the County Refuge were expected to fulfil a similar function. They were encouraged to spin, knit and sew in order that they could make clothes for themselves and for other residents. The Refuge also took in laundry from other institutions and organisations (although none are named in the early records) and charged a fee for this service. The women were paid a small amount of cash for the work they did but most importantly, according to the Refuge administration, the work allowed them to 'keep their heads dry and their bellies full' (Letter from Gentlemen's Committee to the Matron, 6 March 1830). Without this type of work, the Refuge would have faced severe financial difficulties during its early years and, although its primary purpose was to reclaim and reform its female residents, ironically the institution was largely dependent on them for its own survival. This goes some way to explaining the, often desperate, need to retain those women who were extremely productive or had desirable skills. Elizabeth Harris, for example, was admitted in 1826, after her husband had been transported.

> If she behaves well, will make a great acquisition to the Refuge as she makes shoes, weaves fringes and various other works, which are wanted here (Matron's Reports, February 1826).

Ellen Bowden, admitted in 1834, was described as a good seamstress and an industrious and diligent laundry worker. As a result considerable concern was expressed when she requested her discharge from the Refuge in 1835.

> Ladies, the discharge of Bowden was a great loss to the Refuge. Her industrious spirit and keenness were an inspiration to others and *her sewing ability most useful to us throughout these difficult months.* However, our work with her was done and she was restored successfully to her family so we should rejoice in that (Letter from Matron to the Ladies' Committee, 21 February 1835. Emphasis added).

The 'reasonable hope of reform' criterion was most strongly enforced during financially lean years. Letters from the Ladies' and Gentlemen's Committees indicate that the Refuge suffered a great degree of financial insecurity during the 1830s. One letter in particular states that although the situation was not desperate, it did require the assistance of the Matron

> ....to ensure that only the *most deserving and industrious girls* be admitted. We have not the means or desire to support unwilling or idle cases (Letter from the Ladies' and Gentlemen's Committees to the Matron, 21 August 1835. Emphasis added.).

Regardless of the somewhat self-serving practices of the County Refuge, the institution was nonetheless perceived to be a place where, if nothing else, vulnerable women could be 'protected' from corrupting influences. The whole semi-penal movement had been developed on the principle that women, like juveniles, were inherently impressionable and therefore required segregation from dangerous company, hence their removal from the prison system and their subsequent confinement in reformatories, refuges and homes. Of course, not all women at the Refuge were referred from prison. On the contrary, for the nineteenth century woman, the family home and local community could be just as dangerous and corrupting a location as any gaol. Consequently, many women at the Refuge were admitted by their families or husbands as a last attempt to assert some paternalistic control over their wayward females.

Eliza Walton was admitted in 1826 after becoming involved in prostitution which, it was believed, was due to her contact with corrupting influences. Her own family had attempted to 'protect' her from her unsuitable acquaintances but when these informal measures proved ineffective, stronger methods of control were required.

> [Eliza Walton] had been confined in [gaol] for 12 months for stealing a watch in a house of ill-fame. *Was imprisoned by her relations* to keep her from dangerous company having always been wild and worthless (Matron's Reports, August 1826. Emphasis added).

A letter requesting admission for Eliza, written to the Refuge by her father, goes on to state that

> ....we are sure that she will be returned to her family her behaviour having been reformed and her soul reclaimed. We need not remind you of the importance of keeping her apart from bad company as she is very giddy and easily encouraged (Letter to Matron from Mr Frederick Walton, 2 August 1826).

This close contact between the Refuge and the women's families was an extremely significant aspect of the paternalistic philosophy underpinning the institution. A case could be made for admission of almost any woman, regardless of the nature of her offence, as long as it could be assured that discipline could be maintained by an 'appropriate' family member (preferably a father or husband) once her period of reformation was complete. This merging of formal and informal methods of control is highlighted in the case of Mary Ann Roberts who was referred by a prison Chaplain in 1831. In his letter of referral he describes Ann's situation.

> A young woman 22 years old has been six months in prison for stealing money from a man in a public house, and is desirous of admission into the Refuge. It is one of those cases which as far as crime is concerned I would not recommend to the Refuge – she has been two years on the town but she has been well educated and one of the jury stated that he knew her late father who was a most religious man and a Preacher... .She also has an uncle....who is a Preacher and who says he would receive her if he knew that she was reclaimed so far from her bad habits and company as to be an Inmate of the Refuge. She is very modest and retiring in her conversation and keeps aloof from the other prisoners – it is plain she has been a spoilt child and reared by indulgent parents. It is only to say that she is determined to seek for the means of salvation in the Refuge and I hope the good seed which has been sown in her early years will be matured with you and bring forth the fruit of everlasting life (November 1831).

In Mary's case, agents from the whole 'control spectrum' were instrumental in negotiating her future control. Members of her family, the Chaplain of the prison, the Matron of the Refuge, the Gentlemen's Committee and even a member of the jury that originally convicted her, all played some role in deciding how best to discipline, control and thus 'save' this unfortunate woman. The Matron's Reports for February 1832 indicate that Mary was 'successfully reformed' and duly returned to the 'care and protection' of her family.

Close links with the families of the women at the Refuge were essential to ensure their 'total' control and to ensure that the hard work of the institution would not be 'undone' once a woman was returned to her home community. In particular, the forging of these links was deemed to be most necessary for those women who were perceived to pose a 'sexual' threat to feminine 'norms'. Sexuality constituted one of the most pervasive discourses through which the women at the Refuge were constructed and understood. As previously mentioned, the Refuge employed a strict gatekeeping policy with regard to prostitutes up until the mid twentieth century. Experienced prostitutes, viewed as irreclaimable, were rarely admitted and only those with 'special circumstances' (like those women from respectable backgrounds who had been 'led astray' by others) were accepted.

The Matron's Reports record the case of 23 year old Frances Patterson. Referred by a prison Chaplain, Frances was admitted to the Refuge in 1831. Her letter of referral reports that she had turned to prostitution out of desperation when her sailor husband had failed to provide for her and her children. The Matron agreed to admit Frances to the Refuge on a trial period, acknowledging that she had 'fallen into prostitution through no fault of her own' (Matron's Reports, May 1831). However her stay lasted only a few weeks and a subsequent entry in the Matron's Reports records her release.

> After showing much penitence and sorrow for her past conduct she grew tired of confinement and desired to have her discharge. There was much pains taken in pointing out to her the misery she was exposing herself to by prostitution which she did not deny but nothing could restrain her....as is so often the case, the souls of prostitutes are so easily lost (Matron's Reports, May 1831).

As Mahood (1990) points out, the nineteenth century witnessed a dramatic increase in the amount of charitable work carried out with prostitutes and 'fallen women'. In order to financially support this work, the Magdalene Homes and other similar institutions created for the reformation of 'immoral' women, were keen to portray the prostitute as someone worthy of sympathy, pity and charity. Mahood asserts that prostitutes were frequently depicted as luckless, ill-fated women from otherwise 'respectable' families who had been corrupted by unscrupulous company and manipulative lovers. This method of classification, which characterised the prostitute as a non-threatening victim rather than a sexually depraved, inherently immoral offender, served to reduce the sexual and social threat that prostitutes, and working class women in general, posed to 'respectable' society.

In Frances's case, her drift into prostitution was indeed attributed to social circumstances rather than inherent, moral failings. However, her subsequent desire to leave the institution, and thus her obvious failure to reform, was understood and explained through moral discourse. This inability or unwillingness to separate the social and moral dimensions of women's lives and experiences was to become a lasting theme within the institution throughout the nineteenth century.

Another woman, whose immoral behaviour required controlling (first by her family and friends and finally by the Refuge) was Ann Tyrer, who was admitted in 1825.

> Ann Tyrer is of a respectable family....her last husband, Capt Gurnell is now living but has long been separated from his wife, owing to her own misconduct and love of liquor. She has repeatedly left him and associated with depraved characters of both sexes - *her friends have tried every means to reform her conduct...* .She is a desperate character...a Child of the Devil and acts like

> one....is so cunning and immoral....a dangerous and wicked woman (Matron's Reports, September 1825. Emphasis added).

Ann left the Refuge in 1826, and a subsequent entry in the Matron's Reports records that

> ....the Matron has been informed that [Ann] is guilty of every crime but murder and *that* she *attempted*. Is reportedly in bad health, nothing reformed. Most likely dead (Matron's Reports, February 1826, Emphasis in original).

What is particularly significant about this example is that Ann Tyrer was 35 years old on her admission to the Refuge in 1825. The reformist ideology that underpinned the work of the Refuge centred on the notion that women were inherently irresponsible and infantile. Thus women like Ann, a mature woman in her thirties who had been married and was possibly a mother, were still discussed within a discourse that served to 'infantilise' them, reducing them to the status of children. Feminists have argued that the regimes within modern day custodial institutions deny their female inmates the right to take control over their lives, thus inducing a dependency culture which in turn promotes the infantilisation of those women (Carlen, 1983; Rafter, 1983; Faith, 1993; Heidensohn, 1996). This was true for women at the Refuge however it was not *solely* the institutional regime that reduced them to less-than-adult status. Rather the process of infantilisation often began even before admission, with negotiations between families (usually husbands or fathers) and the management of the institution serving to envelop the women within a demeaning patriarchal discourse.

The discourse around sexual immorality and inherent wickedness pervades the historical documentation for the Refuge throughout the nineteenth century. The examples of moral decency promoted within the institution were believed to provide an ideal environment to reform and normalise 'fallen' and criminal women back to acceptable standards of behaviour. Other institutions, such as the Workhouse or the gaol, were not perceived to adhere to the same moral standards as the Refuge, and were thus viewed as corrupting and unsuitable for the reformation of their impressionable female inmates. In his letter of referral in 1831, a prison warden implores the Refuge's Committee to accept 17 year old Catherine Connoly as her prospects in the Workhouse, he claimed, would be bleak.

> I cannot but think if she were so inclined that she would be admitted into the Workhouse but I fear from the lack of circumspection in that building, and in consequence the opportunity of young people of different sexes mating each other, there is little hope of a doubtful or vicious character being reclaimed there (7 June 1831).

The request for 20 year old Margaret Saxon to be admitted in 1855 was based on a similar premise.

> She was a woman of the town and has been in the Penitentiary here but was discharged from thence, *and is now diseased and corrupted...* .I have good hopes that she is now fully convinced of her sinful nature and wicked habits and is in earnest in desiring to flee from such courses in future and of becoming a sincere Christian (Matron's Reports, April 1855, Emphasis added).

The sexual behaviour of another woman, Ann Hassel, was also the cause of much concern within the Refuge but for somewhat different reasons.

> In consequence of an unpleasant intimacy with one of the inmates, felt much inclined to allow her to leave the Refuge....but she saw her error and was thankful to remain longer (Matron's Reports, August 1833).

The 'unpleasant intimacy', although not defined within the reports, undoubtedly refers to a sexual relationship between the two women. Although Ann was originally allowed to stay after acknowledging 'the error of her ways', it was unsurprising to find that one month later the Matron described her as

> Unthankful and disobedient. Expelled without her earnings for bad conduct, immoral behaviour and using improper language (Matron's Reports, September 1833).

Catherine Briggs, one of the first residents to be admitted in 1823, left later that year but wished to return some months later. The Matron's Report indicates that this request was refused.

> Considering her improved health and her sister's perfect willingness to keep her, it is the opinion of the Ladies' Committee that her return is not desirable, especially as she looks for *sinful and shameful indulgences* which are inconsistent with the rules of the institution (Matron's Reports, November 1823. Emphasis added).

'Immoral' or promiscuous sexual behaviour was unacceptable within the dominant discourses of respectability and decency, but sexual conduct which resulted in illegitimate pregnancy was the most intolerable behaviour of all. The case of Ann Cook, aged 17, highlights this. There is only one short entry for Ann in the Matron's Reports which reads as follows.

> Left the Refuge in disgrace - pregnant... .Is not to be allowed back (Matron's Reports, January 1839).

Many women were expelled from the Refuge during the nineteenth century but usually for much less serious 'offences' than Ann's. Whatever the transgression that led to their dismissal (whether it be refusing to work, using bad language or attempting to leave without the permission of the Matron), the behaviour of these women was always explained within a moral discourse. The following examples (all found within the Matron's Reports) emphasise the way in which women were perceived to be intrinsically sinful throughout the whole of the century.

Mary Ann Gilmore, aged 33, was discharged from the Refuge for being 'A wicked depraved character, capable of many sins' (February 1828). Likewise, Ann Johnson, aged 19, 'Would not settle to work....is vile and unprincipled and sinful in character' and was subsequently discharged (July 1847). Ann Birk, aged 23 was 'very artful, sinful and wretched, went out at her own request with bad prospects' (June 1868). Ellen Lynch, aged 19 was described as 'very deceitful and wicked, endeavoured to escape to pursue her former vile habit' (December 1873). Finally Catherine Taylor, aged 22, was dismissed after it was concluded she was 'naturally deceitful and cunning. A woman whose evil tendencies cannot be reformed' (April 1897).

It is apparent from the examples above what constituted a 'failure' at the Refuge. The inability or refusal to submit to and accept the feminising regimes of the institution caused the greatest disappointment amongst, and the harshest response from, the management and staff. By the same premise, success at the Refuge was measured in terms of how closely the female inmates managed to adhere to the ideal model of femininity endorsed by the institution. A failure to return to criminal behaviour or the securing of gainful employment (which would allow the woman to become not only respectable but self-supporting too) was obviously accepted as some measure of 'success'. However the most celebrated form of 'success', and that which proved more than any other that a woman had been effectively reformed, was marriage. Rimmer comments that

> As far as the reformers were concerned, the day on which an old girl produced her marriage certificate in order that she might claim an offered reward of 10 shillings was certainly an occasion for much rejoicing and ample evidence of their job well done (1986: 6).

Marriage was the ultimate confirmation that a woman had been reformed and had willingly accepted and assumed the feminine norms that the Refuge worked so hard to promote. Sarah Hill was admitted to the Refuge in 1835 after the corrupting influence of male companions had turned her from 'a respectable teacher into a wild and unruly woman' (Matron's Reports, October 1835). A year later, after her discharge, a letter from the Matron states that

> Sarah Hill is now married to a steady young man. Much rejoicing....*a better example of the success of our work we could not ask for* (Letter to the Gentlemen's Committee from the Matron, 23 August 1836. Emphasis added).

Catherine Kelly, admitted in 1860, was also a success story for the Refuge.

We are pleased to record that Catherine Kelly, who left the institution in October, is respectfully married and settled at Bangor....a wonderful inspiration for others (Matron's Reports, November 1860).

Likewise Annie Sharpe was 'wonderfully reformed....now married and far from her previous habits' (Matron's Reports, April 1831) and Flora Newgate was 'a true success, married and restored to good health' (Matron's Reports, January 1841). Catherine Smith, although not newly married was still a cause for great celebration when she was 'restored to her husband much reformed' (Matron's Reports, March 1855). Catherine was the ultimate proof that the institution could succeed where all informal measures of control had failed.

> The gentleman [Catherine's husband] would like to thank the Committee for the great improvements in his formerly unruly and ill-tempered wife. Gentlemen, it is so often the case that the women in our care require guidance far beyond that which a loving husband or family can provide and this woman's case should remind us of our duty and function in that respect (Matron's Reports, 1855).

As discussed throughout this chapter, the primary way in which the Refuge attempted to provide the necessary 'guidance' was through the promotion of a range of feminising discourses and practices that served to reaffirm the importance of domesticity, respectability and (legitimate) motherhood. This was primarily achieved through a process of religious and domestic instruction. However, instruction was insufficient without the provision of some 'good examples' to which the female inmates could aspire.

Discipline by Example: Women reforming other women

The Refuge was often perceived as a 'last resort' for the salvation of unruly or immoral women who might otherwise have faced further corruption in prison, their homes or communities. However, once these women were received into the institution, there was no guarantee that they would become impervious to negative influences. As Mahood (1990) points out, it was acknowledged early on by the administration of the Magdalene Homes that there was a greater chance the female inmates would accept the reformist philosophies of the institution if, once there, they remained separated from 'contradictory examples' (1990:78). The Refuge went to great lengths to ensure that those residents deemed to be potentially 'disreputable' were kept apart from their 'respectable' and potentially reformable counterparts. Margaret Roberts and Esther Smith for example, were discharged shortly after their arrival in 1826.

> [Margaret] will be no loss to the Refuge as she is very idle and *sets a very slothful and disagreeable example to the younger females*. The Matron has allow'd (*sic*) her to smoke once a day for a week or two, to wean her off the woe of tobacco

altogether but she smokes till she faints off her chair (Matron's Reports, April 1826. Emphasis added).

The Matron has reason to believe Smith a vile and unprincipled woman dissatisfied with the Refuge *and desirous to make others so...* .She is to be dismissed (Matron's Reports, September 1826. Emphasis added).

Likewise, in 1832, 23 year old Elizabeth Moore was expelled from the Refuge because

[She] continues her wicked practice of contaminating the minds of the inmates by encouraging them to be dissatisfied and discontent *(sic)*. The Ladies....considered it necessary to discharge her immediately (Matron's Reports, June 1832).

Some 26 years later, similar concerns were being raised about Anne Wyn who, again, was quickly expelled.

Anne Wyn, by her influence and bad example, has led on Elizabeth Gascoigne and Sarah Cowley to very ill conduct. The two former have been dismissed from the institution, the latter made her escape but sent back the clothes which she wore which belonged to the Refuge (Matron's Reports, January 1858).

It would appear that the most, or perhaps the only, effective way to protect vulnerable residents from the corruptive influences of 'undesirables' was to dismiss those 'bad apples'. It can be observed from the reports above that decisions to dismiss these 'corrupting' women seemed to have a note of urgency to them. Women who led others astray or who caused others to be dissatisfied with the Refuge were rarely given a second chance and the haste with which they were expelled is a good example of the fear that such women provoked. However it was not sufficient to simply protect the women from negative influences, it was just as important to provide them with some alternative *positive* role models. Thus the appointment of a suitable Matron was felt to be crucial to the success of the institution. As Zedner (1991) points out, women's knowledge of household economics, their background of domesticity and their experiences of caring for the sick and infirm made them an ideal choice for such a role. But, as Sim (1990) argues, throughout the early nineteenth century it was believed that the restoration of *idealistic* moral and social values could be best achieved by setting the inmates of institutions a *realistic* 'feminine' example. Thus, although institutions such as the Refuge aimed to restore women back to a middle class standard of femininity, it was *working class* women who were believed to be most suitable for undertaking this task.

The notion of the respectable and honest working class woman fitted in well with the middle class ideals of 'working class femininity' (diligent, maternal and domesticated). A letter from Nicholas Waterhouse to the newly created

Gentlemen's Committee, prior to the opening of the Refuge, highlights the need for a respectable working class role model. He recommended that the new Matron be

> ....hardworking, clean and sympathetic. The lady appointed must show generosity of spirit *although she need not necessarily be a woman of means* (1 September 1822. Emphasis added).

The Matron was to be responsible for supervising the 'complete' reformation of the female residents and this was to be achieved through two methods. First, she was required to take responsibility for the women's religious instruction thus ensuring their moral reform.

> [The Matron] shall read a chapter out of the Scriptures morning and evening. Each service to begin with a Psalm or Hymn. She shall preside at table during meals, ask a blessing and permit the women to return thanks (First Book of Rules, 1822).

Second, she was expected to supervise their daily household chores, thus guaranteeing their domestic restoration which, in turn, would promote their 'total' reformation. So the Matron played a crucial role in the restoration of women to an appropriate standard of behaviour. It should be acknowledged however that the responsibility of the Matron went far beyond the provision of a good 'feminine' role model. Arguably one of the most significant reasons why the Refuge required a female supervisor was the fact that, as Heidensohn (1996) has asserted, and as discussed in Chapter Two, these women were able to act in a conciliatory role, elucidating and interpreting the 'expert' knowledge of the Gentlemen's Committee (and later other 'experts' such as doctors and psychiatrists) into 'common sense' discourse and practice which, in turn, could be appropriated by the already-failing residents.

Setting a 'good example' was not the sole duty of the Matron. On the contrary, the residents themselves were expected to play an active role in disciplining and reforming their sisters. 27 year old Margaret Downes was referred from Lancaster Prison in 1832 and was described in the Matron's Reports after only a few days as being

> A well behaved woman, very industrious and attentive to the rules of the House. *An excellent example to other inmates* (Matron's Reports, October 1832. Emphasis added).

Similarly, 20 year old Ann Hughes, referred in 1856, was described as

> ....very clean and diligent and likely to set a good example to the other inmates (Matron's Reports, August 1856).

Women who were perceived to be a good influence on others were extremely desirable and, as with those women who offered necessary skills, much effort was taken to keep them in the institution for as long as possible. Maria

Phillips, aged 28, was admitted from Kirkdale Gaol in 1831. She had been abused at home in Glasgow by her stepfather and had decided to walk to Hereford to stay with her mother. She was found in Liverpool in a state of ill health and was sent to Kirkdale for seven days 'in order that her health might be recruited' (Matron's Reports, May 1831). Maria was described as being well educated, articulate and determined and in his letter of referral the prison Chaplain explained that

> Her language is much superior to her station in life and she has evidently experienced very great affliction for she would be thankful to remain in prison rather than go home where she expects to meet with nothing but unkindness from her stepfather whose conduct....drove her from a comfortable home into service. She is very anxious to be admitted into the Refuge and I have no doubt she will benefit by the means afforded by the institution and *also be useful to others by her good example* (12 May 1831, Emphasis added).

Once Maria's health had recovered she expressed a desire to leave the Refuge and continue her journey to her mother in Hereford. The Matron's Reports state that the Matron, Reverend Dawson of the Gentlemen's Committee, Reverend Horner (Chaplain of Kirkdale Gaol) and the members of the Ladies' Committee all tried to discourage Maria from leaving but they were unsuccessful in their attempts and she was eventually discharged in September 1831. Maria had not committed any criminal offence and was, according to the Matron's Reports, only sent to Kirkdale and subsequently to the Refuge, in order to 'regain her health'. She was well educated, from a respectable background and was never once described as being in need of reform. However, she was felt to be such a good example to other residents that this made her a desirable acquisition to the institution, so much so that profound concern was expressed at her request to leave and indeed great efforts were taken to prevent her departure.

Total conformity to accepted standards of femininity was required before a woman would receive the approbation of the Matron and the Ladies' and Gentlemen's Committees. A whole range of 'non-feminine' behaviour such as swearing, drinking and smoking were considered inappropriate and thus attempts were made to control such activities. However, moral judgements were not solely made by the management or staff of the Refuge. Whereas in some cases residents would, by their *good example*, set the standard for acceptable behaviour, in other cases residents would actively determine, by their *disapproval* of other women's actions, what constituted unacceptable, or censured, behaviour. These judgements tended not to concern minor misdemeanours such as using bad language, behaving boisterously or getting drunk. Rather they primarily came into force when a woman was perceived to have seriously transgressed the boundaries of female morality, most commonly when she had been accused or charged with the death, abuse or neglect of a child.[5]

Mary Bennet, for example, was admitted to the Refuge in 1825 after having served nine months in prison for 'stripping children' (Matron's Reports, April 1825). The Matron's Reports state that her youngest child had been admitted to the workhouse and her husband had left her. The Matron goes on to describe Mary as a 'bigoted Roman Catholic' claiming that

> She has not made friends in the Refuge. The other inmates resent her bigoted views and the fact that she so cruelly treated her own children.

Likewise, Bridget Fothergill, admitted in the same year, provoked a similar reaction from the other female residents.

> She was imprisoned for deserting her child... .Fothergill has many good qualities but disgraces them with great violence of temper and bad language... .Is always unhappy, *the other inmates are displeased and allude to her deserting her child* (Matron's Reports, July 1825. Emphasis added).

Although there is no evidence to suggest that these women were subjected to physical violence from their fellow inmates, records do indicate that some degree of verbal abuse was a common response to these 'maternal delinquents'. Bridget for example was described as being upset at the 'spiteful taunts she receives from the other women' (Matron's Reports, July 1825) and Mary requested her leave of the institution after 'becoming weary of hearing the unpleasant names she is so often called' (Matron's Reports, April 1825).

The demarcation and condemnation of 'non-appropriate' behaviour by their fellow residents represents one of the most powerful methods through which many women at the Refuge were policed and controlled. As Smith (1996) argues (in her discussion of contemporary women's prisons) the marginalisation and subsequent 'scapegoating' of particular women, because of the nature of their offence, is a method through which other women can express their own frustrations and emotions by identifying themselves as 'different' and essentially 'superior' to those 'lowest of the low' females (Smith, 1996: 160). Likewise, women at the Refuge would set boundaries between acceptable, 'normal' behaviour and unacceptable, abnormal behaviour, thus segregating and castigating those women who fell into the latter category. Through this process, it could be argued, women who had found themselves deprived of any real status or power (through their admission to such an 'infantilising' institution as the Refuge) could retain some sense of influence and control by separating themselves (both physically and 'morally') from those that they considered to be real 'aberrations' of femininity.

Of course, women did not only police each other. From the Matron's Reports, which provide numerous accounts of women submitting to and accepting the regime at the Refuge, it could be argued that the inmates participated in a form of 'self-policing' too. This issue, along with a discussion of those women who did not accept the regime of the institution and thus rejected or resisted the disciplinary processes and discourses that sought to control them, will be explored below.

Conformity and Resistance in the Semi-Penal Institution

For the most part women *appeared* to readily accept and submit to the disciplinary regimes at the County Refuge. The historical documentation records no incidents of serious collective insurgency and those women who were perceived to display rebellious inclinations were quickly expelled from the institution. The women who remained within the Refuge to complete their period of reformation were, according to the Refuge records, generally tractable and unproblematic. However this apparent passivity needs to be scrutinised closely and examined within the broader context of the situation of working class women in the towns and cities of nineteenth century England.

At this time in history, many women who became labelled 'criminal' or 'wayward', even as children, could find themselves in a persistent cycle of poverty and incarceration. The Matron's Reports (December 1825) highlight this with the case of Helen Malone. She had lived much of her life in the Workhouse but escaped and, in order to avoid starvation, resorted to begging. She was accused and found guilty of theft and was sent to prison. From there she was referred and admitted to the Refuge but left after a few days, as she did not like the regime. Consequently she returned to the workhouse but escaped again and finally ended up back in prison.

The Matron's Reports from 1831 recount another similar case. 16 year old Harriet Pickford was abandoned at a canal in Stockport when she was two months old. She was taken to the Workhouse where she remained until she was ten at which time she went to work in a local factory. However work became scarce and she is described as having frequently gone days without food. She subsequently left the factory and went to work as a servant in the country but after several months of abuse and no pay she left, taking with her an apron belonging to her mistress. She was sentenced to six months imprisonment before she was finally admitted to the Refuge (Matron's Reports, May 1831).

These women, and many others like them, spent much of their lives shunted from one institution to another. In the cases of Helen and Harriet their lives revolved around the workhouse, the prison and the Refuge with periods of poverty and abuse in between. It may have been the case therefore, as Okley (1978) has argued, that many women were willing to participate in their own regulation, by conforming to the disciplinary regimes imposed upon them, as a means of avoiding further and more intense intervention from authority. Thus, women may have submitted to and accepted the regime of the Refuge in order to avoid the more harsh and severe conditions they would face in the Workhouse, the prison or on the streets. Indeed, life within an institution (whether it be a prison, as in Zedner's (1991) argument, or a reformatory as in this case) could be preferable to life at home for some working class women during the nineteenth century. The Refuge undoubtedly offered some women a period of respite from the chronic prison-poverty-workhouse cycle, providing living conditions that they may not have found elsewhere.

Examples of those women who *did* resist the regimes of the Refuge and who consequently ended up in more desperate circumstances were often presented to other residents as a warning of the penalties for bad behaviour. Ellen Partridge was only 17 when she was received at the Refuge in April 1823. She had been tried for burglary and was acquitted whilst her co-accused (her mother and sister) were sentenced to death (Matron's Reports, January 1823).[6] Ellen could not settle at the Refuge and absconded after eight days only to be subsequently charged with another burglary for which she was sentenced to seven years transportation. A letter to the Ladies' Committee from the Matron (20 November 1823) explains the situation.

> Ladies, I have been informed by our dear friend the Chaplain that Ellen Partridge, who absconded several months ago, has since been sentenced to transportation. It is distressing to hear we could not help this poor creature *but this should act as a warning to others who may be thinking of similar action* (Emphasis added).

A similar case was that of Ann Simpson, aged 18, who was admitted to the Refuge in 1844.

> [She was] favourable on arrival. Discontented, left at her own request. Has been since in...prison and sentenced to 10 years transportation (Matron's Reports, October 1844).

A later entry records that

> The women were most upset to hear of the fate of Ann Simpson but are all the more sensible and grateful of the comforts of the Refuge because of it (February 1845).

The staff at the Refuge were well aware that many women only conformed through fear of what might await them outside the institution's gates but as long as the women were hardworking and not disruptive, the motive behind their conformity was unimportant. One such example was 18 year old Ann Shaw, referred in 1845.

> [She is] much addicted to story telling and very bad tempered... .She is very ignorant and dull in all kinds of useful learning. But she takes great pains to behave as she is *quite sensible of her destitute situation and therefore very afraid of being discharged* (Matron's Reports, April 1845, Emphasis added).

29 year old Emma Stubbs, admitted to the Refuge in May 1831, also expressed such fears.

> On first admission very thankful but soon became unsettled and anxious for liberty....she is ashamed of her weak and fickle mind and knows she shall have many difficulties to encounter if thrown upon the world again, without a change of heart (Matron's Reports, May 1831).

Thus, it would appear that conformity was a more common response to institutionalisation than resistance for the women at the Refuge. However, as Bosworth (1999) asserts, there exist other, more subtle, kinds of behaviour in addition to the explicit forms, such as violence or aggression, that are generally defined as 'resistance'. As suggested above, it would seem that many women conformed to the regime in order to avoid further, more severe subjugation or deprivation, rather than to simply satisfy the desires of the reformers. In that sense their conformity could indeed be considered as a form of resistance.

Not all women at the Refuge adopted this approach however. As Sim (1990) argues, institutional regimes established around domesticity and paternalistic surveillance were frequently (and explicitly) resisted by women and he cites several prison protests concerning food and unreasonable punishments as examples. Records do show frequent minor incidents of disobedience and non-conformity within the Refuge but these were seldom collective protests. Rather they were usually incidents of *individual* resistance. Any incidents of collective resistance usually only involved small groups of two or three women and these were, according to the official records, quickly dispelled through the immediate disposal of the 'ringleaders'.

For the most part the women's resistance consisted of verbal protests (using bad language or talking disrespectfully to the staff), general disobedience (refusal to work or disregard for the rules of the Refuge) and leaving without permission (even though the women's stay at the Refuge was not compulsory there are many accounts of women 'escaping'). 21 year old Elizabeth Jones from Holyhead was one of many women who refused to submit to confinement.

> [She is] dirty to a degree, would not be trained, went over the wall April 25th (Matron's Reports, May 1827).

Similar accounts from the Matron's Reports occur throughout all of the nineteenth century records. Susan Campbell, aged 16, was 'expelled for disobedience and other faults' (February 1828); Jane Williams, 16, was described as 'Brought up in the Workhouse and returned to the Workhouse. Troublesome and disorderly and not suitable for the Refuge' (August 1839); 14 year old Mary Pope was 'Discontented, insolent and would not submit to work. Likely to cause unrest amongst the inmates due to her bold and independent manner' (December 1844); Ellen Bradley, 19, was 'remarkably bold, daring and unruly. The Matron expects to have a difficult task to bring her into order' (March 1852); and finally Eliza Gibbons, 23, was 'Bold and rude and independent of all rule. Would not accept help or submit to the rules of the Refuge. Dismissed' (October 1855).

It was usually the extremely structured and disciplined regime of the Refuge that many women would not or could not adapt to. Although living conditions at the Refuge were most likely better than those in prison or the workhouse, and possibly better than those at home for some, the constraints on liberty were a frequent cause of complaint amongst the women. One such woman was 28 year old Elizabeth Collins who was admitted to the Refuge in 1826.

> She has been a woman of the town. Had a child born in [gaol], dead. Has something bold in her manner. Collins has frequently expressed a desire to go out, thinking the Refuge not half so cheerful and pleasant as [gaol]. She expected, she says, that they might amuse themselves as they please (Matron's Reports, April 1826).

Elizabeth was obviously under the impression that the Refuge would be a less restrictive environment than the prison from which she had been sent. Finding that this was not the case, she requested her discharge and was ultimately granted permission to leave. Ann Jane McBride, aged 16, also showed considerable resentment at the restraints on her liberty.

> ....is heartily tired of such confinement and says she cannot bear it much longer (Matron's Reports, October 1826).

According to Mahood insubordinate and unruly women were a great cause for concern at the Magdalene Homes. She argues that these women did not perceive themselves to be immoral or in need of discipline hence 'their refusals may be interpreted as acts of resistance to moral reform and surveillance.' (1990: 101). There is evidence within the Reports from the County Refuge to support Mahood's assertions. Many of the women dismissed for unmanageable or uncontrollable behaviour did not believe they required the strict discipline and structured regime of the Refuge. Mary Evans, admitted in 1860, was described by the Matron as

> ....very unruly and insolent. She refuses to abide by the rules of the Refuge and complains that *she is not a criminal and should not be treated as one.* She is most defiant and ungrateful (Matron's Reports, November 1860. Emphasis added).

Women like Mary, who rather than displaying the gratitude and appreciation so desired by the Management Committee, declared instead feelings of resentment and indignation at, what they considered an unnecessary intrusion into and constraint upon their lives, were deemed to be the most intolerable type of resident. The Matron finally agreed to the discharge of Mary Evans, after her profound discontentment proved her to be 'stubborn, morally unmovable and completely untrainable' (Matron's Reports, November 1860). A letter to the Gentlemen's Committee explains the Matron's decision.

> Gentlemen, this woman, Mary Evans, was beyond our help, indeed it would appear she was beyond help of any kind. Alas she was ignorant to the fact that help was what was offered her, thinking instead that she was being unduly restrained here in the Refuge... .I fear the likes of Evans will never redeem herself and will forever remain bound by her own stubbornness (Letter from the Matron to the Gentlemen's Committee, 2 December 1860).

This chapter has identified and analysed the genesis and development of the County Refuge throughout the nineteenth century in terms of the management and administration of the institution and the dominant ideologies and discourses through which the female residents were disciplined and reformed. In addition the ways in which women responded to their confinement, through either displays of conformity or through both subtle and explicit forms of resistance, have been explored. The following chapter will take up these theoretical debates, scrutinising the history of the institution throughout the twentieth century.

Notes

[1]   This information was found in an undated and unpublished report, entitled *The Church and Social Service*. It was located in the attic of Vernon Lodge during the period of fieldwork for this research. The majority of material used in this, and the following, chapter originated from the same source and is the property of the Church of England Council for Social Aid (CECSA), formerly the Church of England Temperance Society (CETS). The documentation found consisted of unpublished material including Matron's log books, Matron's Reports, rule books, annual reports, minutes of meetings, medical reports and several memos and personal letters. Although the majority of the material was dated, some documents were not and so specific dates will be given whenever possible. For further details of the documents used see the Primary Source Material section in the Bibliography of this book.

[2]   Matron's Report books for the early years of the Refuge provide many examples of the Ladies' Committee meeting with the Gentlemen's Committee in order to gain permission for the reception of inmates and the allocation of funds (for books, games and clothing).

[3]   Women would also be referred by their husbands or families and this issue will be discussed later in this chapter.

[4]   The Matron's Log Book for the years 1835 - 1838 is a record of all admissions to the Refuge. Of the 75 women admitted during this time, 40 are identified as being able to 'read sufficiently', 16 are described as able to read 'imperfectly' and 19 are recorded as 'illiterate'. However although there was a fairly high rate of illiteracy amongst the residents, this was not recorded as a priority in the reform process.

[5]   See Chapter Six for a further discussion of this issue in a contemporary context.

[6]   There is no record to confirm if the death sentence was carried out on Ellen's mother and sister. During this period of history, it was quite common for capital sentences to be commuted.

Chapter 5

Between the Church and the State: Semi-Penal Institutionalisation in the Twentieth Century

Unlike during the nineteenth century when the Refuge was underpinned by a prevailing moral paradigm, the institution during the twentieth century was characterised by two seemingly opposing, but at the same time, mutually reinforcing discourses built around morality/religion and medical science. These two discourses were employed to explain and respond to women's deviant behaviour and although each had periods of influence throughout the century, neither one ever gained total, singular dominance over the other. Because these discourses tended to re-emerge at particular points during the twentieth century, this chapter will be structured differently to the previous chapter. So although I will address similar themes to those addressed in the previous chapter (themes of continuity between past and present, the merging of informal and formal methods of control for women, the way in which women responded to, or resisted, the disciplinary discourses and regimes imposed upon them and so on), a chronological (as opposed to a thematic) structure will be applied here.

In some cases the time periods covered by the sub-sections overlap (the first sub-section for example covers the first two decades of the century whilst the second sub-heading covers the period between the wars). This was essentially unavoidable given that I am examining changes, shifts and modifications in both organisational structure and dominant, disciplinary discourses and, whereas sometimes these two aspects were found to be interrelated, at other times they were not. Hence, the chapter will broadly maintain a chronological 'flow' as far as possible but will 'backtrack' in places where necessary. However, before any discussion regarding the twentieth century can begin, it is first necessary to revisit the latter years of the nineteenth century in order to briefly outline some important changes that occurred with regard to the Refuge.

In 1864 the institution had been re-named The County Female Refuge. It was from this period to the late nineteenth century, that two significant and powerful organisations, namely the Church of England Temperance Society (CETS) and the probation service, became influential in its development.

The Temperance Movement had gained a particular stronghold in England throughout the nineteenth century. However, apprehensions for drunkenness continued to increase and in 1876, on the instigation of Frederick Rainer (generally acknowledged as the pioneer of the English probation service) the CETS began practical rescue work with the intemperate (Jarvis, 1972). Missionaries were attached to police courts in order to 'reclaim' the souls of drunkards who agreed to sign a pledge of temperance.

The police court missionaries had two major objectives. First, through the undertaking of social enquiries into the background and antecedents of offenders at the request of magistrates, they aimed to prevent those who were 'at risk' of incarceration from getting a custodial sentence. This work was extended after the implementation of the Probation of First Offenders Act of 1887 when the missionaries became largely responsible for the supervision of offenders released by the court on probation orders (McWilliams, 1983).

Their second objective was to succour and comfort on their discharge, those released from prison. Missionaries were placed in attendance outside the police courts and gaols. Newly released prisoners would be received by the missionaries daily, given breakfast and then encouraged to sign the pledge. Those who complied (and there were many, in 1898 for instance over 1000 declarations were made in Liverpool alone (*Liverpool Review,* 1928: 31)) were then assisted in finding accommodation or employment.

The Probation of Offenders Act of 1907 increased the powers of the courts to release offenders on their own recognizances or on the sureties of others. What was particularly significant about the 1907 Act, however, was that it finally formalised the system of supervision. On hearing of the appointment of supervising probation officers, the CETS contacted the Home Office offering the services of its missionaries, who by 1907 had many years experience in the supervision of offenders. By December 1907, 120 missionaries had been appointed nationally as probation officers (Jarvis, 1972: 20).

One consequence of these appointments was that from the late nineteenth century women were being referred to the County Refuge via the police court missionaries and then later, by the new probation officers, in addition to those referred by prison chaplains, husbands and families. This new method of referral was to have a significant and lasting impact on the development of the institution throughout the twentieth century.

The First Two Decades of the Twentieth Century

By the first decade of the twentieth century, the Refuge was still operating under the same 'catch them young' philosophy that had been employed during its early years. An article in the Welldoer, the newsletter of the League of Welldoers, records the kind of women targeted by the Refuge during the early 1900s.

> Women 'from the streets' are not admitted, because there are now numerous institutions.... to receive such. Young domestic servants, who have lost their place and character by some act of dishonesty; girls over whom their natural guardians have lost control; first offenders bound over and placed under probation, form the class received at the institution (1909: 2).

The Refuge was still employing the same methods of gatekeeping that it always had. Those women considered incorrigible were generally not admitted. The women referred from both the prisons and the court missionaries or probation officers were young, first-time offenders and a genuine desire to reform was still a desirable criteria. The regime at the Refuge was at this time still based around the combination of moral and domestic reform, as had been the case throughout the nineteenth century. Moral reform, it was believed, could be achieved through religious doctrine. Christian charity was still the overriding philosophy that drove the work of the Refuge and the practice of the inmates attending morning and evening worship was still enforced. However during the early years of the twentieth century the notion of 'training' took on a new significance and for the first time a set training period of 18 months was introduced for the inmates. During this training period laundry work and the duties of domestic service were taught and the 'deserving' women who remained at the Refuge for the allotted time were found employment in this field when they left (Welldoer, 1909: 2). So, although there still existed a strong religious emphasis, the objectives of the Refuge were now not solely concerned with the saving of individual souls. Rather, the creation of an industrious, productive and controllable female workforce had become an important priority. A letter from the Matron to the Ladies' Committee highlights this shift.

> Ladies, we must put our efforts into training and finding employment for our charges. The light of God will still lead their way but the development of useful skills is necessary if they are to lead productive, decent and sober lives upon their discharge (1 September 1908).

With the Refuge regime now emphasising strict and structured training, women were expected to work long hours in the laundry and learn general household duties. The Matron's Reports for December 1902 give an account of a prize giving ceremony held in November of that year. 12 inmates received prizes and 11 received 'encouragement gifts' for categories such as Laundry Work, Washing, Cooking and Sewing which give a good indication of the type of work and training undertaken. In addition to these categories however, and in keeping with the still dominant moral discourse employed, the women were given prizes for Scripture, Honesty, Good Example, Good Conduct, Obedience, General Improvement and Truthfulness.

The strict discipline, structured regime and the concentration on training at the Refuge, coupled with the emphasis on the teachings of religious doctrine, greatly appealed to the magistrates and judicial officials faced with young female offenders who, they believed, were in need of diversion from the corrupting prison system (Leeson, 1914). Hence from 1908, just a few months after the introduction of the Probation of Offenders Act, many women who had been bound over and placed on probation by the courts were referred on to the Refuge by their probation officers, where it was hoped they would be reformed and successfully returned to their families. Given that the majority of the newly appointed probation officers were indeed former police court missionaries (who were still firmly attached to the

Church and the affiliated Temperance Movement) it is unsurprising that the County Female Refuge, with its strong religious emphasis and firm links with the Church of England, was well utilised by the courts for women on probation.

The earliest official records of women on probation being admitted to the Refuge are found in the Matron's Reports of March 1908. Margaret Thomas and Almenia Richardson are reported as having been 'sent from police court under the Probation of Offenders Act'. However this development had actually begun some years earlier. The Register of Residents indicates that from as early as 1898 the number of women being referred via the court missionaries was already increasing whilst the numbers referred from prison was decreasing. In 1898 for example, of 17 women admitted that year, only two came directly from prison and similarly in 1900, of 16 women admitted, only three were referred from prison (Register of Residents, 1898-1948). Although the Register does not state where the remainder of the referrals came from, it is reasonable to assume, given that women were only referred through three main sources at the time – prison, family and probation - that a significant proportion of women admitted to the Refuge from the late nineteenth century onwards were probation referrals.

By the end of 1908, however, concern was growing in the Refuge as to whether the acceptance of women on probation was indeed a positive development. Although it was acknowledged that probation officers were a most productive source of referrals, several reports describe the probationers as being more unruly and badly behaved than the other inmates. An entry in the Matron's Reports highlights this.

> Maggie Asbridge absconded. She was one of the....probationers. *All the probationers have been most unsatisfactory* (Matron's Reports, December, 1908. Emphasis added).

Up until the Probation of First Offenders Act of 1887, all admissions to the Refuge were classed as 'voluntary'. As discussed in the previous chapter, prison chaplains would generally only refer, and the Refuge would only accept, those women who had a genuine desire to reform their lives. However after the Act, women were sent on orders by the courts and, although the Refuge still had the authority to refuse a referral if they did not deem the woman to be suitable, the philosophies behind both the Refuge and the Probation Act were so similar it would have been difficult to justify the non-acceptance of referrals. Also as stated previously, the number of referrals from prison chaplains was falling and therefore, in order to stay financially viable, maximum residency had to be maintained. Consequently the Refuge became home to large numbers of women who did not necessarily have a desire to be there but possibly only agreed to a period of residence in order to avoid the probable alternative, a custodial sentence. Although the Refuge had experienced, throughout its history, some resistance from its female inmates, these new compulsory referrals were seen as a particular cause for concern.

I am concerned that those women sent by the courts will be more troublesome than those.... who have a genuine desire to reform their characters... .Our greatest fear is that these women will have an unsettling effect on the others (Letter from the Matron to the Ladies' Committee, 8 November 1908).

The female probationers were viewed as disruptive and disorderly and from 1908 onwards, possibly in response to this perceived unruliness, 'internal' punishments began to be enforced. This constituted a definite shift in philosophy for the Refuge. Primarily it represented a move towards a more formal type of institutional regime and although there is no record of any widespread, collective protest at the Refuge during this time, the introduction of 'punishments' indicates that the legitimacy of the social order within the institution was not always automatically accepted and tolerated by the female residents.

Throughout the previous century bad behaviour had been generally punishable by immediate discharge from the institution. After 1908, however, women could be punished through a variety of methods, including withdrawing their allowance (given for productive laundry work), vetoing visits from friends and families and banning the writing and receiving of monthly letters (Matron's Reports, 1908, 1910, 1918). In addition to the need to deal swiftly with troublesome inmates, there is another reason for this change. The Refuge was not as economically buoyant as it had been throughout the early to mid nineteenth century. Indeed, during the first decade of the twentieth century, it suffered a series of major financial crises and therefore the Management Committees could not afford to discharge women at the rate they once had as the Refuge now depended financially to a great extent upon the industry of the residents.

Around the same time another change occurred, this time in relation to explanations of the women's offending behaviour. During the early years of the 1900s a new and oppressive paradigm emerged within which the women at the Refuge, and indeed women offenders more generally, were viewed and categorised.

The appliance of science

The scientific / medical claim to understand Woman and render her intelligible was part of science's wider project: the understanding and controlling of Nature (Bland, 1995: 53).

The end of the nineteenth century had seen a rise in 'scientific' and medical explanations of criminal behaviour and these explanations gave rise to theories that advocated medical treatment rather than punishment. Zedner (1991) comments that by the end of the nineteenth century social inadequacy and 'feeble-mindedness' had been identified as serious medical conditions, conditions that were believed to be the source of many social problems. Poverty, intemperance and crime, which had previously been blamed on the lack of morality amongst the poor, were now perceived to be the result of 'feeble-mindedness' and mental inadequacy. The Eugenics Movement at the time went further by asserting that these social deficiencies would be bred into future generations and consequently 'feeble-mindedness' (amongst females in particular) became viewed as a dangerous *social* problem (Zedner, 1991).

This shift in thinking had a significant impact upon the regime of the Refuge. However, the growing emphasis on medical knowledge did not lead to the demise of the moral discourse that had driven the work of the institution during the previous century. Rather, what developed was a situation where no single philosophy was dominant.[1] As a result, the classifications of the women at the Refuge became remarkably diverse and they could find themselves and their conduct explained in medical and moral terms at the same time. Faith was placed in both God and science in an effort to modify the behaviour of the women and salvation and 'treatment' existed side by side as the dominant methods of reform.

Zedner (1991) asserts that, as far as women were concerned, the very definition of 'feeble-mindedness' was influenced by both moral and medical debates. Judgements regarding a woman's mental condition were often made on the basis of her moral conduct. In other words sexual promiscuity or immorality was commonly used as evidence of mental inadequacy.[2]

The register of residents (1898-1948) indicates that from 1907 potential residents at the Refuge were examined by a doctor and their suitability for admission was assessed primarily on the state of their physical and mental health. It was the responsibility of the doctor to declare each referral as fit or unfit for training at the Refuge. The assessment of the women's physical health was justified in two ways. First, the women were expected to work long hours in the laundry and therefore they would need to be in a reasonable state of physical health to cope with these demands. There are indeed many accounts of women being refused admittance because they were not deemed well or strong enough to undertake such work. 18 year old Elizabeth Walton for example was restored to the care of her mother in 1900 after serving a prison sentence because she was declared 'medically unfit for work' (Register of Residents, 1898-1948). Likewise, Annie Cooper (1900), Daisy Wright (1900), Jessie Davies (1900), Jessie Bowley (1909) and Lilly Burrows (1919) were all categorised as medically unfit for work or training due to their poor state of health and were returned to their families instead (Register of Residents, 1898-1948). Not all women were returned to their families however. The Register of Residents records cases of medically unfit women, such as Edith Donald in 1902, who, on having no family to receive her, was sent straight to the Workhouse.

In some instances the work itself led to illness and hospitalisation and there are several recorded incidents of accidents in the Laundry. Eliza Brown suffered scalds to her neck and face in 1912 (Matron's Reports, August 1912) and Ruth Carter lost part of her finger in the washing machine in 1919 (Matron's Reports, November 1919). A year previous Lizzie Holt had been sent to hospital after suffering a rupture doing laundry work (Matron's Reports, July 1918). The Refuge accepted no responsibility for any of these incidents. In Lizzie's case the accident was deemed to be of her own making because, as the Matron explained 'Holt [had] never been strong.' (Matron's Reports, July 1918). In the same report the Matron went on to declare that more care should be taken in future to ensure only strong and healthy women, capable of withstanding such laborious duties, be admitted.

The second reason why physical health checks were so important was because, during the first two decades of the twentieth century, sickness and death were commonplace occurrences at the Refuge. Lucy Davies for example, aged 14, died of scarlet fever in 1900 and Mary Connely suffered the same fate two years later (Register of Residents, 1898-1948). The Refuge witnessed six deaths in the ten years between 1905 and 1915 along with 26 admissions to hospital (List of Hospitalisations and Deaths, 1905-1915). Mary Barlow was one of several women who died from Influenza (Matron's Reports, December 1918) but her death was recorded in a very different way to many of the others. For the most part deaths were recorded as routine incidents, in much the same way as an expulsion or an escape. Mary was obviously an exemplary resident and her loss was a significant one to the institution. Her illness and death are mentioned several times in the Register of Residents (1898-1948), the Matron's Reports for 1918 and also in a separate letter from the Matron to the Ladies' Committee, all of which highlight the importance the Refuge attached, even in death, to reformed and grateful women.

> Mary Barlow has died. She was a particularly nice girl and we are very distressed about her... .She was bright and happy to the last and wished me to thank the Committee for their kindness to her (Register of Residents, 1898-1948).

> I regret to inform you of the death last week of Mary Barlow. She was indeed a most kind and pleasant inmate and an industrious and grateful worker. We are all very distressed about her death (Letter from the Matron to the Ladies' Committee, 25 September 1918).

However, it was not only the women's physical health that was routinely assessed. On the contrary, emphasis was also placed on assessments of *mental* health and these 'diagnoses' were used primarily as a form of gatekeeping.

In 1917 Millie Worthington was deemed to be feeble-minded and was subsequently sent from the Refuge to an Institution for the Mentally Defective (Matron's Reports, June 1917). This case highlights the powerless position of those women categorised as 'feeble-minded' or 'mentally defective'. Many of these women, most of whom had not committed criminal offences, or if so, only minor ones, would find themselves shifted between various (semi-penal and custodial) institutions. 16 year old Lillian Bradshaw is an example. She was sent to the Refuge in June 1924 on probation for stealing a bag. In the Register of Residents her behaviour is recorded as 'very strange' and a subsequent doctor's report which labelled her as 'weak minded and medically unfit for training' led to her transfer, firstly to Mill Road Infirmary and from there to the Asylum (July 1924).

As stated previously both moral and medical discourses were employed to explain the conduct of women at the Refuge. This was most often the case if a woman's behaviour was judged to be sexually promiscuous. Molly Kelly, aged 17, was refused admission to the Refuge in 1909. Although there is no record of a doctor's assessment, a letter from the Matron to the Ladies' Committee clearly highlights the concerns regarding her sexual conduct.

> This woman has an *immoral* and unhealthy weakness for associating with members of the opposite sex. This I believe is due to her *low mental ability*. I believe her to be untrainable (Letter from the Matron to the Ladies Committee, 22 March 1909. Emphasis added).

A similar example is Lizzie Dobson, admitted to the Refuge in August 1911. Lizzie was described in the Matron's Reports for that month as being 'weak minded, wilful and wicked'. Again, her behaviour is explained and rationalised by intertwining discourses around morality and pathology.

The Refuge was therefore utilising pseudo-scientific explanations of (criminal and female) behaviour from the very early years of the twentieth century. However, although these scientific models went some way towards explaining the ('immoral') conduct of the women at the Refuge, thus justifying and legitimating further medical *and* moral intervention, they were never used to mitigate or excuse the behaviour of the women. Nonetheless, as Zedner (1991) points out, the prevalence of feeble-mindedness and other forms of mental 'deficiency' amongst the poor and 'criminal classes' *was* used to justify and rationalise the failure of institutions to control and reform refractory inmates.

During the early twentieth century (as had been the case during the nineteenth century) the Refuge took full credit for the successful reformation of its residents. Women whose lives and characters had been amended and restored to an acceptable degree of respectability were seen to be the product of an effective regime of discipline and moral teachings. The role played and the effort made by the reformed women themselves was only rarely acknowledged and the Refuge (in particular the Matron) was given full credit for any positive transformations. Conversely, 'failures' were not seen to be the responsibility of the Refuge. Instead blame was placed on the inherent badness, immorality or mental inadequacy of the individual women themselves. Examples include Catherine Williams who was dismissed after being described as 'lazy and idiotic. An imbecile and untrainable' (April 1909) and Maud Cooper who was 'unruly and untrainable due to her feeble-mindedness' (February 1912). On the other hand Elizabeth Howard left with glowing reports in 1916 but her successful reformation was proclaimed to be evidence of 'yet another example of the fine work of the institution' (January 1916).

It is worth making some further comment here on the way in which success and failure were measured during these early years of the twentieth century. Due to the emphasis on formal training, success was partially measured in terms of the acquisition of gainful employment. However, the most important measure of success was, still, marriage and (legitimate) motherhood. The Matron's records for 1906, 1908 and 1909 make reference to several 'successful' ex-residents.

Visited three girls who are married. It was most gratifying to see how beautifully clean and neat they keep their homes and their children (March 1906).

Two of our girls came back to visit. One is married and the other is in a respectable [domestic] situation. It is most satisfying when one's hard work comes to fruition (October 1908).

The Committee will be pleased to hear that Emma Steed was married to a very respectable young man on the 11th May. She had been a faithful servant in her first situation for over eight years (June 1909).

One might assume that any woman who avoided returning to prison or the courts, and who managed to secure legitimate employment would be seen as a 'good result' by the institution, however this was not the case. Ethel Withnall, admitted in 1921, left the Refuge two years later to enter domestic service. However she only remained in this position for a few months before going to work in a local factory. The Matron subsequently informed the Refuge Committees that

Ethel Withnall has turned out very badly....untruthful in her situation also rude to her mistress. I hear she is now working in some factory. *She is the greatest failure we have had* (Matron's Reports, September 1923. Emphasis added).

The utilisation of both moral and pseudo-scientific explanations of deviant behaviour was to remain a significant feature of the Refuge throughout the twentieth century. The end of the First World War coincided with several changes within the institution. Many of these were related to organisational and financial matters but they are significant as they raise important issues regarding the culture and regime of the institution and its peculiar role within the growing probation service. Most significant though was the increasing influence of the Church of England and the subsequent shift back to a dominant moral philosophy.

The Refuge Between the Wars

Between 1913 and 1919, whilst the country was preparing for, fighting in and recovering from the First World War, there was a steady decline in the number of offenders placed on probation orders by the courts (Jarvis, 1972). However, whilst the probation service in general was witnessing a decline, the Refuge saw a steady increase in referrals and admissions and throughout the duration of the war, its occupancy levels rarely fell below maximum capacity.[3] In keeping with the traditional paternalistic culture of the Refuge, this increase was attributed to the fact that 'The fathers have gone to the War and the mothers are unable to manage their girls' (Matron's Reports, August 1917). However, the high number of admissions brought other problems. The institution experienced a rise in unruly and disruptive behaviour from its residents (although whether this increase was actual or perceived is unclear). The Refuge adhered to the traditional notion that idleness led to unruliness and during the war years a shortage of work was frequently associated with the lack of discipline. As the Matron explained

> It is harder to keep up the discipline when we have not a comfortable amount of work for the girls (Matron's Reports, June 1918).

In addition, a rise in resident numbers coupled with the shortage of work meant that the Refuge had difficulty staying financially viable during this time. Although the institution was utilised more than ever in terms of referrals, funds were becoming scarce and from as early as 1880 up until 1920 it ran into many financial crises. One reason for this was that the Refuge was still a charity and depended largely upon voluntary contributions and donations for its existence. During the early years of the nineteenth century this did not present any problems but by the twentieth century philanthropy had become a victim of its own success and there existed so many charitable organisations and societies in the area that money to fund all of them was sparse (*The Welldoer,* 1909). Also, after the First World War, the industry of the residents, which had in the past kept the Refuge afloat, had largely dried up leaving them financially exposed. At one point the situation became so desperate that the Refuge even considered asking the families of those residents on probation to pay towards the keep of the women. This scheme was proposed by the Management Committee in 1917 and would have meant registering all probation cases with the Council for Voluntary Aid (CVA). A CVA worker would then visit the family homes of the probationers to see if the parents, guardians or other family members could afford to pay a little towards the upkeep of the Refuge (County Female Refuge Annual Report, 1917).

Because of its close links, the Church of England Temperance Society (CETS) found itself bailing the Refuge out of financial trouble on several occasions between 1880 and 1919 with sums of up to £500 each time. Finally in 1919, with the Refuge facing imminent closure, the CETS decided to clear its debts completely and in doing so took full control and trusteeship of the institution. Although this ensured a more pecuniary secure future for the Refuge it would still rely heavily upon voluntary contributions and upon 'the industry of the inmates' for many years to come.

The re-emergence of the 'moral' paradigm

With the powerful Temperance Society at the helm, the Refuge was obviously now seen as a more viable and worthwhile charity. This is reflected in the Annual Report for 1919 which gives details of 186 subscriptions as well as over 40 donations for that year, the total amount of contributions being over £500, a significant increase over previous years (Annual Report, 1919). By the 1920s there were four full time staff, a Matron and three Assistant Matrons (Annual Report, 1927). Those members of staff who had most contact with the female residents were still, of course, all women while the formal management of the Refuge remained predominantly male. This situation, with women acting as the 'mediators of knowledge' between the male 'experts' of the Refuge administration and their 'failing' clients was to change little throughout the remainder of the century.

The 1920s through to the 1940s saw significant changes to the rapidly evolving probation service. As stated previously, since 1908 the majority of probation officers had been closely affiliated to the Church of England Temperance Society. In 1920 the Home Office established a Departmental Committee responsible for the training, appointment and payment of probation officers and in response to growing criticism, this Committee set about re-evaluating the role of the CETS in the probation service. Concern had been expressed about the appropriateness of the association between probation work and a society whose primary aim was to promote temperance. However it was also acknowledged that nationally, the supply of probation officers depended heavily on the CETS, and other similar voluntary organisations. The Committee finally recommended that although links would need to be maintained between the probation service and the CETS, a clear distinction would be drawn between the supervisory work undertaken by the missionaries for the probation service and the temperance work still carried out by the CETS (Jarvis, 1972).

This is a further example of the paradoxical situation of the Refuge with regard to trends and developments in the wider realm of non-custodial penalties. While the probation service was taking steps to separate its work from that of the CETS (in order to 'professionalise' the service and cut ties with the old religious and moralistic philosophy), the Refuge was actually moving in the opposite direction. From 1919 the CETS was in control of one of the few institutions for women probationers and many of the traditional philosophies and values still prevailed.

Although the CETS had openly reported that their take-over would make no difference to the day to day running of the Refuge, the 1920s saw a strong re-emergence of the religious and moral discourses that had been dominant throughout the nineteenth century. Although the religious emphasis had persisted into the twentieth century it had been 'diluted' to an extent by the emergence of medical and scientific theories. However once the CETS had assumed control of the institution, religious and moral discourses began, once again, to dominate the regime. The opening address of the Refuge's annual meeting for 1919 highlights this clearly.

> Never in the history of the [Refuge] was there greater opportunity for such a Home than that which is before [us] today. The growing importance which the Magistrates attach to the work carried on under the Probation Act emphasises the need for *a Christian Institution*, when those who are in danger of developing unruly characters may be brought under wholesome discipline, and trained in habits of obedience, reliability and industry (Annual Report, 1919. Emphasis added).

The CETS placed great emphasis on the importance of the teachings of Christianity and the rite of baptism. From the time it took over trusteeship in 1919 it began, very quickly, to introduce these philosophies into the daily routine.

Compulsory attendance at bible classes and daily prayers were written into the official rules along with a warning that 'untruthfulness, swearing and disorderly conduct' would not be tolerated (Rules for the Matron, 1920). Perhaps one of the most significant changes as a result of the CETS take-over was that from 1920, women were prepared, under the guidance of the Chaplain, for confirmation. The Matron's Reports for the 1920s and 1930s indicate that as many as 13 women were baptised each year and records show that this practice continued until well into the 1960s.

In addition, whereas the probation service was attempting to distance itself from an organisation dedicated to the promotion of temperance, the new administration at the Refuge was busy implementing its doctrine of sobriety. In 1927 four women were awarded the Madden Memorial Prize for essays written on the subject of temperance after a lecture given by the Diocesan Secretary. Another three women were awarded the same prize the following year along with prizes for achievements in scripture, religious knowledge and truthfulness (Matron's Reports, 1927, 1928).

By 1927 the Refuge had moved to a new address. The move to the new building provided accommodation for four more residents and eliminated the overcrowding that was beginning to occur at the previous location. Towards the end of the 1920s, the Refuge housed approximately 26 women per year and the population was now significantly less transient than it had previously been. One reason for this was that the regime was now far more structured and the period of training, usually between 12 months and two years, was more rigorously enforced. Also, during the 1920s the Refuge was particularly well utilised by probation officers seeking suitable supervision and training for their charges. By the late 1920s approximately 50 per cent of the women at the Refuge had been placed on probation by the courts and were required to undertake the necessary 'training' that the institution provided (Matron's Reports, 1927, 1928). Identifying an appropriate period of 'training' was to be the cause of an ongoing disagreement between the Refuge and judicial officials who, by the 1930s, wanted to impose a standard period of six months training upon probationers. The Refuge administration, specifically the Matron, strongly resisted this proposal.

> There are social workers who think that six months training is sufficient for these girls, but the Matron with her many years experience, is convinced that the two years which this Home makes its rule is barely adequate for the necessary training (Annual Report, 1937: 4).

The Refuge staff, having spent many years working with 'a class of girls whose difficult dispositions and temperaments and characters made an incessant demand upon the patience, tact and sympathy of the Matron' (Annual Report, 1928: 7), believed they were inherently more qualified than professional social workers to judge what was best for their residents.[4] This resistance to fall into line with the practices of the probation service did not abate throughout the 1930s. The Refuge remained, to a great degree, firmly unaffected by developments in probation policy, yet was still well utilised by the service in the supervision of women on court orders.

In 1930 formal training was established for probation officers and by 1938 the police court missions began to hand over full control of probation supervision to the Home Office (King, 1969; Jarvis, 1972). Throughout this time though, the Refuge managed to maintain its independent status and its emphasis on moral reform and Christian charity.

> [The Committee] can tell once again of patient and faithful service rendered by the Matron and her fellow workers in a Home which, by the blessing of God, has been fruitful in the task of rescuing and restoring to a place of usefulness, more than one young life that has for the time being missed the right road and fallen on wrong ways....see these young lives in the places and homes where they were living and where they have failed and strayed from the right path, and then see the Home and its workers as friendly hands held out to lift them up to better and worthier living (Annual Report, 1937: 3).

The CETS had incited a move back towards a strong Christian emphasis within the institution. As a result, the Refuge of the 1920s and 1930s provided a deeply religious and moral environment within which fallen and misguided women could repent, and reform their lives and souls. The CETS attempted to ensure that the notions of salvation and reform underpinned all of the work carried out at the Refuge however the dominance of this moral and spiritual paradigm was to be relatively short lived.

The re-emergence of the medical paradigm

As mentioned previously 'psycho-medical' explanations of women's behaviour had been influencing the work of the Refuge since the early years of the twentieth century. However these pseudo-scientific discourses had tended to impact only upon the way in which women were *described* and *categorised* within the institution. In other words, although women were frequently labelled as 'feeble-minded' or mentally deficient within official records, there is no evidence to suggest that these women were offered any form of 'treatment' (other than the standard domestic training programme undertaken by all of the residents). Indeed the assessment of the mental condition of a referral was often used as a method of gatekeeping or 'screening out' particular 'types' of women. So those women found to have any form of mental inadequacy were frequently deemed unsuitable for the Refuge and were quickly returned to their families or the Workhouse. If their condition was judged to be sufficiently severe then they would be transferred to hospital or to the asylum.

The 1930s, however, saw a dramatic change in this practice. Psychological assessments were still carried out on women referred to the Refuge but the purpose of these examinations was no longer to keep the 'feeble-minded' out of the institution, but rather to get them in. Women identified as 'feeble-minded' had become, by the mid 1930s, a target group and mental inadequacy became almost a pre-requisite for admission.[5]

Although women had historically always been subjected to the intense scrutiny of doctors and medical professionals, the 1920s and 1930s represented an exceptionally oppressive period for women diagnosed or labelled as mentally disordered. Despite the rise in the number of female practitioners entering the fields of psychiatry and psychoanalysis after the First World War, promiscuous, criminal or 'wayward' women were increasingly diagnosed as mentally ill. Treatments such as insulin shock, electro-shock and lobotomy were taken up with great relish by British doctors intent on curing female mental illness (Showalter, 1987).

According to Sim (1990) the psychological assessment and treatment of criminal women gained much credibility in the 1930s following the publication of a Medical Research Council report in 1933 which advocated the permanent segregation and sterilisation of mentally defective women. What was so significant about this report was that it supported and validated the notion that psychopathology and immorality, as far as the behaviour of women was concerned, were inherently linked.

Throughout the 1930s and 1940s many of the women referred to the Refuge (either by doctors or by their own families) had never been convicted of a criminal offence. Instead they were categorised as 'preventative cases' and were sent to the Refuge simply because they were 'wayward' or outside of parental control.[6] For example Georgina S.[7] was admitted to the Refuge 'for her own protection' in 1934 (Register of Residents 1898-1948) because her parents were unable to control her behaviour. A year later in 1935 Elizabeth M. was also admitted 'for her own protection' on account of her 'weak spirit and feeble-mindedness' (ibid) and in 1937, 16 year old Nora C. arrived at the Refuge, her 'offence' being that she was 'weak minded' and therefore in need of protection from 'her own defectiveness' (ibid).

The dual paradigms of 'morality' and 'pathology' fitted perfectly with this new focus. The role of the institution, as far as these 'preventative cases' were concerned, was to provide a structured, disciplined and 'wholesome' environment within which young troublesome women could be assessed, contained and 'normalised'. The idea of targeting women *prior* to them having committed any criminal offence was, of course, nothing new for this type of institution. Indeed, as noted in Chapter Three, one of the features that characterised institutions as semi-penal, and indeed underpinned the establishment of the reformatory movement in general, was the fact that they served to expand the methods of discipline and control normally found within formal custodial environments to cases of 'less-than-full-criminality' (Weiner, 1990: 130). Targeting 'preventative cases' served to widen the, already all encompassing, disciplinary net for 'deviant' women.

The regime for 'preventative cases' at the Refuge was both restrictive and oppressive. These women were subjected to frequent medical examinations and regular psychological assessments throughout their stay, and for some this could be many years. Also the Refuge possessed the power to restrain women on the orders of a doctor under the Mental Deficiency Regulations of 1935.[8] Article 35 of this

Act provided institutions that housed certified cases (such as the Refuge) with the power to mechanically restrain individuals for the purposes of surgical or medical treatment or in order to prevent injury to themselves or others. The means of restraint, recorded in the Refuge Medical Journals, included restrictive clothing (for example a dress or jacket with straps fitted to the sleeves enabling the arms to be tied around the body; gloves without fingers which fastened at the wrist making self-removal difficult); the 'continuous bath' (a covered container in which the patient sat with their head through a hole in the cover); splints and bandages; and a 'dry and wet pack' (no explanation is given regarding the purpose of this procedure).[9]

As mentioned previously, women classified as 'feeble-minded' or admitted as 'preventative cases' could often find themselves institutionalised for many years. Individual medical records were found for only two women, Constance B. and Alice C., but these journals provide a detailed and disturbing insight into their lives. Although neither of these women had any criminal convictions, Constance remained at the Refuge for 12 years whilst Alice stayed for eight.

The journals cover the whole period of residency for the two women although entries are spasmodic (for example there are sometimes entries made every few months but often only one or two entries a year are recorded). The journal entries are written, dated and signed by the Refuge doctor and are recorded under the headings of 'mental condition', 'any change since last visit', 'visit of friends' 'state of house and furniture', 'employment' and 'exercise and recreation'. A further category entitled 'condition of wearing apparel' is the first real indication of the importance that the Refuge would later place on the relationship between a woman's physical appearance and the condition of her mental health (see Hunt *et al*, 1989; Zedner, 1991; Chapter Three of this book).

Constance was aged 15 when admitted to the Refuge in 1930 (Medical Journal for Constance B., 1930-1942). In a separate letter attached to her journal she is described as a 'notified case' although there is no further explanation as to the meaning of this term. She had been referred to the Refuge from the Waifs and Strays Society at Scholfield House under whose care she had been placed some years previously due to the poor condition of her home. The letter goes on to state that

> She was recently found too poor mentally to be trainable. She was transferred to the care of Miss Clarke [Matron of the Refuge] some months ago with a view to being placed under her Guardianship. She is well and happy under Miss Clarke's care. She is never likely to be able to earn her own living (Letter from Doctor Russel to the Refuge Committees, 20 February 1930).

The first entry in her journal, dated 17 February 1930, describes Constance as 'very dull and slow' and goes on to state that she 'reads very badly and cannot deal with money'. A month later she had not improved and was therefore not ready to be returned home. Instead she was to be trained at the Refuge until suitably prepared to return to a 'normal', independent life. One of the most striking aspects of Constance's journal is that the only visitors mentioned are two doctors, one of whom was Dr Russel, the Refuge doctor. There is no reference to her ever leaving the confines of the institution. Up until 1936, Constance's 'exercise', 'employment' and 'recreation' are all described as 'housework'. Although defined by the doctor in his letter as 'too poor mentally to be trainable', Constance was nonetheless subjected to the same level of domestic training as the other women in the Refuge. In keeping with the dominant feminising discourses, housework was utilised both as a means of (mental) reform and as a form of entertainment for Constance.

Although there is no indication of any specific 'treatment' or 'training' given to Constance within the Refuge (apart from housework), her condition is nonetheless described as 'improving' over the years. Thus, having been to some degree domestically reformed, she is described in October 1933 as 'a useful worker under supervision' even though she was still 'a feeble minded person of the lower grade'. By the following year she had achieved some progress towards complete reformation, having been restored to a (minimal, but nonetheless acceptable) standard of femininity. In February she was 'well spoken, quiet and amiable' and by May was 'perfectly respectful...reformed in almost every manner'.

There was some discussion around this time as to whether Constance should be found employment but a 'relapse' in her condition in 1935 eliminated this idea. The entry in her medical journal for 16 August 1935 comments that she was acting 'silly and strange' and goes on to state that she was 'occasionally upset like this for no apparent reason'. However by March 1936 she was again 'brighter and more extroverted....happy and contented' and by November 1937 she was 'well behaved and apart from a tendency to quick temper she gives no cause for anxiety'. As a result of this improvement, and given that she had expressed 'interest and satisfaction' in doing housework and had attained six Girl Guide badges, she was found employment as a daily domestic in a nearby house. The final entry for Constance was September 1942, by which time she was still employed and continuing to improve in her 'rather simple, good natured way'.

Alice was aged 19 when admitted to the Refuge in 1938. Her mother had been sent to a mental hospital and Alice had been left to take care of her family. However this was soon felt to be 'beyond her mental capacity' and she was sent to the St. Agnes Home. Once there she was diagnosed, like her mother, as being 'mentally inadequate' and with the agreement of a doctor was placed under the Statutory Guardianship of Miss Clarke, the Refuge Matron (Medical Journal for Alice C., 1938-1946). The first entry in Alice's journal, dated 25 May 1938 states that

> Alice is very simple and childish but she has a very pleasant manner and responds well to simple questions giving quite a fair account of herself. She says she is very happy and that everyone is very kind to her. She seems well placed.

However by September 1939 she had grown tired of her confinement. She is described as being 'very moody, simple and childish' and 'unfit to fend for herself'. By December the following year she was still unreformed having been found to be 'unreliable and slovenly' and suffering from 'outbursts of emotional disturbance'. Little is recorded about Alice after this date until October 1946 when she is reported to have left the Refuge to enter employment in a convalescent home for babies.

During the late 1930s and 1940s the Refuge was described as being '...not at first penal, but preventative, remedial and educative' (Annual Report, 1941). Thus, during this 'preventative and remedial' era many women were subjected to long periods of pseudo-medical supervision. In addition to Constance and Alice, another Board of Control case was Hilda who, after being admitted in March 1933 spent a total of nine years in the Refuge undertaking 'domestic training' (Matron's Reports, January 1942). In 1942 the Chairman of the Committee requested a list of residents who had spent over three years in the Refuge. The list contained a further three names; Eileen, who had been aged 15 on her admission in March 1929 and who had spent over 13 years in the Refuge; Lena, who was admitted in September 1933 aged 17 and had been a resident for nine years; and Polly admitted in April 1937 aged 14 who had spent over five years in 'training' (Matron's Reports, 1942).

What these cases highlight, above all else, is the inconsistent understanding and categorisation of mental illness within the Refuge during this time. Constance and Alice in particular were subjected to frequent medical intervention and psychological assessment. Yet, their journal entries do not provide the clinical discussions one might expect. Instead, the language of the doctors is emotional and paternalistic (describing the women as 'moody', 'childish' and 'silly') and as a result assessments of their mental condition, although assessed and monitored by medical professionals, remained embroiled within the discourses of morality and respectability. The evaluation of the state of their mental health was based on how well behaved, submissive and domesticated they were, or in other words, how closely they measured up to the standard of femininity endorsed by the Refuge.

Some 'feeble-minded' women, however, did not stay long at the Refuge. In the past disruptive women, or those who would not submit to the regime, were usually expelled. By the 1940s however, failing to adhere to the feminising discourses and normalising regimes could have much more serious and possibly permanent consequences. Emily was 16 years old when she was admitted to the Refuge in 1944. She was described as 'troublesome' and

> ....very unreliable and mentally unbalanced. She has never been before the courts. This girl may only be here for a short time to see if suitable... .If not [the Matron] will remove her to be certified (Matron's Reports, August 1944).

Emily *was* found to be 'suitable' and as a result allowed to stay. Although the Refuge environment was oppressive, Emily could be described as fortunate given that the alternative, had she been deemed 'unsuitable', was certification. Another resident, Betty, was not so lucky. She was described as 'disruptive' and consequently certified by the doctor as mentally deficient (Matron's Reports, March 1944). A letter from the Matron to the Committee states that Betty 'could not adjust to the training' and would therefore be transferred 'to a more appropriate institution'.

It is apparent then that, even as late as the 1940s, the Refuge was still operating as a relatively autonomous institution. The end of the decade however was to be a period of increasing state influence and the Refuge consequently witnessed the introduction of a new, more structured and accountable system of administration.

The Institution under Home Office Regulation

By the mid 1940s occupancy levels had reached crisis point. Women on probation were by now rarely sent to institutions not approved by the Home Office (Annual Report, 1946). As a result over half the beds stood empty and the Refuge was in severe debt, ending the year with an overdraft of over £162 (Annual Report, 1946). This provoked a great deal of discussion regarding its viability and purpose. Concern was expressed that the institution could not justify its existence with so few residents and some members of the Management Committee recommended its closure. It was suggested that, because of the difficulties encountered in attracting the 'the class of girl for whom it was originally intended' (Annual Report, 1945: 2) the Refuge should close and re-open as a Home for 'elderly gentlewomen in very poor circumstances' (Annual Report, 1945: 2). This was a popular idea as there was indeed a great need for support for the elderly poor in the area. However the idea was eventually overturned in favour of proposals to apply for Home Office approval. This, it was believed, would not only allow the scope of the work of the Refuge to be widened but it would also overcome the serious financial problems facing the institution.

By the 1940s the Home Office had identified an urgent need for supervised accommodation for young offenders on probation. Home Office guidance notes on *Homes and Hostels for Young Probationers* (1942) state that most young offenders tended to become involved in crime through the corrupting influence of their friends or their families. If any reformation was to be done, it was therefore essential to remove these vulnerable young people from their home environments and expose them to a different, more 'appropriate' way of life. Supervised homes and hostels, it was believed, fulfilled this purpose in that they provided an environment where

> ....young people can live under homely conditions and where they will learn much of value to them in life including cleanliness and decent manners, the wise spending of wages, the use of leisure and the give-and-take of working life (Home Office, 1942:1).

The Matron, however, had reservations regarding the proposed links with the Home Office. She commented in her reports that although she understood the need for Home Office approval, she would prefer to take the Home in another direction as she 'did not like or understand the probation type of girl' (Matron's

Report, November 1946). She was to be disappointed though as in 1948 the Home Office finally agreed to grant approval.

The approval did not come without conditions. First, although the Home Office promised not to interfere with the running of the institution (meaning that it would remain, to a great degree, outside of full state control) they stipulated that 'mental defective cases', epileptics, remand case and pregnant females were not to be admitted (Annual Report, 1948). The second condition was that, as well as the domestic training within the Home (which was still desirable) the women were to receive instruction in 'useful subjects'. The Home Office drew clear distinctions between suitable regimes for males and females. Males were to be encouraged to take up training and employment within fields such as gardening, greenhouse work, woodwork, carpentry, painting or plastering. Females on the other hand, were still expected to undertake domestic duties and laundry work although secretarial work and gardening were also recommended (Home Office, 1942: 2).

The Home Office recommended that hostels be small with a 'homely' atmosphere, and contain at least one recreation room and one 'quiet' room for residents.[10] As discussed in Chapter Three, it went on to recommend that hostels for boys should have some outdoor playground facility 'where high spirits can find an outlet' (1942: 2) although this was not a recommendation for all-female institutions.

The third condition stipulated that all probation cases would be admitted for a specified period, usually a minimum of six months and a maximum of 12 months. No resident was to stay longer than 12 months unless special permission was granted by the Home Office because

> Longer stay than a year in a hostel would tend to defeat the object of 'supervision in the open' - which is to restore the offender to a normal way of life as soon as he (*sic*) is likely to withstand its temptations and difficulties (Home Office, 1942: 2).

Finally, the name of the institution would have to be changed once again, this time in order to emphasise the fact that it was now a hostel (Annual Report, 1948). The CETS and the Management Committee agreed to these conditions and finally, on 1 September 1948 the institution changed its name again and opened its doors as Vernon Lodge Approved Probation Hostel for Girls.

The regime at the hostel changed radically once it had been set within Home Office guidelines. The Christian emphasis still existed, because the hostel was still owned and managed by the Church of England, however it was now solely utilised for 15 to 18 year old females who had been placed on probation with a condition of residence. This meant that only women who had been before the courts would be admitted, there was no longer any place for 'preventative cases'. The new regime was based around the notion of a 'normal, happy family' (Annual Report, 1948:2) with a great deal of emphasis on the teaching of good manners and habits (Home Office, 1942). In order to support these ideals of respectability, a married Matron was employed and both she and her husband were required to live on the hostel premises. This idea was very quickly heralded as a great success.

....the happy relationship which can and should exist between husband and wife has been shown to these girls and has been a gracious influence in putting before them a happy life based on Christian principles (Annual Report, 1948: 2).

However, the CETS Committee still felt the need to emphasise religious and moral reformation as well as 'family values'. The 1948 Annual Report states that

> The spiritual side of the work has been kept in mind - there have been daily family prayers and regular attendance at the House of God each Sunday (1948:2).

Although the hostel was never meant to be a fully penal institution, prior to the Home Office granting its approval it had functioned within strict notions of confinement. One of its basic philosophies was the belief that young women needed to be taken away from the temptations and iniquitous influences within society and placed in an environment where they could repent and reform. The Home Office saw such control as detrimental to reformation and it strongly encouraged hostels to build up links within the local community. It advocated that probationers should attempt to lead as 'normal' a life as possible and this included contact with friends (albeit only suitably respectable ones).

> ....normal friendships with people of a similar age, even if of different sex, need not be discouraged so long as reasonable supervision is maintained (Annual Report, 1948: 3).

Also, all work undertaken by the residents had previously been carried out on the hostel premises (for example in the laundry) and the women were only allowed to enter the external world of employment once it was believed they had been fully reformed. However, Home Office approval meant that from the late 1940s the residents were allowed outside for their employment, working in shops, factories and nurseries, remaining in the hostel only in the evenings and at weekends.

The 1950s and 1960s: Respectability and domesticity

> [The residents] are missing love and care at home, in the hostel they can mature....the home is the greatest training ground and in the hostel they should receive what is missing at home and learn to live with people as part of a community... .They have lost the respect of others and they have lost their own self respect. In the hostel they can learn to earn respect, to respect themselves and to acquire standards. Their own homes are lacking, they are the future mothers and the basics of housecraft should be taught. Having achieved all this they are fit to enter society (Memo sent to hostel staff by Vernon Lodge Management Committee, 11 October 1967).

The 1950s was a period of 'gender readjustment' in Britain. During the Second World War women's lives had changed dramatically and many had left their homes, worked and learned new skills for the first time. Consequently, by the 1950s efforts were being made to return to traditional roles and values, thus discourses around 'normal' gender relations (and in particular 'normal' femininity) were prevalent (see Smart, 1992a). Accordingly, as Sim (1990) has argued, the primary purpose of penal institutions for women during this period was to normalise and domesticate the inmates, ensuring they become respectable wives and mothers. This was also the case for women offenders on probation at Vernon Lodge. The women were by now receiving educational classes from visiting teachers but these consisted mainly of domestic studies, for example needlework and cookery (Annual Report, 1949). The overarching philosophy was to instil in the young female probationers the virtues of housewifery and motherhood. An unpublished information leaflet for Vernon Lodge states that

> Some of these girls will be the future mothers of our race and to place them for a period in a hostel such as Vernon Lodge must give them some idea of right living and something to hold on to when they return to their own homes (1952: 3).

As had been the case during the nineteenth century, female virtue was still perceived to be fragile and the women at the hostel, although they now mixed more freely within the local community, were still thought to be in need of constant protection from the corrupting influences of others. A letter written by the Matron (or Warden as she became known after 1950) to the Hostel Management Committee raises concerns about the dangers facing young women working within the local community. The Warden, a believer in strict discipline and supervision, felt sure that the probationers would benefit from being 'kept apart from other boys and girls, some of whom will no doubt be of dubious character' (Letter from the Warden to the Hostel Management Committee, 4 April 1952). The Home Office may have been of the opinion that employment outside of the hostel would be beneficial to the young probationers but the Warden was not in agreement. In her opinion female morality was too fragile and thus too easily corrupted and she was concerned at the types of social activity the young women would be able to engage in during recreational periods at work. Factories in particular were the breeding grounds of iniquitous behaviour and residents would never be reformed while engaged in 'frivolous' activity (such as playing card games and gossiping) and mixing with 'undesirable company' (ibid).

Even though the Warden strongly objected to 'frivolity', the hostel did encourage the women to participate in respectable supervised leisure events, such as trips to the Blackpool illuminations, Christmas pantomimes, plays, concerts and nature rambles (Annual Report, 1956). Many of the organised events, however, were based around the church and the Annual Report for 1956 informs of the women enjoying church musical evenings, passion plays, Easter Services, Salvation Army Youth rallies and juvenile meetings of the Church of England Temperance Society. An unpublished information leaflet on the hostel emphasises the importance of this contact with religious organisations.

There is close contact with the local church life, which ensures the creation of a spiritual atmosphere which is so vital in the building of character (1952: 3).

Throughout the 1950s there is no documented evidence to suggest that the women at the hostel collectively or overtly resisted the religious regime imposed upon them. On the contrary, Annual Reports provide lavish accounts of yearly confirmations and enthusiastic attendance at church events. The Annual Report for 1956 records that eight women had willingly signed the pledge of total abstinence that year. However, examples of internal disturbances or unruly behaviour were not generally reported in the widely circulated Annual Reports. Instead, such accounts would have been located within the Warden's daily report books but unfortunately none could be found for this period.[11]

By the early 1960s the numbers of referrals had risen dramatically and once more there was a constant waiting list for places at the hostel. The Church continued to be a major influence and in 1960 the institution still had its own Chaplain. That same year the Committee also proposed that £100 be spent from private funds on furnishing a chapel in the hostel (Annual Report, 1960). The notions of respectability and domesticity still prevailed and the CETS strived to maintain a 'family atmosphere' in order that the women might acquire, through experience and observation, the skills and characteristics necessary to look after their own future families and homes. The ideals of the 'respectable woman' went further during the 1960s and an interest in personal appearance, at one time considered sinful vanity, was encouraged. It was not enough that women acted feminine and respectable, they had to look the part too. So women were encouraged to enter the Duke of Edinburgh Award Scheme, taking such subjects as Personal Hygiene and Good Manners. In addition they were allowed to wear make up and visit a local hairdresser (Annual Report, 1963). The Warden's daily logbook for 1963 refers to the women being encouraged to look 'pretty' for special day trips. There is also a reference in December of that year to women being taken to the local hairdresser in order that they 'look their best' for the Christmas church events and their yearly home leave. In 1964 special arrangements were made with a local hospital for the removal of tattoos from those women ready to be discharged (Vernon Lodge Care Committee Minute Book, May 1964).[12]

The women leaving the hostel were expected to be well groomed, well mannered and fully equipped with domestic and maternal skills. However, not for the first time in its history, the hostel clashed with the probation service as to how these goals should best be achieved. The probation service's theory that young offenders could best learn responsibility and self-control if they were allowed to lead relatively 'normal' lives within the community was dismissed by the hostel Warden. It was her belief that the strict supervision, segregation and discipline employed in the hostel in previous years was the most appropriate way to deal with the errant young women in her care. As had been the case during the nineteenth century, idleness was still perceived by the hostel staff to be the root of unruly behaviour. Even though the residents were employed daily, this work was considered to be insufficient to keep the women occupied and content. It was believed that a more satisfied and submissive group of residents could only be achieved through increased discipline. The Care Committee Minutes record this dispute.

> ....[there] ought to be firmer discipline in the hostel. [The Warden] herself would not allow any girl out for a month after arrival - coupled with a system of rewards for good behaviour and added responsibilities for the girls who had been here longest. She fears the girls are aimless and bored and for this reason more rude and tiresome (February 1964).

Discipline problems are recorded as increasing significantly from around 1964 after the Government had raised the school leaving age. This change in the law meant that the age of admission for the hostel was also raised and as a result, those admitted were becoming 'a little more worldly wise each time' (Letter from the Warden to the Management Committee, 15 November 1965). Consequently the discipline problems caused by these new residents were perceived as much more serious and dangerous than those stemming from simple 'idleness' or boredom. Being somewhat older and 'more worldly wise' than their predecessors, concern was now centred on the sexuality of these new admissions. In 1966, the Warden stated that the hostel was facing a 'moral crisis' when it was found that boys had been climbing over the walls and into the residents' bedrooms where they would spend the night (Warden's Daily Log Book, August 1966). It is interesting to note that although this problem was discussed urgently and frequently and several 'solutions' were proposed, for example the fixing of broken glass around the top of the hostel walls (Warden's Daily Log Book, September 1966), the main concern of the hostel staff and Committee was not the protection of residents from physical harm or danger (this issue is hardly mentioned in the hostel records) but rather their protection from sexual corruption, temptation and moral degeneration.

> The girls in residence are mostly at risk from serious delinquency or serious moral danger....(Vernon Lodge Managing Sub-Committee Meeting Minutes, 11 October 1967).

In 1967, the hostel's worst fears were confirmed when a 15 year old resident became pregnant. It was consequently decided that the women should receive some form of sex education. As neither the Hostel Management Committee nor the CETS wanted to be seen to be encouraging sexual activity amongst their young female probationers, it was decided that the best way to approach the issue was to bring in representatives from the Marriage Guidance Council who could not only teach elementary sex education but could also go beyond this and give instruction on the institution of marriage (Annual Report, 1967). Also, that same year permission was granted for the hostel to be extended in order that a Warden *with a family* might be accommodated as this, it was believed, would be an ideal example to set to the impressionable residents (Vernon Lodge Managing Sub-Committee Meeting Minutes, 14 June 1967).

The end of the decade did see some significant changes within Vernon Lodge. First, in 1967, the trustees (The CETS) amalgamated with the police court mission to become The Church of England Council for Social Aid (CECSA), an organisation that retained trusteeship throughout the rest of the century. The most remarkable change though came about in response to the 1968 Government White Paper *Children in Trouble*. This proposed legislation meant that no young people under the age of 17 could be placed on probation and therefore no orders of residency would apply under that age. The subsequent Children and Young Persons Act changed the whole concept of the hostel's approach to its task. It now received only adult probationers and so in response it undertook a large upgrading project and an extension of the hostel facilities. These facilities were to include provision for young expectant mothers and women with young children. By the early 1970s Vernon Lodge had become the first probation hostel in the country to make provision for young pregnant women or women with babies. As the Chair of the Vernon Lodge Executive Committee explained,

> Up to this time I had been prodding for a more humane approach towards these young women for I felt they were not being supported at the time when they were most vulnerable (quoted in Emmanuel J, 1977, unpublished report).

Apart from some physical changes to the building itself, and some efforts to 'update' the regime, relatively little changed *for the women* at the hostel throughout the remainder of the 1960s. In keeping with the medical model employed for many years, the hostel appointed a psychiatrist in 1968 whose role was to examine and assess the probationers during their stay. An inspection report from that year records the case of Paula F. who stole a lighter from her employer whilst resident at the hostel. Given that she would not acknowledge the seriousness of her offence, it was recommended by the Warden that she see the psychiatrist. On examination he recommended that psychotherapy would be of little use as her problem was simply that she was lacking in discipline and moral standards (Vernon Lodge Hostel Committee Inspection Report, 8 May 1968). It is apparent that both the medical and the moral explanations for female offending behaviour were still being employed as mutually reinforcing discourses within the institution as late as the 1960s. In addition the discourses around domesticity and femininity were also still prevalent. The annual report for 1968 proposed a 'new' training programme for the residents. In addition to first aid, music, art and keep fit, the programme would include dressmaking, personal hygiene, etiquette, personal grooming and household management.

> In this way it is hoped that not only would the girls be more able to manage their lives and future lives more adequately but that they would also begin to be less resentful towards authority and to regard it with different eyes (Annual Report, 1968).

As had been the case for over 100 years, success was still primarily measured, not so much on the gaining of employment or the cessation of offending behaviour, but rather on the procuring of a husband and the successful management of a home.

> Sir, I am pleased to inform the Committee that Gladys F. has, since leaving the hostel, married and settled down with a respectable man, a shopkeeper. A success story we should pass on to the other girls (Letter from the Warden of Vernon Lodge to Chair of the Hostel Committee, 14 August 1965).

The 1970s and 1980s: Some concluding issues

It is at this point in history that the detailed records and accounts pertaining to Vernon Lodge begin to dry-up. The original archive documentation found in the attic of the hostel primarily covers the period 1823 to 1970. Records after 1970 were predominantly financial accounts or brief memoranda to and from the Management Committee regarding funding or charitable donations.

During these decades Vernon Lodge continued to accept only women aged 17 and above. The Warden remained the primary role model for the women in the hostel, responsible for their supervision, care and control.

> It is an important duty of [the Warden] to provide a caring environment in which young women can feel comfortable and secure whilst, at the same time, understanding and accepting the conditions of their residency (Memorandum from the Vernon Lodge Management Committee, March 1973).

By the 1980s Vernon Lodge still occupied a unique and autonomous position within the criminal justice system. Analysis of the occupancy figures for 1981 to 1983 indicates that the period of residency in the institution was significantly longer than that at the other (male) hostels in the area. In addition, the same figures indicate that the hostel was breaching the probation orders of residents at a higher rate than any of the other male hostels in the area. This analysis would seem to suggest that two traditional gender assumptions, which had for almost two centuries underpinned the philosophy and regime of the institution, continued to influence its operation in the latter decades of the twentieth century. First, the significantly longer period of residence is reminiscent of past debates between the Home Office and the Refuge / Hostel Management Committee regarding an appropriate length of training for women. 'Deviant' women, it was assumed, required a more intensive form of supervision than their male counterparts. Second, the higher number of breaches at Vernon Lodge is indicative of both the enduring theory that women are inherently susceptible to influence and hence need to be kept separate from other, recalcitrant or 'corrupting' women and the established practice within institutions for women (both penal and semi-penal) of 'zero tolerance' of 'inappropriate' behaviour.

By the mid 1980s the hostel was once again suffering from a lack of referrals and low occupancy rates. In 1984 the average occupancy rate was 27 per cent. The situation improved slightly the following year but by 1985 the hostel had only seven beds occupied from a total of 18 (Burgess, 1985). Possibly in response to the occupancy crisis, the Chief Probation Officer circulated a memorandum that year in which he reminded probation staff that the hostel had widened its referral criteria. Vernon Lodge would now accept women who were already serving a probation order *without* a condition of residence as long as they met at least one of three conditions. Women would be accepted if they found themselves without accommodation as a result of 'either relationship problems or breakdown of family support' (Senior Staff Notice from Chief Probation Officer, 18 April 1984). In addition, women who, on the assessment of the probation officer, were 'at risk'[13] of 'community or cultural problems' (ibid) were suitable candidates for referral, as were clients who after committing a further offence whilst on probation were 'at risk' of committing yet another.

Although the motives behind this change in admission criteria were undoubtedly a mixture of benevolence and self-preservation on the part of the Management Committee, the effect was once again to widen the regulatory net for women offenders. Thus women who had already been sentenced by the courts to a probation order (their original offence not warranting extra conditions such as a period of residence at a hostel) could find themselves, through circumstances not related to their criminal activity, recommended for admission to Vernon Lodge and thus subjected to a much more intensive and regulatory supervisory process. Of course there would be no legal compulsion on these women to agree to such a recommendation but even the existence of such a provision is symbolic of the traditional, unquestioned notion that the hostel (like the reformatory, the refuge and the home) is essentially a positive, protective and even therapeutic environment for women.

It is the intention of this book to deconstruct this assumption and in doing so proffer an alternative, more critical analysis of the probation hostel and other forms of semi-penal institutionalisation. This and the previous chapter have gone some way towards achieving this goal by examining the creation and development of Vernon Lodge from its early years as a nineteenth century reformatory to its more recent history as a twentieth century bail and probation hostel for women. In order to complete this investigation the following chapter will present an in-depth analysis of the fieldwork conducted in Vernon Lodge between 1992 and 1994 and in doing so will draw together those themes of continuity (as well as highlighting those aspects of discontinuity), relating to discourse, philosophy and regime, which link the institution's previous existence with its present one, thus answering the question 'is Vernon Lodge a semi-penal institution for the new millennium?'

Notes

[1]   See Young (1981) for a further discussion of the way in which criminological theories in general do not emerge in distinct historical phases but rather can appear simultaneously as competing paradigms.

2   Zedner (1991a) states that discussions which preceded the Mental Deficiency Act of 1913 went as far as proposing a new category of 'sexually feeble-minded' which referred specifically to 'sexually immoral' women.

3   The maximum capacity of the Refuge during the First World War was 20 (Annual Reports, 1914 – 1918; Register of Residents, 1898 – 1948).

4   Eventually by October 1942 the Refuge had to concede and begin to accept girls on a minimum trial period of six months instead of two years.

5   The term 'feeble-minded' had largely been discarded by medical professionals during the 1930s. However, in accordance with its incongruous position within the wider realms of criminological / criminal justice discourse and practice, the Refuge continued to use this term to describe women into the 1940s.

6   It should be acknowledged that no specific definition of the term 'preventative case' is provided in the records of the institution nor is it explained who was responsible for making this 'diagnosis'.

7   Henceforth in this chapter names will be abbreviated in order to ensure anonymity of persons who may be still living.

8   From 1930 separate medical records (entitled 'Medical Journals for Patients under Guardianship and for Patients under Private Care with provision for Mechanical Restraint and Seclusion') were kept at the Refuge for those women categorised as 'feeble-minded' or as a 'preventative cases'. As mentioned in footnote 6, it is unclear from the institutional records who made these diagnoses.

9   It should be stated here that although the Refuge was afforded the authority to employ such disciplinary procedures, there exists no recorded evidence to suggest that these powers of restraint were ever implemented on women at the institution.

10   It is interesting to note that at the time of research (1992-1994) Vernon Lodge still had both a recreation room and a 'quiet' room.

11   See Bosworth (2000) for a discussion on the inadequacy of historical data.

12   Whether this procedure was compulsory or voluntary is not mentioned and details of how the tattoos were removed are not given.

13   There is no explanation in this document as to the specific definition of 'at risk' although from discussions with the Hostel Warden during the 1990s (see Chapter Six) it is likely this referred to women perceived to be in physical danger.

Chapter 6

Vernon Lodge: The Probation Hostel for Women as a Semi-Penal Institution?

As the previous chapters have shown, Vernon Lodge has developed through a variety of guises and purposes over the past 180 years. As stated in Chapter One, it is the main intention of the book to draw together various themes of continuity and discontinuity between the institution as an early nineteenth century reformatory and the institution as a late twentieth century bail and probation hostel. This was to be achieved through the pursuit of three main objectives. First, it was the intention to identify the meaning of the term 'semi-penal institution'. Second, the nature of the ideological discourses that underpinned the practices and regimes of the institution throughout its long history, and the way those discourses attempted to 'normalise' and regulate the female residents to an appropriate standard of femininity, were to be explored. The final objective was to examine the way in which women adapted to, endorsed or resisted this construction of femininity and the regulatory regimes imposed upon them. I have dealt with these objectives, in an historical context, in Chapters Three, Four and Five. Utilising a series of interviews conducted with staff and residents, and a period of participant observation carried out in the hostel from 1992 to 1994, it is now my intention here to conclude the analysis by examining the three main objectives outlined above in a contemporary context.[1]

The Hostel as a Semi-Penal Institution

Beyond the reach of state control

The first characteristic of nineteenth century semi-penal institutions was that they were usually set up beyond the reach of full and formal state control. Institutions for prostitutes (Dobash *et al*, 1986; Mahood, 1990; Lindfield, 1992), inebriates (Hunt et al, 1989; Zedner, 1991, 1991a) and various other groups of 'deviant' or 'dangerous' women (Dobash *et al*, 1986; Rimmer, 1986; Weiner, 1990) were popular philanthropic projects and consequently were often created and managed by charitable or voluntary organisations. As Chapter Five explained, the County Refuge was such a project, established by a wealthy Quaker family in 1823 as a charitable institution and fully independent of state control. It remained essentially removed from any formal state influence for almost a century until 1919 when the management and trusteeship of the institution were taken over by the Church of

England Temperance Society. However, even with this much larger charity in control, and even though by this time the institution was accepting women released by the court on probation orders, the Refuge still remained relatively free from state interference. By 1948 the amount of state input increased when the institution became an Approved Probation and Bail Hostel for women thus making it eligible for Home Office funding, however, even by 1994 the institution was still a comparatively independent body.

By the 1990s, Vernon Lodge was primarily funded by the Home Office with money being allocated, as with all bail and probation hostels, according to bed space availability.[2] However, although the Home Office managed the overall budget for the hostel, the hostel was managed on local level by the Vernon Lodge Management Committee, a voluntary group set up to oversee the day to day running of the institution. The Church of England Council for Social Aid (CECSA) were still the trustees of the institution and owned the building within which the hostel was located. Consequently CECSA members constituted a significant proportion of the hostel Management Committee (the remaining representatives being made up of probation personnel and including the Warden and Deputy Warden of the hostel).[3]

The retention of this church influence had a considerable impact upon the institution and frequently caused tensions between the probation appointed hostel staff and the CECSA members of the management committee. Many staff members complained of a lack of communication between these two groups and a general lack of understanding on the part of the CECSA with regards to the purpose and function of probation accommodation in the late twentieth century. Home Office National Standards (1992: s8, para 5) identified the purpose of approved hostels as providing 'an enhanced level of supervision' for offenders under non-custodial supervision in line with the 'just deserts' philosophy underpinning the 1991 Criminal Justice Act. The CECSA, however, saw the function and philosophy of Vernon Lodge as somewhat different, adhering strongly to the traditional, 'welfare' based roots of the probation service.

> The philosophy [of the hostel] is Christian in its widest sense. That fits with probation because it has the same Christian background. The objectives for us have not changed or modernised since the 1930s because we want to retain the scope for who we can help (CECSA representative 1).

The CECSA asserted that its philosophy and objectives fitted more with the traditional, rather than the current, aims of the probation service and on this point the hostel staff generally agreed. The majority felt that the work undertaken with women at Vernon Lodge was more akin to the 'advise, assist and befriend' ideals of the early to mid-twentieth century probation service, than to the 'confronting offending behaviour' (Worrall, 1997: 101) philosophy of the 1990s. Worrall has stated that under the punitive climate of the 1990s, probation hostels had become more like custodial institutions and less like the 'sanctuaries' they were perceived to be in the past (1997: 107). However many of the staff did not see

Vernon Lodge in this way, believing instead that the hostel's fairly autonomous position with regard to national developments in probation and criminal justice in general, had left it somewhat 'untouched' by recent, unwanted, changes in legislation and policy.

> I think we fit in well with the *old* style probation service aims. As far as I can make out the emphasis [in probation] now is on punishment and regulation and I don't think we fit in too well with that, at least I hope we don't. I don't think there is anything wrong with 'sitting outside' the probation service, you can't compare what goes on in here and what happens in the field. I think we punish because we have to, that is the nature of these institutions but the difference is we try to help while we are doing it (Staff Member 8, emphasis made in interview).

> We sort of fit in [with the probation service] but we might do things differently from the other hostels. Like we are the only hostel that isn't totally   run   by   the probation service and so although [all hostels] work along certain lines we sort of have a bit of leeway and we can use our own initiative and we have our own way of doing things (Staff Member 3).

For many of the staff this autonomy and 'removal' from full probation control was a positive aspect of the hostel. However, not all staff saw this independence as completely beneficial. One commented that such independence had the potential to create a totally arbitrary system within the institution and thus the introduction of National Standards in 1992 was welcomed as a way of reducing this inherent problem.

> National Standards [are] trying to standardise things instead of having idiosyncratic hostels with idiosyncratic managers doing whatever they like, so it stops Vernon Lodge having this cranky system, and its good. It is very difficult because the Church of England likes to see this as their hostel with a bit of probation involvement out of necessity for funding but they do not like to see the necessity of probation input and there is a possessive side to it as though the hostel is *theirs*. Difficulties can occur and there are often tensions (Staff Member 5, emphasis made in interview).

Although the majority of staff felt there were advantages to be gained by remaining outside the realms of full probation control, the trepidation of the member of staff quoted above, regarding the input of the CECSA, was mirrored by several others who felt a similar anxiety regarding the level of power held by this group. They saw the CECSA as out of touch and unenlightened, with regard to the hostel client group, and agreed that this could be problematic.

> The general feeling though is that the Management Committee's influence is out of proportion to their actual involvement with the women. They take a lot of decisions and they don't know the women at all (Staff Member 6).

I can't believe that in the 1990s we still have a hostel like this which is basically being run by the Church. It just astounds me. Those people on the Management Committee still see the women here as either fallen harlots or poor misguided girls who need to be shown the error of their ways. I don't think they have any idea of the reality of this place, how dangerous it can be, the violence we see, the horrendous abuse some of these women have suffered, the horrendous crimes some of them have committed. I think they'd be shocked if they knew (Staff Member 9).

Some staff indicated a sense of isolation enhanced by the fact that even the Home Office was reluctant to challenge decisions taken by the CECSA.

The Home Office....the people you deal with are civil servants and their knowledge of hostels is minimal and so they are kept informed through people like [the CECSA representatives] I think they are quite happy [not to interfere] because the accommodation is provided by the CECSA so it's quite economical for them. But it is a tension (Staff Member 5).

[The CECSA] wield the power here. I think even the Home Office and the probation committee are reluctant to challenge them because they own the building you see (Staff Member 9).

So the concern was that the power of the hostel Management Committee and the relative independence from full probation control served to enhance the potential for arbitrary decisions and strategies to be employed by the hostel. This problem of 'dual control', the tensions between having to accord to some degree with state regulations and yet wanting to remain independent of state interference at the same time, was not new for Vernon Lodge nor indeed for the probation service in general. As Brownlee (1998: 67) states, the probation service has always 'operated within a range of contradictory aspirations'. McWilliams (1983) noted that the history of the service has always been a history of conflict: conflict between the ideologies of religion and science, conflict between the ideals of punishment and welfare and conflict between the church and the state. He went on to assert that the Church of England Temperance Society missionaries began their work, which was rooted in the concept of clemency, with magistrates who were entrenched within a harsh and punitive system of justice. Hence, it was in many ways inevitable that the probation service would have to deal with the juxtaposition between their conflicting philosophies. In order to reconcile this conflict of ideals many missionaries saw their role as combining 'the grace of God with sensible treatment according to the state' (Holmes, 1913, cited in McWilliams, 1983: 137), perceiving themselves as a kind of intermediary body which could temper the punitive ideals of the formal system with Christian philosophies of benevolence and mercy. The CECSA trustees of Vernon Lodge perceived themselves in a similar way.

The [CECSA] is trying to maintain the original philosophy of the probation service. We think we are not just here to contain women or indeed to punish them, although of course we are still part of the whole system. We think part of the role is to provide a place of care and support for the women here. We want to provide an environment where women can look at themselves and change their outlook on their own (CECSA representative 1).

We are a church based organisation. We obviously have a religious conviction for this work. We understand that we are dependent on the Home Office and probation service for the funding of this hostel and we admire a lot of the work the probation service does. But there is a movement [in probation] that we don't really agree with, away from the idea of helping those in need. We like to think that here at Vernon Lodge we can provide an element of Christian charity that is missing from a lot of other types of work with offenders (CECSA representative 2).

Of course, this desire to retain some element of care and support in an otherwise punitive criminal justice system is not a negative ideal. It is not the intention of this book to argue in favour of a move towards a more regulative and disciplinary regime in probation hostels for women. However, these ideals of Christian charity should be examined within a broader context. The way in which these ideals were applied in reality, and consequently the way in which they impacted upon the women at Vernon Lodge, needs to be carefully addressed. As has been highlighted in previous chapters, the Christian philosophy underpinning the Refuge (and other similar institutions) during the nineteenth and twentieth centuries actually served to *increase* the levels of discipline that women were subjected to, as well as expanding the net of control to encompass those cases of 'less than full criminality' (Weiner, 1990: 130). Similarly, as subsequent sections of this chapter will show, for women at Vernon Lodge these Christian ethics frequently served to entrap them within particular moralistic and feminising discourses that, in turn, created a very specific and uniquely gendered regime, a regime which, it will be argued, was more oppressive and regulative than those to which their male counterparts were subjected.

A unique position on the social control continuum

This conflict of ideals and the attempts to reconcile the, often competing, philosophies of the church and the state lead on to the second major characteristic of the semi-penal institution. One obvious criterion which identifies institutions as semi-penal is the fact that they are indeed *semi*-penal, in other words although they are not formally penal, or custodial establishments, they cannot be described as 'informal' or 'domestic' either. Instead they occupy a place somewhere towards the middle of the 'domestic-custodial' spectrum. As discussed in Chapter Four, the County Refuge occupied such a position during the nineteenth century and it can be argued that Vernon Lodge was situated within a similar space on the social control continuum during the 1990s. As described above, Vernon Lodge had remained beyond the reach of total state control and thus was necessarily removed from the formal penal sphere. However, due to the fact that it was part-funded by the Home Office, and the fact that it received women on court orders, it was, at the same time, necessarily entrenched within the criminal justice system. Thus, it could not be considered as an 'informal' environment in the way that, for example, a local neighbourhood, a workplace, a social club or the family home could be.[4] As a result, it appeared to occupy a unique position within the 'control continuum'. This unusual status (neither formal nor informal, neither custodial nor communal) was highlighted by three issues that emerged from this research. First, as discussed above, the hostel was neither totally within, nor completely without, state or penal, influence. Second, as will be discussed later in the chapter, the hostel attempted to combine formal (state legislated) rules and regulations with informal (*ad-hoc*, unofficial and often questionable) systems of control and punishment and in doing so created an environment that was a curious hybrid of penal and 'familial' discipline. The third issue, which will now be discussed, was the fact that there existed no consensus or agreement amongst the Management Committee, the staff or the residents as to the 'overarching' function or purpose of the hostel. With regards to the Committee and the staff group, some members located the hostel at the 'benign' end of the control spectrum, perceiving it as a place of sanctuary and support. Others, however, perceived it to be situated at the opposite, more punitive and penal, end of the spectrum, acknowledging its focus on punishment, containment and control. Some members of staff placed it squarely in the middle of the spectrum commenting that the purpose of the hostel was to attempt to combine a variety of roles and functions.

> We are here to help and support those who need it. A helping hand, a refuge, for some women it's a sort of retreat (CECSA representative 1).

> I see [the hostel] as a support agency, or just a roof over the head for some women. It's everything apart from punishment. I don't see us as being here to punish at all (Staff Member 4).

> I think I'd say [the hostel is a] sanctuary, but certainly punitive in that it is a big restriction on liberty, a very large restriction on liberty and I don't think [all of the residents] recognise it. I think it's also rehabilitative because of the set up we have here. It is a multi-purpose and multi-functional place (Staff Member 5).

> The main role is to provide an alternative to custody and in those who are on orders or on bail assessment, to reduce the risk of offending (Staff Member 7).

> The hostel is a last refuge in the custodial system. In a sense it is still a custodial institution (Staff Member 9).

This lack of consensus regarding the function of the hostel served to emphasise the ambiguity of institutions such as Vernon Lodge and the impact of years of dual control by two authorities. Barry (1991) highlighted that amongst 21 hostels he studied in the 1980s and early 1990s, there existed no real consensus in the aims, objectives and regimes of the institutions. So, while some were very punitive, others were much more liberal. In addition, they all appeared to be extremely resistant to changes in national policy and practice. Some of the staff at Vernon Lodge saw this multiplicity of ideas and views regarding the purpose of the hostel as positive:

> I think having a diversity of views is healthy. It means we can satisfy many different needs and roles (CECSA representative 1).

However, it could be considered as extremely problematic. Problems mainly arose due to the fact that, in spite of residents being made fully aware on arrival of the rules and regulations of the institution, they did not receive consistent information with regard to the *purpose* of their residency and the *function* of the hostel, primarily because there was no agreement on these issues amongst the hostel staff. Indeed, the diversity of opinions amongst the staff was reflected by the residents who also described the hostel in a variety of ways, with some women likening the institution to prison whilst others saw it, almost, as a 'home from home'.

> It's just a lock-up, this place. I don't care how they dress it up, that's what it is. I get told when to sleep, when to eat, when I can go out…I live in a lock up (Sarah).

> Well it's just part of the system isn't it? I mean I know you've got some freedom here but it's still part of the same system….prisons, police, courts, probation, just part of the same system. I mean I'm not here because the police or courts feel sorry for me am I? They say I've done wrong, committed a crime and so you have to be punished for it. If they think you're really bad you might get banged up, if they think you're not dangerous then they might send you here (Leanne).

> [Coming to this hostel] is like going from home to home because you can sit and talk to somebody as if you are at home. You have your own bedroom, or you might have to share but you still have a home environment around you. It's not as if you are shut in a room and told you have to stay there all day. You have a radio, TV, pool table, table tennis, you can go out and do your shopping. I think hostels are a good thing for people who really want to keep themselves out of trouble and start afresh (Maureen).

> [The hostel] is a bit of everything really. I think the main purpose is to try and help people sort themselves out. If you take drugs then they try and get you on Meth[adone]. If you need to see a drugs counsellor or a psychiatrist or whatever then they sort that out too. I think the main purpose is to help people. I don't think it's punishment really because you can come and go during the day as much as you want really and there are no real rules and regulations. People learn to live with each other and get on with each other here, it's like a big family sometimes….it's not like that in prison, you just get on each other's nerves (Debbie).

It could be argued that likening the hostel to a 'home from home' was a basic coping strategy for many women, almost a way of avoiding the reality of being embroiled within the formal criminal justice system, something which perhaps cannot be achieved as easily in a prison environment. Similarly, for other women, treating the hostel as a custodial institution also provided them with an, albeit different, coping mechanism. By responding to the hostel regime as they might to a custodial regime they set for themselves definite boundaries that were otherwise seen to be missing in an institution with no obvious coherent function. These coping strategies will be discussed more fully in the final section of this chapter. However, it has to be acknowledged that the lack of consistency amongst the hostel management and staff with regards to the purpose of the hostel did filter down to the residents of the institution and seemingly created uncertainty amongst the women with regards to how they were expected to relate to hostel staff and the regime in general.

Combination of formal and informal methods of control

One factor which possibly aggravated this situation was the way in which the hostel attempted to combine both formal and informal methods of control and discipline. This is the third semi-penal criteria and is, in many ways, an inevitable consequence of both the unique non-custodial / non-communal status of the institution and the lack of consensus amongst the staff as to the purpose of the hostel. As with the nineteenth century County Refuge, Vernon Lodge could not be described as either a custodial or a 'communal' institution but had developed a regime which attempted to amalgamate methods of control and discipline from both those arenas. Some methods of control and punishment were set by government legislation and thus the hostel was required to abide by these rules. These formal rules included the set curfew times of 11.00pm to 7.00am, during which hours residents had to be on the hostel premises. The hostel was required by law to breach bailees who missed the curfew.[5] These women would be required to leave the hostel, the police would be informed that they were no longer adhering to the conditions of their bail and a warrant would be issued for their arrest. With women on probation the situation was different as only the supervising probation officer could breach a probation order. The staff of the hostel could however recommend that Vernon Lodge was unsuitable for any probationer who regularly broke curfew and she could then be required to leave.[6] Other formal rules included no drugs or alcohol on the premises and no violence towards staff or other residents. The penalty for breaches of these rules was always exclusion from the hostel and, for the most part, residents understood, accepted and adhered to this formal regulation.

In addition to these formal rules, however, were other, much more 'informal' methods of regulation which were determined 'locally', within the hostel itself. One such rule was that residents had to be out of bed by 8.30am or they not only missed their breakfast, but were also subjected to an informal 'punishment' known as sanctioning. This involved either forbidding the woman concerned from leaving the hostel premises for a period of one day, or requiring her to complete some set chore or task around the hostel (for example doing dishes, cleaning floors or, on one occasion, picking up litter from the grounds of the building). Sanctioning was such a significant and controversial aspect of the hostel regime that it will be discussed again in the following two sections of this chapter. The way in which it was used to 'infantilise' the female residents will be discussed in the next section of the chapter and the way in which women resisted or conformed to this form of discipline will be examined in the final section. The concern here though, is the inherent 'informality' or familial nature of this form of discipline.

Many semi-penal institutions during the nineteenth and early twentieth centuries attempted to combine 'familial' style control with more formal rules and regulations. As previously discussed, institutions for prostitutes, 'wayward girls' or inebriates frequently employed domestic labour as a form of social and moral training for women. Women at the County Refuge were expected to fulfil domestic chores in order to 'learn the way of ordered home life' (CECSA, undated and unpublished report) and as Rafter (1983) states, women in reformatories were frequently subjected to a 'benign' form of discipline, not dissimilar to that found within the family home, with the aim of encouraging (rather than imposing) conformity. So what were essentially 'punishments' could be in some ways concealed under the guise of personal responsibility, care and protection. At Vernon Lodge, this combination of 'domestic' style discipline with more formal methods of regulation was relatively successful and residents often accepted these informal rules as part of 'normal' life. However, some methods of sanctioning were considered unreasonable. One particular form - whereby residents were requested to wash up after tea and if they refused then none of the residents would be given supper that night - did appear to take to the notion of 'parental disapproval' to extremes.

> If they don't do the dishes then no-one gets supper that night so they get peer pressure then off the others to do them (Staff Member 1).

Many of the staff were themselves unhappy about the use of sanctioning as a means of discipline but they felt there were few options available which would allow them to keep a sense of 'order' in the hostel. During the first week of fieldwork for this research, a new practice was developed with the aim of getting residents out of bed in the morning without having to resort to sanctioning. This new procedure involved the Warden taking all of the staff and all of the residents who were already up, into the bedrooms of those women who were still in bed. There she would ring a large hand bell until the woman woke up and the entourage would be requested to remain in the room until the woman agreed to get up. Unsurprisingly this method did not last long as both staff and residents blankly refused to take part in such an undignified and intrusive procedure. However, what this serves to highlight is the way in which the hostel attempted (albeit unsuccessfully in this case) to merge authoritative discipline with a family style form of chastisement through a display of united disapproval and the use of 'sisterly' peer pressure.

'Voluntary' status of admissions

The fourth semi-penal characteristic concerns the 'voluntary' status of admissions. As previously explained, in the early semi-penal institutions, women generally had to provide their consent before they could be admitted as this consent indicated a desire to reform which was often considered an important admission criterion. Given that many of these institutions depended heavily on both charitable donations and inmate labour for their existence, they had to ensure that residents were likely to be a 'success' (in other words inclined to conform and reform) and likely to want to work. Although Vernon Lodge no longer depended on the labour of its residents for its funding, it was still felt that the most useful and 'successful' work carried out within the hostel could only be done with those women who *wanted* to be there.

> As far as this hostel goes....the main problem is women who are here but don't want to be here, they want to be at home with their children. There are women here who want to continue their lives as much as they can as if they were living outside and so find it difficult to abide by certain hostel rules (Staff Member 7).

> I think the main obstacle [to the social work function of the hostel] is the people themselves, whether they are prepared to co-operate or not. You can't work with somebody who is not prepared to tackle their offending behaviour (Staff Member 6).

Prior to the 1991 Criminal Justice Act probation was identified as an 'alternative to custody' (Brownlee, 1998) and as such individuals had to consent to a period of probation supervision. The 1991 Act established probation as a sentence in its own right and thus negated the requirement of the offender's agreement to such a sanction. For individuals on probation with a condition of residence however, consent was still required.

> When the probation officer is writing the report they put in their conclusion 'I believe that a period of residence at [Vernon Lodge] is suitable' and then at the bottom of the report you say 'and I've discussed this with Ms so-and-so and she has agreed'. So she would have agreed beforehand. No magistrate will actually put someone in a hostel without there having been some process of assessment, they would always ask for an adjournment so she could be assessed at the hostel (Staff Member 5).

So in theory women would have to be willing to reside at the hostel before they would be referred and accepted there. This process of gaining consent and requesting a period of assessment obviously served the interests of the hostel as well as the residents. The management of Vernon Lodge had no desire to take referrals for women without an assessment period. Generally, they preferred to take women who had been bailed to the hostel prior to their court appearance.

If somebody is coming on probation there has got to be a four week assessment period beforehand. So they will be referred here before their probation order is issued and so they will actually be here on bail for four weeks. [This is because] it's technically difficult to move somebody on once they are on probation so we like to see what we are taking on first. You see while they are here on bail they can just be breached but with probation you are sort of, to an extent, stuck with them once they are here (Staff Member 6).

The hostel staff believed that the requirement of consent and, more importantly, the process of assessment was beneficial to the residents as, in theory, they were thus provided with the opportunity to decide for themselves if they actually wanted to spend a period of probation within such an institution. The hostel staff frequently reminded residents that it was *their choice* to be at Vernon Lodge. In reality though the 'choice' that women had was somewhat limited. As previously discussed, many women admitted to nineteenth century semi-penal institutions only agreed to a period of confinement because the options offered to them were often much worse than a stay in a reformatory (see Rimmer, 1986). Similarly, it could be argued that the element of 'choice' open for women regarding a condition of residence in the hostel was an artificial one. All of the residents, and many staff, were fully aware that a refusal of a condition of residence meant only one alternative.

I had nowhere to live but I didn't have to come here....well I'd have been on the streets and I'd have had to go into custody. It was here or prison (Nikki).

I think if I'd said I didn't want to come here I might have been sent to prison (Debbie).

Likewise women on bail faced a similar lack of real choice.

They have a choice [about coming here] but they don't at the same time. If someone was coming up for bail and the magistrate was asking for a hostel then they would have a choice - they could either come here or [be remanded]. So really they don't have a choice (Staff Member 2).

I was just told I was being bailed to a hostel. I suppose I could have said no but it would have meant I'd have had to stay in Styal (Joanne).

I could've said I didn't want to come here but I would have ended up in prison. There wasn't really any choice (Maureen).

Even when some women tried to assert their right to say no, they were often strongly encouraged to consent by their solicitors or probation officers. For women like Billie, who definitely did not want to be sent to a hostel, the weight of professional discourse against her was too much to resist.

My solicitor really pushed for this. I argued with the magistrate saying I'd rather be remanded and that I didn't want to go that far from home. I said I'd end up on heroin if I went to [Vernon Lodge] because I was only on speed before and I was right. They kept on and on at me... .I gave in. Look at me now. Everyone said it was best that I came here so I agreed. I thought that when my case finally came up the fact that I hadn't been remanded might look better and I'd just get probation. Then my probation officer went and recommended I come back here as a condition of probation. The magistrates agreed. I didn't really want to. I told them I'd have been better off in prison because at least your remand time comes off your prison sentence. Your time on bail here doesn't come off your probation order you know. And at least in prison I'd have got a visit from my kids occasionally.

Billie's case is a depressing example of how professional or 'expert' discourse can be utilised to 'silence' women who wish to articulate an alternative understanding of their situation. As Worrall asserts, women's accounts of their behaviour or situation are frequently only listened to if they are communicated through the 'dominant modes of expression' (1990: 11). As women are often not expected to be able to construct a coherent account or explanation for themselves it becomes necessary for professionals to construct that account for them. Billie's solicitor, her probation officer and the magistrates that dealt with her case did not 'hear' Billie's own account. She attempted to communicate throughout her case that she would rather be in prison for good reason. She argued that given the small number of female only probation hostels she would undoubtedly be sent a considerable distance from her home. Prison, therefore, would have been preferable, as she would probably have been held closer to home. Being closer to home would have meant more regular contact with her family and children and finally, being in prison, she argued, would leave her less likely to succumb to the temptation of hard drugs like heroin. Instead of 'hearing' this account Billie's professional representatives constructed an alternative understanding, adhering to the liberal notion of probation as a 'benign' and supportive alternative to prison. They decided they knew what was in Billie's best interest, even if she did not know herself. According to Billie, the magistrate who bailed her to Vernon Lodge stated that it was 'for her own good'. He wanted to move her to another part of the country in order to 'protect' her from the 'bad company' she was keeping in her home town and from the same corrupting elements she would encounter in prison. For Billie, the consequences of her account being 'muted' (Worrall, 1990: 11) and reconstructed through professional discourse were disastrous. As she had predicted, she very quickly became a heroin user and eventually the separation from her children proved too much and she committed suicide in February 1993. This issue of suicide, and Billie's case in particular, will be discussed in more detail in the final section of this chapter.

Unlike Billie, the majority of women interviewed stated that, even if they did not want to be at the hostel, it was still preferable to a prison sentence. However, ironically, sometimes women who were keen to be accepted at the hostel found themselves excluded due to the gatekeeping procedures of the institution. As this member of staff explained

> [Vernon Lodge] will not accept women who are clearly mentally ill. Or if somebody has been at another hostel and wrecked the place. We won't necessarily say no but we will want to interview them ourselves. We don't have women with their children and we don't accept those drug users who use ampoules, in other words inject themselves by prescription. Also those women whose record of violence is such that we consider they are almost certain to be violent again....but that's when you get into the area of measuring risk (Staff Member 7)

Carlen (1990) has argued that women's hostels are frequently too selective with regard to their gatekeeping procedures and she goes on to suggest that by being this selective hostels 'manage to exclude those most in need' (1990: 43). It was of course totally understandable that the management of Vernon Lodge would wish to protect the hostel staff from any risk however even some members of staff stated that the gatekeeping procedures were verging on excessive and were consequently problematic, particularly with regards to the drug quota. This recently introduced measure meant that the hostel would only allocate 25 per cent of its beds to registered drug users. Once this quota was reached, any further referrals for drug users would be rejected. Not only was this considered to be unworkable by some of the staff but it was also perceived to potentially cause long-term problems with regards to under-occupancy. As Carlen (1990) has stated, rigid gatekeeping in women's hostels leads to under-occupancy which in turn can mean hostels are closed and provision for women is lost. Similar concerns were expressed at Vernon Lodge.

> I think having a drug quota is discriminatory practice. If [there are large numbers of drug users in] prisons or within groups of offenders we have got to reflect that otherwise we become a dinosaur in the system. We can't be choosy and say 'okay 75 per cent of offenders are drug users but we don't want this reflected in our figures'. I think if we keep doing that then we won't survive. We can't manipulate and block people out (Staff Member 1).

The gatekeeping criterion of the hostel, in particular that which focused around potentially violent women, raises another important issue. As Zedner (1991) points out, during the nineteenth century, institutionalised women were frequently considered to be more disruptive and undisciplined than their male counterparts and Faith (1993) argues that this is still the case today, with women prisoners being perceived as a greater threat to authority and more unmanageable than male prisoners. At the time of research, although Vernon Lodge actively attempted to screen out those women with a 'potential' for violent behaviour, this hostel was the only one out of a total of four in the area (the other three being men only) which had 'double cover' as standard practice. In other words, it was the only hostel for which it was deemed necessary to have more than one member of staff on duty overnight. Given that this hostel often had the lowest level of occupancy, this meant that the staff-resident ratio was considerably higher in Vernon Lodge (sometimes 1:5) than in any of the other male only hostels. When asked why this was the case, one Assistant Warden explained that

> It's the nature of the cases we deal with. We have women here with a lot of problems. I wouldn't like to be here on my own at night, you don't know what you might face. Like [Mary] is always trying something, usually cutting herself, and people like [Alice], well she's so unpredictable you just need two people here, or actually three would be better I think (Staff Member 9).

'Non-criminal' admissions

The fifth and final feature which identified institutions as semi-penal is the practice of admitting women who had not been convicted of any criminal offence. During the nineteenth century many non-criminal women were declared to be in need of a reforming influence due to their 'immoral' or 'wayward' behaviour. As Weiner (1990) points out, semi-penal institutions were often promoted as offering 'protection' to young girls 'at risk', offering a means of reform which would prevent their otherwise inevitable progress towards incarceration. However, as Dobash *et al* (1986) assert, this targeting of non-criminal women who were deemed to be 'at risk' had the effect of extending the formal social control of women from the prison into the community.

Although Vernon Lodge only dealt with women who had already formally entered the criminal justice system (in other words those who had been *charged* with criminal offences) it did accept women who had not been *convicted* of criminal offences. The hostel catered for women on bail as well as probation and, linking back to the issue discussed above (that of the hostel preferring to deal with women who *wanted* to be there), this was occasionally perceived to be a problem by the staff.

> One major problem is that if you have got women who are here on bail and are pleading not guilty then you have got nothing to work with. They come here and you can only work with what they tell you because obviously they are innocent until proven guilty and we can't go assuming anything. So we have a lot of women who just come and go and there is not a lot we can do with them or for them really (Staff Member 3).

Perhaps more significant than the problems of attempting to 'work' with women pleading not guilty was the issue of the potentially discriminatory practice of subjecting bailees and probationers to the same set of rules and regulations. National Standards made it clear that hostel staff were to ensure 'residents (on bail) [were] offered a place on any programme on how to avoid offending' (Home Office, 1992: s8, para 23), in other words they were to be treated in the same way as convicted offenders on probation orders. However, a thematic inspection of approved hostels (Home Office, 1993) raised serious questions regarding the appropriateness of accommodating bailees and probationers in the same environment and requiring unconvicted bailees to take part in offence focused work. As a 1998 thematic review states, this meant that many hostels were dealing with bailees 'on the basis of a presumption of guilt' (Home Office, 1998: s6, para 7). Although the member of staff quoted above stated that the hostel could not 'assume anything', many of the bailees in Vernon Lodge felt that there was a 'presumption of guilt' and this was a cause of frustration and contention.

> Sanctions... .I think they are a waste of time and they are not fair. You see I'm here on bail so technically I'm innocent till proven guilty yet I've got to be up at a certain time or else I can't go out that day. Who dreamt that one up? I may as well be on remand. I can understand there being rules for women on probation but it should be different for bailees (Frances).

Rather than there being fewer rules for women on bail, as Frances suggests should be the case, bailees often found themselves subjected to a more intense and regulatory regime than those convicted women on probation. As mentioned previously, they could be excluded from the hostel more readily than women on probation for breaching the curfew rules. However it was the 'informal' regulations that caused the greatest displeasure amongst women on bail. These women complained of being subjected to a greater level of coercion with regards to attending particular group activities (such as programmes aimed at confronting offending behaviour) and often felt under greater pressure to conform to the petty regulations of the hostel regime (getting up at a particular time, attending meetings, obeying sanctions) than probationers. The reason for this was that, unlike those women who had already been convicted, bailees still had a trial to face and thus felt compelled to conform as they were told this would improve their chances in court.

> It looks better in court if you go with a good record from the hostel (Sharon).

> I try to attend the meetings and get involved with all the activities here because they've told me it will go in my favour at my trial if I do (Kate).

Occasionally, women would be accepted to Vernon Lodge under the 'emergency accommodation' facility.

> We do have another facility which starts off with emergency accommodation. Say I was working in the field and I had a client on probation and something had happened in her life which caused her home life to be a bit of a danger, I could ring up the hostel and ask if she could come and stay for up to three days. During that period her probation officer would see if it would be possible for her to stay for a longer period and [the hostel] would then be part of her supervision plan (Staff Member 5)

The member of staff justified this process, stating that this facility allowed women already on probation to take 'time out' from the often difficult or dangerous circumstances of their everyday lives. Undoubtedly there was some merit in this facility however, once a woman entered the hostel, and it became part of her 'supervision plan' she would be subjected to an altogether more regulative and restrictive environment than that to which she was originally sentenced. Although her home life may have become too impoverished or hazardous for her to remain there, being offered alternative accommodation in a probation hostel would mean she could then be informally disciplined (through practices such as sanctioning) for actions or petty infractions which, under her original sentence, she could not be disciplined for, such as getting up or coming home late.

So, the five criteria, previously utilised to identify the nineteenth and early twentieth century semi-penal institutions could be equally applied to Vernon Lodge, a late twentieth century bail and probation hostel for women. What is missing from this analysis is an examination of the feminising discourses that underpinned this modern day institution. The next section of this chapter will attempt to redress the balance and present an analysis of the extent to which similar feminising discourses underpinned regimes which, in turn, were utilised to normalise and discipline the female residents.

Discourses of Discipline

Once women entered the reformatories and refuges of the nineteenth century they were expected to conform to a middle class construction of femininity and consequently in order to achieve this goal women were subjected to a range of 'feminising' discourses and controlling regimes based on domestic and moral training. The County Refuge unreservedly endorsed such discourses and regimes.

By the mid 1990s such explicit ideologies had been generally suppressed and it would be unfair to claim that Vernon Lodge was in the business of training women to be 'good' wives and mothers. However, discourses around 'appropriate' or expected behaviour for women, although not explicit, were not entirely absent either in that the regime and practices within the hostel were still constructed around a set of, albeit moderated, discourses which implicitly served to construct, regulate and control women as gendered beings.

One of the primary ways in which these discourses were astutely administered was through the utilisation of sanctioning as a method of discipline. Sanctioning, as discussed previously in this chapter, was a form of informal punishment imposed for minor rule infringements (such as getting up late or missing meetings). The assumption, amongst some of the staff, and in particular members of the CECSA, was that requiring women to undertake chores or tasks around the hostel was not really a form of 'discipline' but rather just part of a 'normal' disciplined life for women.

> It depends how you define discipline. Is discipline having to get up and do jobs? I don't see it as discipline because that is just a way of life and in many ways it is easier because they might only do the dishes once a week here whereas at home they might do them three times a day (Staff Member 3).

Well I think it's a bit pathetic, making out that doing the dishes is a punishment for the women here. It's not about that, it's only doing the dishes, they'd do that at home anyway. Most of them here have it easy because at home they'd be doing more than a few dishes and making their beds. They'd be running around after husbands and families as well (Staff Member 9).

We expect the women here to treat this hostel like they would their own homes. They have to do the dishes, sometimes they help to make the tea and they are expected to keep their own rooms tidy. It's nothing new for them, they'd be doing that at home (CECSA representative 2).

Expectations of femininity were also found to underpin some of the activities and recreational facilities available for the women at the hostel. Of course some activities (such as abseiling, archery and bowling matches) were original, stimulating and, as many women explained, empowering. But it could be argued that the more day-to-day recreational activities (such as the cookery and hairdressing sessions) functioned to endorse an 'appropriate' standard of femininity deemed necessary in order for true 'rehabilitation' to take place. The CECSA representatives in particular saw such gendered activities as a means of normalising the women back to an acceptable role in society.

Rehabilitation is attempted through assertiveness courses, drug work, even the hairdresser coming in once a week. This gives the women pride in their appearance (CECSA representative 1).

As discussed in Chapter Two, the constant demands placed upon women to adhere to particular standards of external 'beauty', or appropriate standards of outward appearance, leads eventually to the absorption of such images by women themselves. Consequently, constant reassertion of these idealised images would eventually lead to a self-regulating and, it could be argued in the context of the semi-penal institution, a fully 'rehabilitated' female subject.

This association of outward appearance with internal (mental and/or moral) well-being has long been an integral part of the reformation and rehabilitation of 'deviant' women. Records from the County Refuge during the nineteenth century highlight this alliance. Elizabeth Jones was described in the Matron's Reports as being 'dirty' and 'untrainable' (Matron's Reports, June 1829). Ann Hughes, on the other hand was described as 'very clean and diligent' (Matron's Reports, October 1865). In both cases the notion was that outward, physical appearance (in these cases cleanliness) and internal health were mutually reinforcing concepts. This idea remained prominent in institutions throughout the twentieth century.[7] It could be argued that this was still the belief of the CECSA. When asked why the hostel had a hairdresser coming in every week, the same CECSA representative explained that

... it gives the women something to look forward to. They get their hair done and they look better, they feel better and I suppose you could argue that they *are* better. What I mean is if they start caring about themselves, that's good, that's part of the process towards getting on their feet and making a go of their lives again. It's a step towards independent living (Emphasis made in interview).

In addition to being self-disciplined about their appearance, residents were also expected to be self-disciplined with regard to their timekeeping. They were expected to be up by 8.30am (when breakfast was served) and dressed by 9.00am. If women did not adhere to these rules they not only missed their breakfast but could also be sanctioned. Many of the residents objected to having to be up at this time, complaining that, as they often had nothing to do, it made the day seem much longer for them. The hostel staff claimed that this rule was in the women's best interest and served to introduce an element of order into, what they perceived to be, disordered lives.

[The residents] usually have really disorganised lives and part of what is expected at the hostel is they get some order out of it. In the past they were allowed to sleep in all day and go around in their nighties but I actually don't think that's appropriate because it's not giving them an opportunity to change their behaviour and then in turn change their internal behaviour. It encourages an element of self-discipline. We don't expect total changes in behaviour, it's just basic stuff (Staff Member 5).

As Okley (1978) has argued, although females are often not allocated the level of adult responsibility that is afforded to their male counterparts, there is still a greater expectation placed upon them for self-regulation and self-discipline. Bartky (1988) asserts that this creation of disciplined or 'docile' bodies is achieved through deliberate apportioning of women's time, space and movement. It would appear that in Vernon Lodge, the external regulation of time and movement was utilised as a means to produce an internally regulated subject.

We are stricter [than the men's hostels]. When it comes down to medication we have set times and we have set times for visitors, whereas in [the men's hostel] they can come and go all day and they can have medication whenever they want (Staff Member 2).

As Worrall (1997: 9) has argued, the inference of any form of punishment based around the notion of supervision is that the offender is in some way inadequate and is therefore incapable of redressing his or her own behaviour without some external intervention. Consequently the practice of supervision is a dynamic one and its purpose is to instil in the individual the characteristics of 'normal' behaviour whilst setting the boundaries between appropriate and censured behaviour (see also Harris and Webb, 1987: 75). Hostel supervision may therefore have been considered salutary by hostel staff, in that its primary aim was believed to bring about positive effects, but it can undoubtedly be seen as an intrusive process, the objective of which is to control and instruct the individual to a pre-determined (but discretionary) standard of behaviour. What appeared to be happening at Vernon Lodge was that the boundaries between acceptable and proscribed behaviour were set beyond a criminal/non-criminal agenda, instead they were set according to a gendered agenda, creating a demarcation between 'respectable' and 'non respectable' behaviour. Staying in bed beyond 8.30am or walking around in nightclothes was not considered 'appropriate' and women were encouraged to change their 'internal' behaviour and become 'self-disciplining' subjects, thus adhering to more conventional or respectable norms.

> We have a set routine where we will have something planned for the day or the week. They all have to get up early, they all have to get up as if they are going to work so it is important that they are not allowed to stay in bed and waste the whole day. They have to start addressing their problems and keep themselves busy (Staff Member 3).

> They have a structured day, that is often the thing that is most difficult for residents but I think it is the one thing that can be most helpful in the long run because it does help break the previous pattern of disorganisation. I think that daily routine is a form of discipline, it encourages a sort of self-discipline (Staff Member 5).

The expectation that residents should be self-disciplining and self-regulating is a particularly gendered notion. At the time this research was conducted no similar rules existed within any of the three men's hostels in the immediate area.

> We have the rule that you have to be dressed before 9.00am and I know [the men's hostel] don't....its more sort of free and easy there, the lads can stay in bed all day if they want to (Staff Member 1).

Faith (1993: 165) has argued that even at the end of the twentieth century female prisoners were seen to pose a greater threat to prison authority than men. Consequently institutionalised women have found themselves disciplined and punished for often very minor rule infringements and for behaviour which was not deemed to be 'deviant' or worth regulating in men's institutions. At Vernon Lodge this appeared to be the case.

> I've heard that some of [the men's hostels] let lads roll in till about half past 12. We seem to be stricter here. I don't know if that's because it's a female hostel or if it's just the individual management or what (Staff Member 1).

The staff even admitted that women were often 'disciplined' out of proportion to their misdemeanours.

> Sanctioning has changed now. The previous method of residents having to stay in was rubbish and none of us liked it. It used to get the staff in a total state and it

seemed so punitive compared to what the 'sin' was, like not getting up for breakfast. It was so minimal it was ludicrous (Staff Member 5). [8]

The utilisation of sanctioning as a method of discipline within the hostel highlighted the often contradictory expectations and assumptions made about the female residents. On the one hand women were required to be self-controlled and self-regulating and this requirement was encouraged through particular regimes and rules aimed explicitly at encouraging a degree of personal responsibility. However when women failed to achieve this level of personal responsibility, albeit through very minor infringements (such as failing to get out of bed on time) they were disciplined through a process which inferred a total inability for self-governance. This member of staff admitted having serious reservations about this procedure.

> In my opinion sanctioning is nonsense. There are two reasons, one is it doesn't work and two is it seems rather ironic, trying to get the women who come here to behave independently, inviting them to come here so that they have got some liberty and responsibility and then telling them they can't go out because they got up late. It just reminds me of school (Staff Member 7).

As has been argued throughout this book, women's behaviour is frequently understood and explained through two conflicting sets of discourses. It is assumed that women should be self-governing and they are expected to assume high levels of responsibility (not only for themselves but for their partners and families too). However, simultaneously they are assumed to be lacking in the ability to be self-governing and thus require levels of external supervision that reduce them to a child-like status. Together these opposing sets of expectations form the paradoxical nature of 'normal' femininity. Carlen (1983) described how these expectations were inherently present within prison regimes for women and how they, in turn, managed to reduce the female inmates to a less-than-adult status, denying them the rights and responsibilities that are frequently attributed to adult males. Within Vernon Lodge these inherent assumptions had similar consequences and this left some staff feeling uncomfortable.

> [Sanctioning] is crap. It's like you would treat kids from a primary school, you know 'you are grounded you naughty girl'. I don't agree with it (Staff Member 4).

Yet although it was criticised for being inappropriate and although staff acknowledged that they were creating a paradoxical situation through its use for such minor rule violations, sanctioning was still believed to be the only suitable way in which to instil appropriate standards of behaviour in residents.

> I don't think sanctioning is the answer because you are treating them like children but it's the problem of finding a good alternative. Everyone needs to know that misbehaviour is not acceptable and the only way you get this across is to let people know that if you do something wrong you get punished for it. We choose

sanctioning because it's the most lenient way we have to do it (Staff Member 3).

Historically 'deviant' women have been categorised as either 'mad' or 'bad'. Often, as Carlen (1998) has argued, this categorisation has very little to with the offence a woman has committed but all to do with the extent to which she may or may not conform to dominant gendered expectations. In general the staff of the hostel resisted the allocation of such labels to the female residents and indeed were well aware that these stereotypical classifications have traditionally served to construct an ideal of femininity and to punish those who fail to adhere to such ideals. However, although the hostel staff recognised and stated strongly that they deplored the stereotyping of female offenders in this way, they admitted that to some degree these stereotypes were inherently entrenched in the criminal justice system and, consequently, in the hostel regime. This was manifest in the fact that Vernon Lodge had weekly visits from a psychiatrist, a practice that some members of staff found problematic.

> We have a psychiatrist who comes in once a week and none of the male hostels have that so I question that. I have questioned that. That is the one difference that stands out (Staff Member 2).

> We have a psychiatrist who visits once a week. Usually there is a queue of women waiting to see him and I think that is symptomatic of the way women are made to feel about themselves in the system. They are treated like there is something wrong with them and so they take on those ideas and sometimes, I think they start to believe them. I would never encourage any of these women to see the psychiatrist. Well some of them need more professional help than we can give, [Mary] for example who cuts herself a lot, but the rest....no I wouldn't want to encourage them to get involved in the psychiatric system (Staff Member 9).

Several staff members in the hostel recognised the potential problem of women becoming embroiled within the medical/psychiatric system. However because of their inability to deal with particular 'problematic' women, sometimes these members of staff found themselves endorsing or advocating the very discourses or practices that they were actively seeking to reject. One example was Mary, the resident mentioned in the quotation above. Mary frequently cut herself and although these wounds were never life threatening her behaviour left staff feeling angry and frustrated and they readily admitted they were not equipped to help her. Eventually Mary was advised to see the psychiatrist and was consequently hospitalised. Of the 16 women interviewed approximately nine had had some psychiatric intervention, either prior to their arrival at Vernon Lodge or during their stay.[9] It should be acknowledged that most of the women who saw the psychiatrist at the hostel appeared to do so of their own choosing. Women like Mary (who became too much for the staff at the hostel to deal with and was thus encouraged to seek psychiatric help) were relatively uncommon. However, the relative power of 'experts' such as psychiatrists and the dynamics of their relationships with both the residents and staff were important issues and do require some discussion.

The overwhelming majority of staff at Vernon Lodge were women. Out of nine hostel staff interviewed, only one was male. Indeed, apart from this member of staff, a CECSA representative (who had an office in the hostel) and the caretaker, all other staff (Warden, Assistant Wardens, secretaries and auxiliary staff - the people who had most day to day contact with the residents) were female. In contrast, the majority of the CECSA representatives were male and, perhaps more significantly, *all* of the professional and medical 'experts' who regularly visited or were utilised by the hostel (for example the psychiatrist, the doctor, the drug counsellor and the dentist) were male. As I argued in Chapter Two, historically women have been expected to take responsibility for providing an appropriate role model for their 'deviant' sisters. At the same time they have acted as intermediaries between male professionals or managers and female clients, interpreting professional, male discourse into 'reasonable', common-sense ideas. In Vernon Lodge, as one resident articulated, female staff could legitimatise and justify practices and procedures in ways that male staff could not do.

> I think there should be more male staff here. I know some women here, including me, have had bad experiences with men in the past but I just think it's unhealthy for us all to be shut up here with a load of women staff. I bet you the rules would be different if there were more men on the staff. I bet you wouldn't have to get up at half past eight or get sanctioned. *And no way would a bloke come into your room in the morning to get you up out of bed, no way* (Sarah. Emphasis made in interview).

At Vernon Lodge the medical / professional 'experts' were essentially removed from the day-to-day reality of the hostel and the residents but simultaneously retained a considerable degree of power within the institution. This was starkly highlighted by the practices of disclosure of information. Generally residents could request to see all written information kept about them in their hostel files. However, all medical and psychiatric records remained confidential.

> If we had a psychiatric report on a resident, I couldn't show her that. I'd have to get permission from the psychiatrist. Or a medical report, I couldn't show her that (Staff Member 5).

> [The women] are allowed access to most of the files unless certain parties have asked for them to stay confidential. The psychiatrist for example, he might say 'I don't want the resident to see this document' and we can't argue (Staff Member 3).

> The residents can see most of what we write about them, they are entitled to see everything I think apart from the log book, that's our record. But with regard to the psychiatrist and the doctor and so on, they don't have to show anything. They have more control over those things than we do. They can distance themselves from the women in a way that we can't. If a resident is pissed off with the doctor or the drug counsellor or the psychiatrist they don't usually have a go at them. They can make a sharp exit and they usually do, leaving us to deal with someone

who's kicking off because they've been recommended for hospitalisation or a reduction in their Meth[adone] or something. We are usually the ones who have to try and explain why a decision has been made. The doctor or the psychiatrist....they just leave us to it (Staff Member 9).

Regardless of the relative power of the medical professionals within the hostel, and despite the fact that sometimes the hostel staff felt compelled to refer women to these 'experts', the staff in general resisted classifying or discussing women within these discourses and rejected the 'mad / bad' dichotomy. However, in keeping with the welfarist origins of the probation service, what was apparent within the hostel, was the mobilisation of discourses that tended to categorise the female residents as 'sad'. The majority of the staff appeared reluctant to attribute the women with full responsibility and agency for their behaviour. This attitude starkly contrasted with the overarching philosophy of the hostel which aimed to ensure women took some control over their lives, underpinned by the notion that women should be self-regulating and self-governing. So whilst the women in the hostel were expected to take full responsibility for very minor aspects of their lives (such as getting up early, getting dressed and so on) and could be disciplined for not adhering to these expectations, they were not perceived as responsible for the more significant aspects of their lives, such as their offending behaviour. One member of staff acknowledged this problem, commenting that

Sometimes [women] are looked upon as needing help, they are not afforded a sense of responsibility like men are (Staff Member 6).

However, for the most part the hostel staff endorsed the idea of women as victims.

I think most of them are probably victims of some sort. Victims of circumstance. If you look at a lot of their Pre-Sentence Reports and their backgrounds it's really obvious. It's all circumstances (Staff Member 2).

The majority seem to be victims of circumstance in that a lot of them have suffered abuse. In that sense I think their criminality could be defined as being victims of circumstances. A lot of their offending spins out from the fact that they don't get the love and care they should and so they look for an alternative. I know that sounds like an excuse but I think that is why a lot of them adapt and sort of like being in prison because they get the support and the attention that they haven't had outside and that makes for re-offending as an excuse to go back to an environment that is stable (Staff Member 1).

Some [of the women] I would categorise as victims. Victims of other people's actions or victims of circumstances, whatever. I don't think any of them are bad but some are definitely sad. I think female offenders have a lot more psychological problems than men. They have often been abused and so are victims as well as offenders (Staff Member 4).

Of course it *was* the case that many women in Vernon Lodge had suffered terrible abuse throughout their lives and this had sometimes led *directly* to their offending behaviour. Debbie, for example, was charged with the attempted murder of her husband. She stated that because of the level of his violence, and the fact that the police had failed to assist her in the past, she was left feeling she had no alternative.

> I felt I was driven to it in a way. I didn't know what else to do, that's how desperate I was. You see [my husband] used to beat me up, he was a wicked bastard and in the end I couldn't see any way out of it. I thought 'it's either me or him' and I wasn't going to let him kill me first. When the police arrested me I said to them 'can't you just caution me?' and they all laughed. One of them said 'we can't give you a caution for attempted murder love'. I don't see why not, they'd cautioned my husband once when he tried to choke me and you could say that was attempted murder couldn't you?

However, even women like Debbie often did not perceive themselves to be 'victims' of their circumstances. Debbie talked of her actions as 'taking control' and in fact complained that she had only attained the status of 'victim' once she had entered the criminal justice system. Her involvement, she stated, had *intensified* her feelings of powerlessness.

> [Being at the hostel] takes a lot of control away from you, like I have no control about what happens to my kids now. I can't go and visit them whenever I want to. I've got no control over what I do myself, I can't stay out after 11 o'clock, I've got to be up by 8 o'clock....no control any more.

It would be unfair to claim that the staff were the only group able to mobilise discourses around appropriate and inappropriate behaviour within the hostel. As Foucault (1980) articulated, power is dynamic and does not reside with one particular group. Thus feminising discourses that served to regulate and discipline the women within the hostel were not always imposed upon them. Rather the women were sometimes actively engaged in the regulation of each other through the employment of discourses which set boundaries between permissible and censured behaviour. The most obvious example of this was the general consensus amongst the residents towards women who had abused, neglected, injured or killed children.

> We advise women who have committed offences against children to tell the others that they are here for shoplifting or something. Although some of their crimes are pretty horrendous, we [staff] try not to make assumptions, but the women here....for them it's a real taboo subject. Like in prison, hurting children, especially a woman hurting children, well that's just not allowed to go unpunished (Staff Member 9).

We don't like women who have hurt their kids. We don't accept bitches like that. I've never seen any real violence but I suppose we make life difficult for them but I've got no sympathy (Billie).

Children should be able to trust their mothers and it always seems worse if a woman hurts her children because she should be the one to protect them (Debbie).

If you are in prison for a sex-offence the other women soon find out about it. They give you a really hard time. In the hostel they still give you a hard time but there was no real violence, it was really only verbal (Joanne). [10]

For many of the women this intolerance was intensified by the separation from their own children. Women like Billie and Debbie, who cherished their status as mothers, even though (or possibly because) they saw their children very infrequently, were particular bitter about living with women who, in their opinion, had effectively relinquished any rights to motherhood.

Being in here has made me realise that there are a lot of women who commit the sorts of things that I used to think only men did, like child abuse and sexual crimes. I was really shocked when I found out. What really annoys me is that they bend over backwards to let those women keep in contact with their children even if they abused them and the likes of me just gets forgotten. If I had abused them or something then they'd all be running round making sure I saw them once a month. It really makes me sick (Debbie).

So far this chapter has examined the structure and regime at Vernon Lodge and the dominant discourses which underpinned the administration of discipline and constructed an appropriate standard of femininity to which residents were encouraged (either by staff or by each other) to adhere to. However, as previously argued, women are not simply passive subjects upon whom such disciplinary discourses are imposed and who acquiesce without some form of response or resistance. Rather they frequently assume a strong sense of identity which enables them to assert their agency and thus manage, and cope with, their experiences of institutionalisation. The final section of this chapter will take up these debates.

Responding to Semi-Penal Institutionalisation

From their own accounts, it was apparent that the women in the hostel utilised a variety of coping strategies in order to manage their period of residence. Some women responded to their institutionalisation through apparent 'conformist' strategies, for example some consciously decided to fully comply with the rules and regime of the institution in order to avoid further scrutiny whilst others tended to separate themselves from the other residents, seeing isolation as a method of staying out of trouble. For some women, more explicit strategies were used, strategies which may be commonly described as methods of 'resistance'. [11] So, for example some women might disobey the rules of the institution and contest the authority of the staff. Others would assert a sense of agency by taking control of and responsibility for their lives and their actions, including their offending behaviour, thus challenging the 'victim' status often ascribed to them by the staff and rejecting the feminising discourses that underpinned the regime. Conversely, rather than rejecting these discourses and regimes, some women wholly embraced and endorsed them, seeing their feminine and maternal status as a source of empowerment rather than disempowerment.

In addition to these strategies the women often described examples of, what they termed, 'not-coping'. These included self harm and ultimately suicide or attempted suicide. Each of these strategies will be discussed below however it should be acknowledged at the outset that these responses are not mutually exclusive or 'fixed' in any way. As Smith (1996) found in her study of female prisoners, women would employ different methods of response at different times depending on what they perceived to be the most appropriate strategy in any given situation. Alternatively, they might employ more than one strategy at any particular time. What links these strategies and in many ways makes them mutually reinforcing, is the fact that they represent the plethora of ways that women, in everyday life as well as within institutions, attempt to deal with and negotiate the construction of the 'feminine' subject.

Conformity as resistance?

Due to their charitable status, institutions like the County Refuge for the Destitute depended heavily upon the compliance and co-operation of their residents for their successful operation. As Chapters Four and Five highlighted, for the most part women appeared to outwardly conform to the disciplinary regimes imposed upon them. However, rather than this being perceived as passive submission, it could be argued that conformity may have been a conscious decision on the part of women who wanted to facilitate their period of confinement. Conformity to discipline was a more common response than explicit resistance at Vernon Lodge but this was not necessarily a passive form of compliance. Women on bail in particular claimed that they deliberately chose to conform as a means of improving their chances at trial.

> I think hostels like these are like a second chance because if you get bailed here then you have got less chance of going away at your trial especially if you get a good report from here. I don't keep in with the staff or nothing but I don't get in trouble. I'm all right with the staff. I keep well in with [the warden] anyway. I do loads of posters for her and the hostel (Roxy).

> I just do as I'm told really, if I'm sanctioned then I don't go out. I don't go out of my way to make trouble like some do because I want a really good report for my court appearance. I just keep my head down and get on with it (Sarah).

Women like Roxy and Sarah were prepared to co-operate and comply with hostel rules and regulations as they saw their compliance as a strategy which would benefit them in the long term. Other women, like Sandra, took a similar approach. Sandra openly admitted that she was totally prepared to conform to any rules, not because she expected this to help her at her trial (as she frequently commented how she had 'the best barrister money could buy' to do that) but rather because she equated conformity with freedom. Having her own car, she could leave the hostel on a daily basis and go and visit her children, family and friends as long as she was back for the 11.00pm curfew. Her total conformity meant she was never sanctioned and thus had the freedom to go out every day. So rather than making it difficult for her to abide by hostel rules, Sandra's desire to continue a 'normal' life actually fostered her compliance.

There were other women, however, who did not have the personal (strong family connections) or financial resources that Sandra had. Neither did they have as much to gain from conformity as Roxy and Sarah did, yet they still adopted this approach more frequently than any other. Rosie and Belinda were both on probation so were not reliant on a good report for trial, yet both adhered to sanctioning even though this meant on one occasion Rosie missed an appointment to visit her son and on another Belinda could not turn up to her part-time job as a shop assistant and was consequently sacked. When asked why she had not just ignored the sanction and gone to work, Belinda explained that it was not worth getting into even more trouble and that she just wanted to get through her probation as quickly and as painlessly as possible. As Okley (1978) discussed in her study of a girls' boarding school, total conformity often meant a reduction in the amount of attention that the girls would otherwise be subjected to. In other words, as Belinda suggested, conformity was a means of avoiding or resisting further, more intensive scrutiny and regulation.

However, what women like Belinda did not appear to be aware of was the fact that, because disciplinary measures like sanctioning were informally imposed (in other words they were methods of regulation designed by the hostel management and staff and were not part of any probation or bail requirements), they could not be formally administered. Thus, as one member of staff explained, the hostel had no real power to *enforce* a sanction even though it had *imposed* one.

> There is mild objection to sanctioning [amongst the residents] but they will never just say 'well I'm going out' if they are sanctioned. Well some of them have done. There was one woman in the past and you just couldn't sanction her, she would just go out anyway and what can you do about it? The women here haven't cottoned on to it yet that if they go, well so what? If they ever caught on to it that we can't force them to abide by a sanction....[laughs] (Staff Member 1).

When asked why they did conform to rules so readily the residents usually answered that they wanted to avoid being labelled as 'trouble-causers' and thus make their time at the hostel as unproblematic as possible. Some members of staff however, had a different explanation for the compliance of the residents. In contrast to the notion that incarcerated women have traditionally been seen as more recalcitrant than their male counterparts (Carlen, 1983; Zedner, 1991; Faith, 1993), some members of staff claimed that the women conformed primarily *because* they were women.

> ....whereas men often tend to fight the system, women seem to submit to rules more quickly. I know that is probably a gross generalisation because we do have women in here who will go out of their way not to conform but I think looking at prisons, the protests always seem to occur in men's institutions (Staff Member 8).

> The women tend to conform quite quickly. They generally just accept things like sanctioning. I think maybe the women here are keener to please than the men in other hostels. I think women are more conformist than men. I don't think we'd get away with sanctioning for things like getting up late in a men's hostel....they'd just ignore us (Staff Member 9).

As discussed previously, there was some confusion amongst both residents and staff with regards to the real purpose and function of the hostel. Some women complained that they were often unsure as to what was expected of them and consequently total adherence to the written set of hostel rules was one method of laying down boundaries for themselves in order to facilitate and clarify their position within the institution. As women like Sam and Billie articulated, treating the hostel more like a prison, where rules and regulations are clearly defined and imposed, made for an easier life.

> I suppose it's easier to just follow the rules....like in prison. You know where you are then (Sam).

> I think it's best just to behave like you would in prison. Just abide by the rules, don't question them, just accept them. That's the easiest thing to do. I've got other, more important things to worry about than whether the staff were right to sanction me or whether its my turn to do the dishes. Do you know what I mean? (Billie).

In addition to adhering to the rules, many women attempted to navigate through their period of institutionalisation by a process of segregation. This occurred in two ways. Some women would physically separate themselves from either the staff or the other women in the hostel, believing the most constructive way in which they could facilitate their time at Vernon Lodge was to 'keep themselves to themselves'. These women perceived that by removing themselves from any real involvement with other residents, they had developed a means of avoiding potential trouble and this would thus help to expedite their time in the hostel.

> I just try and stay out of the way if there is trouble, I just keep myself to myself. Don't take sides (Debbie).

I try to keep my head down and keep out of it. You know who the trouble causers and the grasses are and so you try to keep away from them (Kate).

I just keep out of it, it does my head in. If [other residents] start having a go at someone I'll say something like 'leave her alone' but anything more serious then you should just stay away (Carrie).

I just come in and go straight upstairs. The new girls now are really cocky, you ask them not to sit on the pool table and they tell you to shut your face. I just go about my own business (Maureen).

This strategy of 'shutting out' is in some ways similar to what Goffman (1961) termed 'situational withdrawal'. For the women quoted above this withdrawal took the form of physical removal from others. Other women however separated themselves on a more metaphysical level, distancing themselves from the reality of their situation and developing a 'them and us' mentality, allocating themselves an almost 'non criminal' status thus separating themselves from other women who they perceived to be the 'real criminals'. These women developed strategies that allowed them to distance themselves from, or even totally deny, the reality of their situation. Margaret, for example, was a middle-aged woman convicted of business fraud. She was from a wealthy background and was well educated, well dressed and noticeably 'different' (mainly in terms of her age, her accent, her mode of dress and the nature of her offence) from other residents in the hostel. This 'difference' provided Margaret with a mechanism through which she could isolate herself from her reality in the sense that, because she looked different, Margaret asserted that she *was* different to the other women in Vernon Lodge. Informal discussions with Margaret highlighted the way in which she had set herself apart from her fellow residents. Margaret would frequently assert that the hostel was a 'stop gap' in her life, insisting that she was only there because she was temporarily homeless. Often this was a strategy employed by women who had committed the most serious offences. So women like Maureen (who was on bail for aiding and abetting the attempted rape of a child), Joanne (on bail for sexually abusing her son) and Mary (on probation for threatening behaviour) would constantly stress how they were at Vernon Lodge 'for their own good' or 'for their own protection' and very rarely acknowledge their status as 'offenders' or their period of confinement as a form of punishment. As quoted previously, Maureen (and several other women) perceived the hostel as a 'home from home' rather than as an institution entrenched within the criminal justice system. Thus, through the utilisation of such strategies, these women would not only minimalise the severity of their offences but also avoid the reality of their situation. However for some women (Maureen and Joanne in particular), the continual claims of being in the hostel for their own protection had the effect of intensifying the reality of their situation as the other women quickly realised the nature of their offences and made life considerably more difficult for them. When asked about the difficult, and sometimes dangerous situation that women like her were in, Maureen's response was surprising. Far from denying her involvement in the crime she was charged with, as was her usual response to her situation, her whole strategy altered and instead she asserted a strong sense of agency indicating that she 'knew the score' and was therefore prepared to deal with whatever situation she found herself in, even if that meant physical violence. Maureen's change of attitude here is indicative of the way in which women could utilise, sometimes very contradictory methods of coping depending on the situation and thus highlights the complex ways in which the residents navigated and negotiated their period of institutionalisation.

Explicit resistance

At Vernon Lodge there were no episodes of collective protest during the fieldwork period and only a few instances of resistance in the form of violence. The women did, however, utilise other strategies of 'resistance'. Bosworth (1999) utilises the concept of resistance in its broadest sense, moving beyond an examination of large-scale protest and serious rebellion, and instead provides a wider frame of reference for understanding women's responses to institutionalisation.

> ....resistance remains an extremely useful concept because of the way in which it illuminates small-scale attempts to disrupt power relations (Bosworth, 1999: 130).

Bosworth analysed how incarcerated women frequently utilise their own race-class-gender identities to disrupt power relations and thus manage or resist the construction of themselves as gendered beings. A similar strategy was used by some of the women in Vernon Lodge to deal with the gendered expectations imposed upon them.

During an informal discussion with a group of residents, one member of staff commented that the women should accept the requirement to undertake domestic chores around the hostel because this was something they would be 'doing at home anyway'. Most of the women agreed that this would indeed be part of a 'normal' routine for them however two women were visibly shocked at this supposition and employed their own class based experiences to negate the gender based assumption being made of them. Sandra explained that at home she had a dishwasher to do her dishes and a cleaner to do her housework and consequently was insulted at the way in which she had been stereotyped on the level of both gender (as a woman) and class (as a typically 'working class offender'). She stated that she had no real objection to doing chores but wanted it acknowledged that she only submitted to this requirement as she saw it as an inevitable part of the regulatory mechanism that constrained all women embroiled in the criminal justice system, not as something she should undertake willingly just because she was a woman. In addition, as discussed previously, Sandra stated that she undertook these tasks as a means of avoiding further, more intense regulation (such as a sanction) as this would restrict her ability to make her daily visits to family and friends and thus prevent her from leading as 'free' a life as possible. Margaret also objected to these assumptions and supported Sandra's point that every task or chore she undertook in the hostel, she did in order to comply with her probation order and to stay out of trouble and not because she accepted that this was part of her 'natural' role.

Perhaps the most common method of resistance was complaint. However, although the women would often complain about various aspects of hostel life to each other, it was only occasionally that they voiced their grievances in a more public or formal way. The daily residents' meetings were set up in order that women would have a platform to air their complaints or discuss any issues of general concern. For the most part women were reluctant to complain at these meetings. Some women stated that this was because they had nothing to complain about but others commented that they were worried that complaining might label them 'trouble causers' and this might be recorded in their files and thus influence their chances in court.[12] In addition, many women commented that they felt fairly powerless and resigned to the fact that it was not worth complaining, as it would have no real effect.

> There have been times I've really wanted to complain about something but I just don't. I want a good record for my court appearance so I don't do anything that might make me seem difficult. Anyway, complaining gets you nowhere because nothing ever changes. Well I suppose they changed the sanction so instead of not being allowed out you now have to do a job in the hostel but really, nothing changes. No one is going to listen to us (Sarah).

Ironically, although the residents' meetings were established for the purposes of airing complaints, the compulsory nature of these meetings was one of the most frequent complaints made by the women. Because generally the residents were not convinced that their complaints would be taken seriously, they felt the meetings to be a waste of time and so some would refuse to attend. This of course was met with the usual response - sanctioning.

> I objected to the curfew and the house meetings. I hated [house meetings] and you get sanctioned if you don't go. So I spent most of my life sanctioned (Mandy).

Because of her usual absence from residents meetings, Mandy developed her own, less formal, method of airing her grievances and asserting her rejection of authority. Mandy, who was 20 years old at the time of interview, responded to her 'less-than-adult' status by behaving in a less-than-adult manner. For example, she would spend her time pulling faces, calling names, throwing food, or pulling chairs away from other women as they sat down. She claimed that she found the process of 'winding people up' a great source of amusement and thus this was a strategy she used to manage her time at Vernon Lodge.

> I'd get up about 9 o'clock have breakfast. If you don't get up you get sanctioned. Then about half past nine you have a house meeting and if you miss them you get sanctioned as well. That's it for the day. Then I'd either play pool or give shite to the staff for the rest of the time (Mandy).

'Giving shite' to the staff usually meant verbal insults or 'answering back' and Mandy was not alone in employing this strategy. Many women articulated their resentments by arguing with, or swearing at, members of staff and although the staff complained that they found this form of behaviour intimidating and sometimes frightening, it rarely escalated beyond verbal threats. However, violence was used against the staff on three occasions during the period of fieldwork. On one occasion Mandy swung a pool cue at an Assistant Warden and, although she claimed she was not seriously trying to hit her, her action left the Assistant Warden extremely shaken and Mandy was asked to leave the hostel. In another instance some weeks later, another resident did hit an Assistant Warden across the head with a pool cue and she also was required to leave. The third incident involved two members of staff who were taken hostage by a resident armed with a knife and a broken bottle. This resident threatened to harm both the staff and herself and the incident only ended when one Assistant Warden managed to get to the panic alarm which alerted the police to the situation. The resident was subsequently arrested.

There are few accounts of collective protest in women's institutions (Madaraka-Sheppard, 1986). However some women at Vernon Lodge did engage in a form of collective behaviour as a coping strategy. Although, as discussed earlier in this chapter, some women felt inclined to distance themselves from other residents, for many women 'sticking together' was the most beneficial and positive way of managing their institutionalisation and challenging authority. These women employed a strategy more commonly associated with custodial institutions and had developed a set of informal rules between themselves that had the effect of adhering them to each other whilst separating them from the staff. The most common of these rules involved 'keeping quiet' or 'not grassing'. Informing on fellow residents was something most of the women agreed they would not do, either because they disagreed with the idea on principal or because they believed that 'keeping quiet' was the best way to avoid trouble.

> Well I wouldn't grass on anyone. You get girls in here who'd grass about anything, they just like crawling to the staff. Another reason why you don't grass is because it's not worth getting yourself into trouble with the other girls. We've all got to live here (Kate).

> You don't grass to the staff. No going back to the staff if anyone does anything wrong. You sort it out yourself (Mandy).

> I had two quid missing and I said if I find who did it I'm going to break their hands because we are all in this situation, we have all committed criminal offences. You just don't do that, same as you don't do it in prison....you don't nick from your own (Roxy).

Sorting problems out informally, without involving members of staff, was a strategy that most of the women adhered to. Although violence sometimes erupted between residents, mainly with regards to thefts, 'sticking together' was still a preferable response to 'grassing'. But not all of the women conformed to this informal strategy. Mary, for example, was known as a 'grass' because she consistently resisted the idea of 'sticking together' stating that she would rather place her trust in the staff than in the other residents.

> Some of the girls say you don't grass but it depends on what's been done. When the fire started in the TV room I had an idea who did that so I told [the Warden] because people could have been killed. I'd also tell the staff if I saw anyone bringing drugs into the hostel (Mary).

The other women did not appreciate Mary's attitude and she was frequently ostracised and verbally abused for her actions.

> In my opinion you shouldn't go running to the staff and grassing on other people, that's out of order. There's one girl here and she is always running in to the staff moaning and complaining and looking for excuses to grass on people. She is going to get into trouble one day. Anyway I don't think the staff like people like that either (Frances).

Frances' comment that the staff did not appreciate Mary's behaviour any more than the residents did was fairly accurate. Generally the staff perceived Mary as an 'attention-seeker' and a 'trouble-causer' who, by constantly informing on the activities of other residents, which inevitably led to frequent friction amongst the residents, made not only her own life at the hostel, but also the life of staff members, much more difficult. Consequently Mary found herself becoming isolated from all parties. Throughout the period of fieldwork for this research, Mary slowly became increasingly angry but at the same time depressed and her growing isolation appeared to reinforce her desire to 'grass' on other women which, in turn, amplified her 'outsider' status within the institution. Mary was eventually hospitalised on the recommendation of the hostel psychiatrist after successive periods of self harm and threats of suicide, which both the residents and the hostel staff asserted were all part of her 'attention-seeking behaviour'. This decline into, what many of the residents described as 'not coping' will be discussed in the final section of this chapter.

Endorsing discourses

Bosworth (1999) states that the formation of the female identity is an inherent aspect of women's resistance to control and discipline. She states that although institutionalised women are subjected to feminising discourses and regimes, this does not necessarily mean that they render women powerless or passive. Rather, the construction of 'femininity' can be negotiated and utilised in order for women to achieve their 'own ends'. Although Bosworth's study focuses specifically on women in prison, a similar analysis could be applied to women confined in semi-penal institutions.

Bosworth provides an example of the women in her study using bodily aspects of femininity to win disputes within prison. A similar scenario emerged during the period of fieldwork at Vernon Lodge. Margaret was a resident who was in her late fifties and was thus considerably older than the other women in the hostel. As discussed previously, Margaret considered herself to be different from the other women, perceiving them to be the 'real criminals' and consequently she objected to sharing a room with any of them. In order to assist her case for a single room Margaret employed 'feminising' discourses pertaining to 'appropriate' body shape, claiming that, because of her age and the condition of her body, she felt uncomfortable undressing in front of much younger women. Margaret won her case and was allocated a single occupancy room, something that Debbie was not allowed. When stating her case, Debbie had not resorted to such feminising discourses but rather had articulated an account that emphasised her strong objection to drugs and the fact that she was sharing a room with a heroin user. She was informed that many of the women in Vernon Lodge were drug users and as long as the other woman was not using drugs on the premises she would have to 'put up with it'.

The majority of women in Vernon Lodge did not perceive 'femininity' as a negative aspect of their lives or identity. Indeed generally they were proud of their feminine status. This was emphasised through the fact that many of the younger women in particular would not even enter the recreation rooms within the hostel without their make-up on. Hair and clothes were also a source of pride and pleasure with frequent changes of hairstyle and clothes-swapping sessions. Frost (1999) has asserted that women often conform to acceptable standards of feminine beauty, through clothes, hair and beauty regimes, because, in addition to providing pleasure, this process can actually improve self-esteem and mental well-being. Thus it could be argued that for the women at Vernon Lodge, this adherence to conventional standards of appearance was a means of avoiding the 'outcast' status often attributed to women with alternative looks whilst at the same time promoting feelings of self-worth which served to empower women who may otherwise have felt relatively powerless through their period of confinement.

> You have to make the effort don't you? If you just sit around in slippers and a nightie, no make up or nothing, well then you're beat. At least it's something to think about when you get up in the morning, 'what am I going to wear today?'. It's a bit pathetic but it's better than just giving up on yourself (Sarah).

As in Bosworth's study, the most commonly endorsed aspect of femininity, and one of the most common ways in which the women maintained a sense of identity, was through their status as mothers. As mentioned previously, women in the hostel who were mothers generally did not accept women whose offences involved children. Often though, as Bosworth stated, even women who would not ordinarily be considered as 'good mothers' were keen to be perceived as such. In Vernon Lodge, those women whose children were either adopted or in care would go to great lengths to explain and justify why this was so, all the time reiterating that their status as 'mother' was the most significant and important aspect of their lives.

[My daughter] is with adoptive parents. She's really well looked after I know, they've got a really big house and they can give her everything but I still wish things had been different so she could be with me. People think if you give your kids up for adoption then you mustn't care about them but I gave her up because I do care about her. It's no life for a little girl to see her mother on the gear and being farmed out when I'm in and out of prison. [My dealer] who beat me up, he threatened that in future if I couldn't pay then he wanted to sleep with [my daughter]. That scared the shit out of me so I finally made the decision although I'd been thinking about it for a while (Kate).

I fucking hate [my son] being in care. That's my fucking social worker for you, I hate her, could kill her....her and her big ideas. She just took him from the nursery, took him away because of the drugs and that. I didn't neglect him or nothing like that, I didn't hit him, it was just the drugs (Nikki).

Apart from justifying why their children had been taken into care, for many women, the most effective way of endorsing their own 'good mother' status was through a rejection of other female figures in their children's lives, in particular foster or adoptive mothers. Roxy in particular had a passionate hatred for her son's foster mother and after every visit would spend hours criticising almost every aspect of her 'mothering' ability.

I don't like [my son's foster mother], she's a tramp. When I went up to see him I asked for his coat and the one she brought out, I said 'you are not putting that on him'. Me and [Nikki] went out and bought him a whole new outfit. Also she said he is always being sick. I've told her it's because she's giving him baby food. He's too old for that (Roxy).

In contrast to women like Kate, who had deliberately distanced herself from her daughter for the sake of her child, Roxy had no intention of relinquishing her role as a mother, even though she was physically separated from her son. For many of the mothers in Vernon Lodge, maintaining their presence in the lives of their children was a priority, primarily as this gave them a strong sense of purpose and identity that facilitated their time at the hostel. This was of course easiest for those women whose children were not in care. Sandra, for example, saw her children almost every day. Another woman, Jean, also saw her daughter every day. Indeed Jean's daughter was not even aware that her mother was not living at home with her father. Jean, who was on probation, would leave the hostel every morning and go to the family home in time to get her daughter up for school. She would stay at home until her daughter went to bed and then return to the hostel in time for curfew. Through this method, Jean not only provided herself with a goal and a purpose but also caused as little disruption as possible for her family.

Overall, it can be seen that the women at Vernon Lodge utilised various strategies through which they could ease the 'pains' of their confinement (Bosworth, 1999). Some conformed to the rules, some segregated themselves from others, some grouped together against the staff, some embraced idealised images of themselves as 'feminine' subjects and some rejected disempowering discourses and took control of their lives, expressing a strong sense of agency. Some women utilised several of these methods depending on the situation. Whatever method they selected, for the most part the women at Vernon Lodge managed to find a coping mechanism that enabled them to negotiate their period of institutionalisation with the minimum of harm to themselves. However, not all women managed to do this. For some women, described by their fellow residents and staff as 'poor' or 'non' copers, confinement (often in addition to other, extra problems and difficulties) was not something that they 'successfully' navigated.

'Not coping'

> There are some girls here who have never lived on their own, they've been in care or in other hostels and I don't think this place prepares them to look after themselves at all. All they seem to do is move them on to other hostels (Frances).

Although the staff and Management Committee of Vernon Lodge were keen to portray the institution as one which attempted to 'empower' women, and although (as discussed previously) many of the rules and practices within the hostel functioned to encourage a degree of personal responsibility and self-governance, in reality the hostel (like the reformatories of the nineteenth century) often had the effect of 'infantilising' the women therein. Consequently, in contrast to those residents who rejected, resisted or consciously conformed to the regime, a small number of women became reliant and dependent on the hostel structure to such an extent that they found it difficult to live independently after their period of residency had finished. Some of these women would persistently visit the hostel once they had left and indeed at one point this became such a problem for the staff that they established set visiting times to which even ex-residents had to adhere.

> We had one resident and she got a flat....but she's totally isolated now, she has contact with a probation officer but she has no support network like she had here (Assistant Warden 1).

> Coping with the outside world is the major problem they face. I mean this place is like a world within a world and can sometimes give a false image of reality (Assistant Warden 4).

Although many residents did continue to regularly visit the hostel after they had left, the number of women who became completely dependent was relatively small and only two obvious cases were observed during the fieldwork. Another form of, what was described as, 'not coping' was much more common. Incidents of self harm, suicide attempts or threats of suicide were fairly regular occurrences. Of course it should be acknowledged that self harm and suicide are not essentially related behaviours. Women who self harm do not necessarily go on to attempt or commit suicide. Billie, who did commit suicide, had not, to my knowledge, harmed herself previously and, indeed, until the actual day of her suicide, had apparently never threatened or discussed killing herself. However, these two, albeit separate, issues will be discussed together as they represent the most extreme responses of women to institutionalisation.

Much of the literature on the subject of suicide and self harm pertains to women who are formally incarcerated in custodial institutions (Liebling, 1992, 1994; Heidensohn, 1996; Smith, 1996) but these analyses were found to be useful when examining self harmful behaviour within a hostel setting. Apps (1988, cited in Smith, 1996) identifies the ways in which the construction of femininity contributes to incidents of self mutilation and injury arguing that because women are entrenched within a society which focuses heavily on the importance of bodily appearance, their anger or frustrations are frequently aimed towards their own bodies. The body is a site that women are made to feel constantly aware of, sometimes to the point of self-detestation. As Eaton (1993) argued, even behaviour such as amateur tattooing can indicate a sense of self-loathing. Amateur tattooing was relatively rare in Vernon Lodge and was mainly apparent amongst those women who had previously been in prison. One woman, Rosie, had numerous tattoos over her body, a mixture of both professional and amateur designs. Although she took great pleasure in showing them off to other residents she stated that she was not proud of them. When asked why she wanted to leave such permanent marks on herself Rosie stated that it meant nothing to her as she felt no affinity with her own body. Indeed she stated that her body was almost alien to her and thus it did not matter if she damaged or scarred it.

Most of the cases of self-mutilation witnessed at Vernon Lodge were more serious and potentially harmful than amateur tattooing. Women like Mary bore the scars of many episodes of 'cutting' and was labelled, by both staff and residents, as an attention-seeker. As Apps argues, some women might injure themselves as a means of gaining and receiving attention and this may have been the case with Mary. However, the way in which her actions were responded to simply seemed to reinforce her behaviour. As Liebling (1992) has noted, women can find themselves in this vicious cycle whereby 'cries for help' or 'attention-seeking behaviour' are actually responded to with little sympathy and the 'help' that is so desperately sought is often not provided. The staff at Vernon Lodge admitted that they felt frustrated with Mary's behaviour and, over time, were losing patience with her. Over a period of several months less and less attention was paid to her behaviour, behaviour which in turn was becoming a greater cause for concern.

Mary's label as an 'attention-seeker' appeared to be reinforced by the fact that she could not reasonably explain why she wanted to hurt herself. Maureen, on the other hand, was able to provide an articulate explanation of her own self harmful behaviour, asserting that she felt unable to outwardly express her feelings of anger and frustration which stemmed from previous episodes of sexual and physical abuse, and therefore turned them inwards onto herself.

> At this moment I see the doctor down at [the hospital] because I tried to slit my wrists. I just felt that no one would really want to listen to me because I'm just

classed as a criminal. I didn't do it to hurt myself, I did it to get rid of myself. It doesn't matter how much you talk about it, you've still got that experience and you've got a lot of anger with it. But the anger, half the time, you can't let it out. You hurt yourself (Maureen).

The most extreme form of self harm is, of course, suicide or attempted suicide. Apps asserted that incarcerated women often lose their self-identity and are frequently deprived of their social status. The most obvious social role that institutionalised women are stripped of is that of motherhood given that they are physically separated from their children. Although Apps is talking about causes of self injury, this analysis can be applied to the case of Billie's suicide. Billie originated from Cumbria and her children were placed in local authority care on her being sent to Vernon Lodge. Due to the long distance between them, she was unable to see them regularly however she was still able to assert her status as a mother through letters and phone calls and utilised this as a coping mechanism, constantly looking to the future when her family could be reunited. Towards the end of her probation order she began to actively fight to have her children returned but encountered a problem that she considered insurmountable. Billie was informed that she could not obtain custody of her children until she had a house of her own. At the same time she was informed that she would not be considered as a priority for re-housing because her children were still in local authority care. In other words, without her children she would not get a house and without a house she would not get her children. Billie felt she had been deprived of her primary status. She commented to a member of staff on the day before she died that she had come to the conclusion her children would be better off if she was dead as it would, ironically, introduce a sense of stability into their lives that she did not feel she could provide. Billie hanged herself in the hostel bathroom in February 1993, on her son's birthday.

It is of course debatable whether the women discussed above are indeed the 'poor' or 'non-copers' that they were often described as. Incidents of self-mutilation, although harmful and dangerous, could be seen as a manifestation of feelings that women are expected to repress. In other words, self harm can represent a form of resistance to 'silencing' and controlling discourses and regimes (Liebling, 1992). Eaton (1993) has argued that even suicide can be perceived in this way, representing as it does the final indication of control over one's own life, the ultimate decision that women are able to make in relatively 'powerless' situations. Billie's suicide could be seen as her way of retaining some influence over, not only her own life, but the lives of her children who, she argued, would be able to lead a more stable life without her. This argument needs to be dealt with carefully however as equating self harm and suicide with resistance and self-determination could potentially lead to a glamorisation and trivialisation of such incidents. Instead, emphasis should be placed on uncovering and deconstructing those discourses, regimes and practices which eventually evoke such extreme responses from women.

This chapter has examined the three primary objectives of this book, building on the historical analysis of the County Refuge presented in Chapters Four and Five, with a contemporary analysis of the institution as it existed in the 1990s. Through an examination of its structure, regime and the discourses that underpinned its administration of discipline, this chapter has highlighted the way in which Vernon Lodge, a bail and probation hostel for women, could indeed be perceived as a semi-penal institution for the late twentieth century. In addition it has shown how, far from being passive and powerless, women continue to develop strategies of coping and resistance, strategies that enable them to negotiate their periods of confinement. But how is this analysis useful for our understanding of the control of women as we enter the twenty first century? The major themes and issues of this book, and a discussion of the way in which this analysis can be utilised when examining the position of institutionalised women in the new millennium will be presented in the next, and final, chapter.

Notes

1   Interviews were conducted with 16 residents, nine members of staff (including the Warden, Deputy Warden and Assistant Wardens) and the Chairman and the Executive Officer of the CECSA. All of those interviewed were women except for the Deputy Warden and the two representatives of the CECSA. In order to maintain anonymity the staff interviews will be referenced as Staff member 1, 2, 3 etc. and CECSA representative 1 and 2. The residents are given false names.

2   Funding for approved hostels comes from various sources. At the time of research the Home Office was responsible for a direct grant of approximately 80% of the total running costs. The exact amount of this grant was based mainly on the number of bed spaces provided by the hostel. The remaining 20 per cent of costs would be provided by local authorities and residents own contributions (rent). For further details of this breakdown in funding see Probation Service Act (Home Office, 1994) and the Hostels Handbook (Home Office, 1995).

3   Some description of the way in which the hostel was staffed is necessary here. In 1993 Vernon Lodge was staffed by a Warden, Deputy Warden and between seven and ten full time, and relief, Assistant Wardens. In addition there were two administrative staff and several auxiliary staff. The CECSA appointed an Executive Officer who maintained day to day contact with the hostel.

4   It should be acknowledged here that these 'informal' environments and institutions can also be restrictive and disciplinary with regards to women (see the discussion in Chapter Two regarding the informal regulation of women through discourse). However, they occupy the opposite end of the control continuum to very formal and regulative institutions such as prisons or special hospitals and for this reason they are classed here as 'informal'.

5   Obviously there was some flexibility regarding this issue. If there were exceptional circumstances which meant a woman was unavoidably delayed then the member of staff on duty would use his / her discretion as to whether breach proceedings were necessary.

6   This issue of the different status of bailees and probationers at the hostel will be discussed in more detail later in this chapter.

7   See Chapter Three for a discussion of this issue.

8   Although, as this member of staff states, the *method* of sanctioning had changed (from requiring the woman to stay on the hostel premises for one day to requiring the woman to complete some chore around the hostel) what had not changed was the reasons for the sanction. In other words women were still being disciplined, albeit in a different way, for the same 'sins' (staying in bed late, not getting dressed etc).

9   The term 'approximately' is used here because it was impossible to say exactly how many women had really had contact with psychiatric services as some women refused to answer the interview questions relating to this subject.

10   Joanne was on bail for sexually abusing her son.

11   See Chapter Two for a discussion of the complex and subtle nature of 'resistance' and the difficulties inherent in describing particular acts or behaviours as such.

12   It should be acknowledged here that the staff completely refuted the idea that any complaints or grievances would be 'used against' individual women either during their period of residence or at their trial.

Chapter 7

Conclusion

The first aim of this book was to fill a theoretical gap in the existing feminist literature by examining the development and establishment of the semi-penal institution as a significant arena of social control for 'deviant' women over two centuries. As mentioned in Chapter One, although there already exist some very comprehensive and critical analyses of various types of semi-penal institutions for women, these studies primarily focus on distinct and specific nineteenth and early twentieth century establishments.[1] Thus, what these studies have generally failed to do is explicitly identify the common theoretical issues and discourses that make the development of such institutions for women a *history* rather than *events in history*.

In constructing this history this book has illustrated that there is indeed considerable historical consistency between the institutions of the nineteenth century (reformatories, refuges, homes and asylums) and twentieth century establishments such as homes for unmarried mothers, halfway houses for 'delinquent' girls and contemporary probation hostels for women. Continuity was found in three ways. First, several of the distinguishing structural and organisational characteristics of the nineteenth century reformatory were found to be present in specific twentieth century semi-penal institutions, most significantly in Vernon Lodge during the 1990s. Second, an element of permanence was uncovered in the discourses and processes through which women were *labelled* as 'deviant' and deemed to be in need of institutionalisation in order that they might be subjected to a process of reformation and 'normalisation'. Finally, and most importantly, the discourses and strategies mobilised within the nineteenth century semi-penal institution, to facilitate the process of reform of 'deviant' women, were found to be similar to some of those employed within a women's probation hostel nearly two hundred years later.

Once the issue of historical consistency is acknowledged, as it has been in this book, it is possible to re-assess the discipline and social control of women in two ways. First, as mentioned above, continuity can be found historically. Second, this study highlights how the mechanisms of social control and discipline are 'all encompassing', not just historically but contemporarily too. In other words, the social control of women in modern society is not confined to two polarised arenas, namely the formal custodial institution and the informal domestic sphere. On the contrary, these two sites could be seen as the extremities of one single 'continuum'. Although this term has been utilised previously[2] it has usually been used to refer solely to the relationship between those methods of discipline imposed in the prison and those used in the home. The fact that a whole range of other, semi-penal, formal institutions have also existed, and continue to exist, has been insufficiently acknowledged.

The second aim of this study was to analyse the ways in which women were disciplined according to dominant feminising discourses. As this case study has emphasised, the dominant, hegemonic discourses constructed around idealised images of femininity played a consistent role in the regulation and discipline of a whole range of 'deviant' women during the nineteenth century. In addition, these discourses endured well into the twentieth century and could in fact be found unperpinning the regimes and practices of the modern day probation hostel studied in this book.

For over two centuries women deemed to be unruly, wayward, immoral or criminal have found themselves subjected to institutional regimes aimed at 'normalising' them back to appropriate standards of femininity. More significantly the condemnation of 'inappropriate' or 'unfeminine' behaviour and the practice of utilising feminising regimes and discourses to 'normalise' that behaviour does not appear to be abating as we enter the twenty first century. Although, as mentioned above, it is not valid to generalise the findings of this case study to the experiences of *all* institutionalised women, other recent studies do support the assertion that women's 'deviant' behaviour continues to be defined through dominant discourses of femininity and these in turn continue to reinforce 'normalising' and 'infantilising' regimes.[3]

It should be acknowledged however that the majority of these recent studies have focussed on the experiences of women within formal custodial institutions. There have, of course, been several pieces of research conducted on women in probation hostels. However, these studies have generally been concerned with one of two issues. First, there exist several investigations that aim to espouse the benefits of probation hostels as credible and indeed necessary alternatives to prisons for women offenders. Carlen's (1990) study, for example, examined the way in which certain 'alternatives' to imprisonment might be utilised in order to prevent women entering into the 'revolving door' scenario in prison. Second, writers such as Buckley (1987), Wincup (1996) and Worrall (1997) have examined the probation hostel by focusing on the advantages of single-sex hostels for women over mixed-sex institutions.

It was never the intention of this book to denounce the use of probation hostels for women. On the contrary, given the rapidly growing numbers of women in prison in England and Wales and given that the majority of these women are incarcerated for non-violent offences, the probation hostel would indeed appear to be a viable and, it could be argued, an essential facility which could assist in reducing the numbers of women in custody.

In addition, it was never the intention to reject the important issues around female-only institutions. As Worrall (1997) argues, placing women in mixed hostels is wholly inappropriate as, due to the small numbers of female referrals, the reality is a very small number of women in an overwhelmingly male environment. This, she states, is problematic with regard to the safety of the female probationers but any attempt to segregate or 'annex' the women to particular areas of an institution can result in a 'feeling of entrapment' (1997: 109). Also, as Buckley (1987) points out, women are often not 'heard' in mixed, or more specifically, male dominated, groups and are consequently ignored. Finally, many women may have previously had negative experiences with men and would therefore want to avoid mixed hostels. This, Buckley asserts, is especially significant for women wanting visits from children.

Thus, a good case can undeniably be made for the retention and expansion of a system of female-only probation hostels. However, as important as they are, these studies have focussed quite specifically on the general issues of practicality, financial viability and 'effectiveness'. Consequently little or no consideration has been given to either the long-term experiences of women within hostels or to the theoretical and ideological assumptions that underpin the existence and utility of these institutions. Nor has the fact been adequately addressed that hostels, contrary to the 'popular' belief, might not represent an environment which is totally dissimilar to the custodial one in terms of dominant assumptions and feminising regimes. One important conclusion of this book is that many of the critical arguments made by feminist writers about the patriarchal, feminising regimes and practices within custodial institutions can also be made about the supposedly 'empowering' probation hostel environment.

Several studies have presented the probation hostel as an 'empowering' or even therapeutic environment for women. Wincup (1996) argued in favour of women-only hostels stating that they are able to provide a 'specialist' service for their clients. She articulated that the women in her study had often shared similar experiences such as emotional, physical or sexual abuse, unemployment and poverty and as a result many suffered problems such as low self-esteem, drug use, eating disorders and the tendency to self-harm. Consequently, two of the hostels in her study had developed links with specialist agencies that could deal with these issues. Wincup raises an important point here with regard to the personal and social difficulties that many women offenders face, a point that is in fact supported by the findings of this book. However, it is not enough to simply accept as unproblematic the idea of women in hostels requiring 'help' for such 'problems'. Rather it is crucial that such issues are examined within the broader theoretical debates around the medicalisation and pathologisation of women's behaviour. If these issues are not examined within a more theoretical framework this could lead to the perpetuation of the image of 'problematic' women (that is, women faced with particular social and material problems) requiring excessive medical, psychiatric or psychological intervention. This image is certainly still being perpetuated within the women's prison estate. The Home Office's *Strategy for Women Offenders* (2001) maintains that the appropriate way to respond to the particular problems faced by many women offenders (such as poverty, homelessness, addictions or abuse) is through *psychological* programmes in prison aimed at altering the way women *perceive* such experiences. According to the Home Office, these problems can lead to offending because they cause women to *believe* they have limited options so all that is required is some intervention to alter this '*criminogenic and faulty thinking*' (Carlen, 2003: 34).

Buckley (1987) presented the probation hostel as a site where women could potentially be 'empowered'. She argued that the rapid escalation of women through the criminal justice system is partly due to their failure to live up to or adhere to dominant stereotyped assumptions around femininity. Again, this book would wholly support that contention. However, she then goes on to argue that the women-only probation hostel could be seen as a 'powerful antidote' (1987: 13) to sexist practice and a possible site of retaliation against stereotyped attitudes. In theory this may well be the case. The women-only probation hostel certainly has the *potential* to challenge the dominant assumptions about 'deviant' women however, given the findings of this book, it is debatable whether this is the case in reality. As far as Vernon Lodge was concerned both its entrenchment within, and its partial removal from, the criminal justice system served to produce a regime that, whilst claiming to 'empower', actually led to the 'infantilisation' of its residents. To be fair to the institution in question, some practices did appear to be sincere attempts to 'empower' women. Activity days (which involved abseiling, archery, assault courses and other types of physical exercise), artistic pursuits (for example painting sessions), assertiveness courses and even the key-worker sessions (in which women were encouraged to discuss problems, issues or concerns individually with a designated member of staff) could all be described, to a greater or lesser degree, as methods to encourage self-awareness and self-confidence, or even just as 'time out' from the worries and concerns of everyday life. However, these activities were only part of a regime in which women were heavily monitored, surveyed and supervised. Add to this the existence of powerful, dominant discourses, assumptions and expectations regarding 'appropriate' feminine behaviour within the institution and it becomes apparent that, rather than being an 'empowering' environment, Vernon Lodge in many ways functioned to 'disempower', 'infantilise' and subjugate its residents.

Of course, this is not to suggest the women tolerate such regimes without question. On the contrary, as the third aim of this book uncovered, women employed a range of methods through which they were able to cope with or resist the disciplinary regimes and discourses that sought to explain, control and discipline them. In support of the studies of resistance within custodial institutions (see in particular Bosworth, 1999) it was found that through a range of processes women were able to re-assert a sense of agency and responsibility that the institutional regime sometimes functioned to remove. Indeed it could be concluded that the very regimes and discourses that sought to transform women into passive subjects produced, in some cases, the opposite outcome. Thus, rather than accepting a submissive and powerless status, many women were able, through their strategies of challenge, to rediscover a sense of authority. In this sense it could indeed be argued that Vernon Lodge served to 'empower' its residents, albeit through the very processes that sought to subdue them. This investigation into women's resistance to institutionalisation is important as it facilitates an understanding of the dynamics of power relations that are frequently overlooked. As Worrall argues, power is not simply a one-way relationship between 'experts' or 'professionals' and those they seek to 'understand'. Rather the imposition of power can often produce a forceful reaction that can then redistribute that power.

Thus far this conclusion has re-visited the main aims of the book and has argued that women have been subjected to, and in turn have managed to cope with or resist, a range of feminising disciplinary regimes and discourses that have, to a great degree, remained constant from the past to the present. But it would not be appropriate to conclude this book without some mention of the future.

Worrall (1990) has argued that although it is imperative for feminist writers to be constantly looking to uncover and deconstruct dominant structures, institutions and practices, it is also important not to become too 'obsessed with debunking' (1990: 164). Thus the dilemma Worrall identifies could, with regard to this book, be articulated like this. Is it at all possible (or even desirable) to construct 'solutions' to problems exposed by critical, theoretical studies such as this? Alternatively, is it satisfactory to undertake such studies but then respond to those individuals who were the inspiration / subjects of the study that there is no 'solution' to the problems uncovered as there is no form of discourse or knowledge construction which would allow things to be different? Or indeed, to respond that there is no 'solution' as it was not the intention of the study to provide such 'answers'.   .

As I have already stated it not the intention of this book to 'debunk' the use of hostels. Neither was it the intention to generalise its findings to all institutions nor to produce a policy-orientated conclusion. However, it was the objective to question the popular notion that hostels are unproblematic institutions which have traditionally been accepted as positive environments simply because they are 'not custodial'. In doing this, the book does indeed raise issues for the future of this form of institutionalisation.

One of the major findings of this study is that the methods of discipline employed within semi-penal institutions for women, and the discourses that underpin those methods, have changed only superficially over the last two centuries. Therefore, it could be assumed that if these processes continue to remain unchallenged, such feminising, 'normalising' strategies will continue to be perceived as 'appropriate' for women well into the twenty first century.

The Prison Reform Trust report, *Justice for Women* (2000) highlighted the dramatic increase in rates of women's imprisonment and made recommendations with regard to dealing with this urgent problem. One way in which rates of imprisonment could be reduced, it proposed, was through greater use of existing community penalties such as probation. In addition the report recommended that

> ... community penalties should be *refocused* so as to make them *more relevant* to women offenders (para 5.15. Emphasis added).

But no discussion followed regarding what makes community penalties (or indeed any sanctions) *more relevant* to women. This book has highlighted that 'relevant' regimes and practices can mean feminising and infantilising regimes and practices. As has been argued, such strategies are extremely problematic and simply perpetuate a whole range of stereotyped gender assumptions about what women 'do' and what women 'need'. They have traditionally been taken for granted and are rarely deconstructed and contextualised.

The report went on to assert that forms of accommodation were required for those women offenders whose homes were, for various reasons, unhealthy and unsafe environments. It argued that

> ...accommodation is needed which is capable of imposing the necessary restrictions on liberty whilst offering *reintegrative and restorative* opportunities. Traditionally *hostels have provided this type of accommodation* (para 5.48. Emphasis added).

Once again, the presumption is that hostels for women provide an environment which is at once restrictive but also 'curative', uplifting and enriching. This book has challenged the taken-for-granted perception that these institutions are inherently beneficial and argues that whilst there is indeed a place for probation hostels in a future system of punishment and justice for women, these institutions must not be uncritically accepted as salutary, unproblematic environments.

In 2001 the probation service dismantled its fifty-four local services and a national service was established. This nationalisation was undertaken with a determination to increase the emphasis on consistency and standardisation with the introduction of accredited programmes for challenging offending behaviour (Home Office, 2001). Nationalisation means a reduction in power and discretion at a local level. As this book has highlighted, the relatively autonomous or 'semi-penal' position of probation hostels can lead to unique regimes and, sometimes, arbitrary decision making which even hostel staff find problematic. The hostel in this study existed very much within the criminal justice sphere, but at the same time was curiously removed from full state control. Thus, the move towards standardisation could have the potential to dismantle such idiosyncratic procedures. However, the emphasis on accreditation indicates that decisions will have to be taken regarding which practices or programmes are permissible or, indeed, 'appropriate'. As Pat Carlen points out, just like in women's prisons, it is primarily the cognitive behavioural programmes that are seen as 'appropriate', whilst

> Non-custodial programmes holding to the notion that women suffer more from economic deficits than cognitive deficits, and which attempt to show women how to cope practically and lawfully with their daily problems, do not receive official accreditation (2003:35).

Also, although it is *assumed* that these shifts will eventually impact upon probation hostels, informal discussions with probation personnel have indicated that whilst nationalisation has impacted upon probation fieldwork, it has yet to really influence the day to day practice within hostels. It appears that even in the twenty-first century probation hostels can manage to remain relatively untouched by state influence *and* academic critique so reinforcing their semi-penal status.

Through a focus on the broader theoretical issues and on the long-term (as well as day-to-day) experiences and standpoints of the staff and residents, this book has provided an alternative understanding and conceptualisation of semi-penal institutions for women. As such it has gone some way towards dismantling the dominant liberal notion that the 'non-custodial' institution is a healthier and more progressive environment than the prison simply because it is *not* a prison. Striving to retain the liberal philosophy that traditionally underpinned such institutions and resisting falling in line with the increasingly punitive, standardised philosophy of contemporary probation practice can certainly be perceived as a genuine concern for women within hostels on the part of staff and management. However one of the problems with such 'liberal' regimes is that, as Chapter Six highlights, they can serve to deny women many of the rights they should be able to take for granted. If women are to receive a form of justice that does not revolve around their adherence to, or deviation from, dominant gendered assumptions then attempts must be made to actively deconstruct (theoretically and practically), and make obsolete, the feminising regimes and discourses that reinforce institutions for women. With regard to semi-penal institutions, these methods of control and discipline have for two centuries been accepted as unproblematic. This book has attempted, in some measure, to redress the balance.

Notes

[1]   See for example Hunt *et al*, 1989; Mahood, 1990; Zedner, 1991.
[2]   See Carlen, 1983; Howe, 1994.
[3]   See for example Faith, 1993; Howe, 1994; Smith, 1996; Carlen, 1998; Bosworth, 1999.

Appendix: Methodology

Researching the Experiences of Women in a Semi-Penal Institution

Three distinct methods were utilised for this study, namely participant observation, semi-structured interviews and historical documentary analysis. The research project consisted of two equally important parts, these being a historical and a contemporary analysis of the experiences of women within a particular institution and the discourses and ideologies that impacted upon those experiences. The institution under scrutiny was Vernon Lodge, an all-female probation and bail hostel. The women at the hostel were either on bail awaiting trial or sentenced to a period of probation with a condition of residence and their length of stay varied from a couple of days to, in once case, almost 18 months. The research was conducted in a three major stages, first a period of participant observation, second the completion of a series of semi-structured interviews and finally an analysis of original historical material found in the attic of the main building. These 'stages' were not as distinct as the sentence above would indicate. The period of participant observation for example did not end when the period of interviewing began. Rather, due to the constant changes in residency at the hostel (with women constantly leaving and arriving) it was necessary to continue the observation period throughout the interview period in order to build up relationships with the newly arrived residents and maintain a relationship with existing residents and staff. Also the historical data were discovered before the interviews began and so analysis of this material was undertaken whilst the interviews, and participant observation, were being conducted.

Building bridges: the participant observation period

The participant observation stage involved a total period of 24 months, from February 1992 to February 1994 (although, as stated above this overlapped the interview period which lasted from March 1993 to March 1994). This initial stage involved visiting the hostel on average three times per week for periods ranging from three to eight hours per visit. Each day varied with regard to the timing of the visit, and the visits would be alternated in order to observe the hostel during morning, afternoon and evening hours. In order to comply with requests from the staff and management committee, and to fit in with the hours of curfew for residents, a visit never began earlier than 9.00am and never ended later than 10.00pm (apart from special events at the hostel, for example Christmas parties, birthday celebrations, or other organised activities).

 The particular time of day, and the particular day on which visits took place would determine my activities that day. On Thursday mornings, for example, a full staff meeting took place and, as I was not permitted to attend, the majority of this time would be spent solely with the residents in the recreation room. On particular afternoons when the doctor, drug workers, psychiatrist or hairdresser visited, most of my time would be spent with the staff as the majority of the residents would be otherwise occupied. My visits were usually restricted to the recreation room (a room with sofas, chairs, a public phone and a pool table), the TV lounge, the 'quiet room' (used as a private meeting room for visits from probation officers, solicitors, families and children and also for individual 'key-worker' sessions with hostel staff), the main staff office and the kitchen/dining area. Other staff rooms were out of bounds as were the private rooms of the residents.

Also, in addition to spending time within the hostel, the observation period also included my participation in other external activities, for example abseiling, archery and bowling competitions, all of which assisted considerably in 'breaking down' barriers and balancing the power relationships. In addition I was invited to several parties within the hostel and on a few occasions accompanied women to court for trial (at their request and in a supportive capacity only).

The period of participant observation was crucial to the research as it afforded the opportunity to develop a deep understanding of the dynamics of the institution, both formal and informal, and to gain an awareness of the relationships, conflicts and struggles amongst and between staff and residents. Most importantly, it allowed me the opportunity to develop as credible and trusting a relationship as possible with all participants and additionally, gave them the opportunity to ask questions about, discuss and criticise the research thus increasing their role within it. In addition, the diary kept of this period of observation (which was written up from memory immediately after leaving the hostel on each visit) was just as useful to the final analysis as the interviews. This diary was analysed by thematic content in a similar way to the historical documentation (this process will be discussed later). Finally, this period of observation facilitated the construction of, and influenced the direction taken by, the interview schedules for both staff and residents and this method of data collection will now be discussed.

Hearing women: the interview process

Although participant observation is a useful technique for feminist research it generally does not 'stand alone' as a research method. This study, like a great deal of feminist research, was multi-methodological and the second stage of this research consisted of 25 in-depth, semi-structured interviews conducted with staff and residents. This period of research lasted for approximately 12 months, from March 1993 to March 1994.

The interviewees were not randomly selected and nor is it assumed that they, or their opinions, were in any way representative of a wider population. Given the relatively small number of staff and residents within the hostel who were available to participate in this research, any attempt to generalise findings to a wider population would have been invalid.

All nine full time members of staff were interviewed along with 16 residents. In addition, two further interviews were arranged with the Executive Officer and the Chairman of the Church of England Council for Social Aid.

For the most part the selection of residents depended on simple availability. Although many more women had agreed to take part, by the time the interviews took place some had left the institution, or had been sent to prison or had simply changed their minds about participating.

With regard to the specifics of the interview process, each interview began with an introduction reminding the participant of what exactly the research was about and of my responsibilities (to ensure participants' complete confidentiality and anonymity and to ensure their own stories would be accurately and sincerely recounted). Participants were informed that they could refuse to answer any questions posed to them and were encouraged to ask questions during the interview process. The interviews took place for the most part in the 'quiet room', apart from on one occasion where, having left the hostel suddenly but still wishing to participate, a resident requested that the interview take place at her new home. All interviews were tape recorded apart from one where the interviewee expressed concern at being recorded on tape. In this case the interview was recorded on paper.

The interviews lasted anything from half an hour to three hours, with the average length of time being two hours. It was hoped that, in accordance with feminist methodology, the women could be interviewed more than once however due to the rate of turnover of residents and the time constraints on staff, this was unrealistic. With regard to structure, both interview schedules (staff and residents) began with some introductory questions that were factual in nature (for example, age, ethnic origin, educational and employment background). These questions were useful if, for no other reason, they highlighted the diversity (at least with regard to age and employment/educational background) of the interviewees, particularly the residents, as well as some notable examples of consistency (for example, none of the women interviewed or indeed encountered during the whole period of fieldwork were black). In both interview schedules the subsequent questions were more open-ended and semi-structured in nature.

Looking backwards to look forwards: historical documentary analysis

The final stage of the research consisted of an analysis of original historical documentary material. This material was originally thought to have been lost during a World War II bombing raid that destroyed the previous hostel site. Out of simple curiosity, and with the permission of the hostel warden, I, along with the hostel secretary, searched the attic of the hostel and discovered several boxes of original records, ledgers, accounts and letters pertaining to the institution from its creation in 1823 up until the 1970s. This material included unpublished reports charting the history of the institution, matron's log books (ledgers which recorded general information regarding the referral, arrival and departure of residents throughout the nineteenth and early twentieth centuries), matron's reports (ledgers which recorded more detailed information about each individual resident's stay), rule books, annual reports, minutes of meetings of staff and management committees, medical reports and a selection of memos and personal letters. The overwhelming majority of this material was hand-written and much of it (being over 100 years old) was barely legible. However most of the reports and documents were dated and this facilitated the production of a chronological history of the institution. More importantly the wealth of information about individual residents and the, often frank and emotional, language used to describe and discuss them, provided a wonderful opportunity to uncover a previously hidden history of (semi-penal) institutionalised women.

The historical data was analysed through a similar process to that employed in the analysis of the interview data. The idea of coding the material in the traditional sense was rejected and instead the records, ledgers, reports, letters and minutes were deconstructed and re-assessed within the context of the feminist theory set out in Chapter Two. Theoretical themes, similar to those identified for the contemporary study, were specified and the historical material was used to develop these arguments.

In conclusion, given the multi-methodological approach taken in this research, it is important to make some mention here of the search for validity. Although this research was underpinned by a particular methodological approach and theoretical perspective, it did not hinge around the concept of hypothesis testing. Therefore with no hypothesis there was no argument for representativeness. Although it was the intention of this study to identify any themes of continuity and discontinuity that may have existed with regards to the discourses that have underpinned the semi-penal institutionalisation of women, past and present, it was *not* the intention to examine the experiences of particular groups of women at particular moments in history and then generalise conclusions to *all* women and to *all* periods of history. Therefore the methodological aim was for *validity* rather than *reliability*. With regard to the contemporary fieldwork undertaken, because replicability was not a realistic criterion (as the accurate replication of fieldwork is impossible) this made the issue of validity even more important. Validity in this case relates to the extent to which the researcher's data and analysis authentically represents the social arena under study. It was anticipated that the approach adopted (participatory, multi-methodological and involving the elevation of the subjects to the centre of the inquiry) would assist in the production of credible and valid data. Also, the extensive period spent in the hostel (regular visits over two years followed by another two years of less frequent, but still consistent, visits) provided me with a comprehensive understanding of hostel life from both the perspective of the staff and the residents (recorded in the form of a day-to-day diary). This presented me with a source upon which to draw in order to validate claims made by the participants during interview.

With regard to the historical aspect of the research, data must be accepted as both *internally* and *externally* valid in order to be legitimate. First, the researcher must determine whether a source material is authentic (external validation). In the case of the historical data utilised in this study the authentication of the material was in no doubt. The fact that its existence had not previously been known, the circumstances under which it was discovered (by myself in the hostel attic), the apparent age of the documents, the accuracy of information contained within them when compared with other authenticated sources (newspaper and local history records for example) and the fact that the Church of England Council for Social Aid (the trustees of the hostel) were extremely keen to take possession of the documents once they had been discovered, left me assured that they were genuinely what they appeared to be.

Second, and more difficult to ascertain, is the accuracy of *meaning* within the material (internal validation). In other words, was it possible to be sure about what was meant by particular comments within the documents and was it possible to accurately predict or 'know' the impact of specific statements or testimony? Of course, when examining any primary source documentation retrospectively it is difficult, even impossible, to claim to 'know' and understand meaning and there was no real way of 'checking' particular comments or assertions (for example, it was not possible to interview the authors of the documents nor the people about whom the documents were written in order to confirm that my interpretation of a record was an accurate one). So, the material used was critically evaluated in the light of a rigorous theoretical framework and as such a complacent and 'face-value' acceptance of the data was avoided.

Bibliography

Vernon Lodge Archive Material

The following are the primary sources of material found in the attic of Vernon Lodge Bail and Probation Hostel. In addition to the sources listed below were numerous letters and memos (including letters of referral for residents, letters to and from the matron and the Management Committee and various form of correspondence with resident's families). These were usually found loose in other documents. As they are referenced fully in the body of the thesis they are not listed separately here but they are all property of the Church of England Council for Social Aid and the Vernon Lodge Management Committee.

Church of England Council for Social Aid, *The History of Vernon Lodge*, undated
    and unpublished report
Church of England Temperance Society, *The Church and Social Service: Vernon
    Lodge, The Oldest Diocesan Charity*, undated and unpublished report
Emmanuel J (1977) *A History of Vernon Lodge*, unpublished report
Lancashire County Refuge for the Destitute, *First Book of Rules 1822*
Lancashire County Refuge for the Destitute, *Record of Residents 1823-1844*
Lancashire County Refuge for the Destitute, *Matron's Reports 1823 – 1916*
Lancashire County Refuge for the Destitute, *Matron's Log Book 1835-1838*
Lancashire Female Refuge, *Annual Reports 1914-1917*
Lancashire Female Refuge, *Matron's Reports 1917 - 1946*
Lancashire Female Refuge, *List of Hospitalisation and Deaths 1905-1915*
Lancashire Female Refuge, *Medical Journal for Constance B. 1930-1942*
Lancashire Female Refuge, *Medical Journal for Alice C. 1938-1946*
Lancashire Female Refuge, *Register of Residents 1898-1948*
Lancashire Female Refuge, *Rules for the Girls 1942*
Lancashire Female Refuge, *Rules for the Matron 1920*
Vernon Lodge *Information Leaflet 1952*, unpublished report
Vernon Lodge *Warden's Daily Log Book 1963 - 1966*
Vernon Lodge *Care Committee Minute Book 1964*
Vernon Lodge *Hostel Committee Inspection Report 1968*

Liverpool City Records Archive Material

County Refuge, *Annual Reports 1917 - 1968*
Horner W (1848) *Kirkdale Gaol Chaplain's Annual Report, November*, unpublished report
Liverpool Review (1899) *Liverpool Slum Life No 17: At the Jail Gates*, October 21st, p11
Liverpool Review (1928) *Police Court and Prison Gate Mission*, Vol III, Jan – Dec, p31
Shimmin H (1856) *Liverpool Life: Its Pleasures, Practices and Pastimes*, Egerton Smith
    and Co, Liverpool

Smithers H (1825) *Liverpool, Its Commerce, Statistics and Institutions*, Thos. Kaye, Liverpool

The Welldoer: The newsletter of the League of Welldoers (1909) 'A Critical Record of Benevolence', Jan-Feb, No.9, Vol.2, League of Welldoers

Probation Service Records

Chief Probation Officer (1984) *Senior Staff Notice regarding Vernon Lodge*, internal memorandum, April 18th

Vernon Lodge (1967) *Management Sub-committee Meeting Minutes 1967*

Vernon Lodge (1973) *Memorandum from the Vernon Lodge Management Committee 1973*

Books and Journal Articles

Andrews J (1979) *Hostels for Offenders*, Home Office Research Study no 52, HMSO, London

Apte R Z (1968) *Halfway Houses: A New Dilemma in Institutional Care*, Occasional Papers on Social Administration, No 27, Bell, London

Ardener S (ed) (1978) *Defining Females: The Nature of Women in Society*, Croom Helm, London

Arthurs J and Grimshaw J (eds) (1999) *Women's Bodies: Discipline and Transgression*, Cassell, London

Ballinger A (1996) 'The Guilt of the Innocent and the Innocence of the Guilty: The Cases of Marie Fahmy and Ruth Ellis' in Myers A and Wight S (eds) *No Angels: Women Who Commit Violence*, Pandora, London

Barry K J (1991) *Probation Hostels and their Regimes: A Comparative Study,* University of Cambridge, Cambridge

Bartky S (1988) 'Foucault, Femininity and the Modernisation of Patriarchal Power' in Diamond I and Quimby L (eds) *Feminism and Foucault: Reflections on Resistance*, Northeastern University Press, Boston

Barton A (2001) *Fragile Moralities and Dangerous Sexualities: A Case Study of 'Deviant' Women and Semi-penal Institutionalisation 1823-1994*, unpublished PhD thesis, Liverpool John Moores University

Baudrillard J (1987) *Forget Foucault*, Semiotext, New York

Bland L (1992) 'Feminist Vigilantes of late-Victorian England' in Smart C (ed) *Regulating Womanhood: Historical Essays on Marriage, Motherhood and Sexuality*, Routledge, London

Bland L (1995) *Banishing the Beast: English Feminism and Sexual Morality 1885 – 1914*, Penguin, London

Bochel D (1976) *Probation and After-Care: Its Development in England and Wales*, Scottish Academy Press, Edinburgh

Bordo S (1988) 'Anorexia Nervosa: Psychopathology as Crystallization of Culture' in Diamond I and Quimby L (eds) *Feminism and Foucault: Reflections on Resistance*, Northeastern University Press, Boston

Bordo S (1993) 'Feminism, Foucault and the Politics of the Body' in Ramazanoglu C (ed) *Up Against Foucault*, Routledge, London

Bosworth M (1999) *Engendering Resistance: Agency and Power in Women's Prisons*, Ashgate Press, Aldershot

Bosworth M (2000) 'Confining Femininity: A History of Gender, Power and Imprisonment' *Theoretical Criminology*, Vol 3, No 3, August, pp265 – 84

Brook B (1999) *Feminist Perspectives on the Body*, Longman, Harlow

Brown W (1995) *States of Injury: Power and Freedom in Late Modernity*, Princeton University Press, New Jersey

Brownlee I (1998) *Community Punishment: A Critical Introduction*, Longman, Harlow

Bryson V (1999) *Feminist Debates: Issues of Theory and Political Practice*, Macmillan, London

Buckley K (1987) 'Why We Should Keep Women's Hostels', *Social Work Today*, Vol 19, No 8, p13

Burford EJ and Shulman S (1992) *Of Bridles and Burnings: The Punishment of Women*, Hale, London

Burgess B (1985) *Approved Probation and Bail Hostels Statistical Digest 1984*, Home Office, London, (HG(85)2)

Cain M (1993) 'Foucault, Feminism and Feeling: What Foucault Can and Cannot Contribute to Feminist Epistemology' in Ramazanoglu C (ed) *Up Against Foucault: Explorations of Some Tensions between Foucault and Feminism*, Routledge, London

Carlen P (1983) *Women's Imprisonment: A Study in Social Control* London, Routledge and Kegan Paul, London

Carlen P (ed) (1985) *Criminal Women,* Basil Blackwell, Oxford

Carlen P (1988) *Women, Crime and Poverty*, Open University Press, Milton Keynes

Carlen P (1990) *Alternatives to Women's Imprisonment*, Open University Press, Milton Keynes

Carlen P (1998) *Sledgehammer: Women's Imprisonment at the Millennium*, Macmillan, London

Carlen P and Worrall A (eds) (1987) *Gender, Crime and Justice*, Open University Press, Milton Keynes

Carter A (ed) (1986) *Wayward Girls and Wicked Women*, Virago, London

Christie N (1978) 'Prisons in Society or Society as a Prison: A Conceptual Analysis' in Freeman, J.C. (ed) *Prisons Past and Future*, Heinemann, London

Cohen S (1983) 'Social Control Talk: Telling Stories about Correctional Change' in Garland D and Young P (eds) *The Power to Punish: Contemporary Penality and Social Analysis*, Heinemann, London

Cohen S (1985) *Visions of Social Control*, Polity Press, Cambridge

Connell R (1987) *Gender and Power*, Polity Press, London

Cooper D (1995) *Power in Struggle; Feminism, Sexuality and the State*, Open University Press, Buckingham

Dahl T S and Snare A (1978) 'The Coercion of Privacy' in Smart C and Smart B, (eds), *Women, Sexuality and Social Control*, Routledge and Kegan Paul, London

Daly K and Maher L (eds) (1998) *Criminology at the Crossroads: Feminist Readings in Crime and Justice*, Oxford University Press, Oxford

Davies H (1996) *West Midlands Probation Service Hostel Survey*, West Midlands Probation Service, Birmingham

Davies M (1969) *Probationers in their Social Environment*, HMSO, London

Davies M and Sinclair I (1971) 'Families, Hostels and Delinquents: An Attempt to Assess Cause and Effect' *British Journal of Criminology*, Vol 11, No 3, July, pp213-29

Davis K (1997) 'My Body is My Art: Cosmetic Surgery as Feminist Utopia?' in Davis K (ed) (1997) *Embodied Practices: Feminist Perspectives on the Body*, Sage, London

DeBeauvoir, S (1953) *The Second Sex*, Landsborough, London

Deveaux M (1994) 'Feminism and Empowerment: A Critical Reading of Foucault' in *Feminist Studies*, Vol.20, No.2, Summer, pp223-47

Diamond I and Quimby L (eds) (1988) *Feminism and Foucault: Reflections on Resistance* Northeastern University Press, Boston

Dobash RP, Dobash RE and Gutteridge S (1986) *The Imprisonment of Women*, Basil Blackwell, Oxford

Eaton M (1993) *Women After Prison*, Open University Press, Milton Keynes

Edwards S (1981) *Female Sexuality and the Law*, Martin Robertson, Oxford

Ehrenreich B and English D (1979) *For Her Own Good: 150 Years of the Experts' Advice to Women*, Pluto Press, London

Elder PD (1972) 'House for Ex-Borstal Girls: An Exploratory Project', *British Journal of Criminology*, Vol.12, No 4, October, pp357-374

Evers H (1981) 'Care or Custody: The Experiences of Women in Long-Stay Geriatric Wards' in Hutter B and Williams G (eds) *Controlling Women: The Normal and the Deviant*, Croom Helm, London

Faith K and Davis N (1987) 'Women and the State; Changing Models of Social Control' in Lowman J, Menzies R and Palys T S (eds) *Transcarceration: Essays in the Sociology of Social Control*, Gower, Aldershot

Faith K (1993) *Unruly Women: The Politics of Confinement and Resistance*, Press Gang, Vancouver

Faith K (1994) 'Resistance: Lessons from Foucault and Feminism' in Radtke H L and Henderikus J S (eds) *Power / Gender: Social Relations in Theory And Practice*, Sage, London

Ferrari-Bravo G and Arcidiacono C (1989) 'Compounded Misunderstanding: Relations between Staff and Girls in an Italian Juvenile Prison' in Cain M (ed) *Growing Up Good: Policing of the Behaviour of Girls in Europe*, Sage, London

Finnegan F (1979) *Poverty and Prostitution: A Study of Prostitution in York*, Cambridge University Press, Cambridge

Foucault M (1972) *The Archaeology of Knowledge*, Tavistock, London

Foucault M (1977) *Discipline and Punish: The Birth of the Prison*, (trans. A Sheridan), Penguin, London

Foucault M (1980) *The History of Sexuality Vol 1: An Introduction*, Vintage, New York

Frazer E and Lacey N (1993) *The Politics of Community: A Feminist Critique of the Liberal-Communitarian Debate*, Harvester Wheatsheaf, Hertfordshire

French, M (1992) *The War Against Women*, Hamish Hamilton, London

Frost, L (1999) 'Doing Looks: Women, Appearance and Mental Health' in Arthurs J and Grimshaw J (eds) *Women's Bodies: Discipline and Transgression*, Cassell, London

Fry E (1827) *Observations on Visiting, Superintendence and Government of Female Prisons*, Hatchard and Son, London

Garland D (1985) *Punishment and Welfare: A History of Penal Strategies*, Gower, Aldershot

Genders E and Player E (1987) 'Women in Prison: The Treatment, the Control and the Experience' in Carlen P and Worral A (eds) *Gender, Crime and Justice,* Open University Press, Milton Keynes

Goffman E (1961) *Asylums: Essays on the Social Situation of Mental Patients and Other Inmates,* Doubleday and Co, London

Green E, Hebron S and Woodward D (1987) 'Women, Leisure and Social Control' in Hanmer J and Maynard M (eds) *Women, Violence and Social Control,* Macmillan, London

Grimshaw J (1993) 'Practices of Freedom' in Ramazanoglu C (ed) *Up Against Foucault,* Routledge, London,

Grimshaw J (1999) 'Working Out with Merleau-Ponty' in Arthurs J and Grimshaw J (eds) *Women's Bodies: Discipline and Transgression,* Cassell, London

Hanmer J and Saunders S (1983) 'Blowing the Cover of the Protective Male: A Community Study of Violence to Women' in Gamarnikow *et al* (eds) *The Public and the Private,* Heinmann, London

Harris R (1995) 'Probation Round the World: Origins and Development' in Hamai K, Ville R, Harris R, Hough M and Zvekic U (eds) *Probation Round the World: A Comparative Study,* Routledge, London

Harris R and Webb D (1987) *Welfare, Power and Juvenile Justice: The Social Control of Delinquent Youth,* Tavistock, London

Harrison B (1971) *Drink and the Victorians: The Temperance Question in England 1815 - 1872,* Faber and Faber, London

Heidensohn F (1996) *Women and Crime, 2nd ed,* Macmillan, London

Henning M (1999) 'Don't Touch Me (I'm Electric): On Gender and Sensation in Modernity' in Arthurs J and Grimshaw J (eds) *Women's Bodies: Discipline and Transgression,* Cassell, London

Hester M (1992) *Lewd Women and Wicked Witches,* Routledge, London

Hirschon R (1978) 'Open Body / Closed Space: The Transformation of Female Sexuality' in Ardener S (ed) *Defining Females: The Nature of Women in Society,* Croom Helm, London

Home Office (1927) *Report of the Departmental Committee on the Treatment of Young Offenders,* Cmnd 2831, HMSO, London

Home Office (1942) *Notes on Homes and Hostels for Young Probationers,* HMSO, London

Home Office (1949) *Approved Probation Hostel and Home Rules,* HMSO, London

Home Office (1988) *Punishment, Custody and the Community,* Cmnd 424, HMSO, London

Home Office (1990) *Crime, Justice and Protecting the Public,* Cmnd 966, HMSO, London

Home Office (1992) *National Standards for the Supervision of Offenders in the Community,* Home Office Probation Service Division, London

Home Office (1993) *Approved Probation and Bail Hostels: Report of a Thematic Inspection,* HMSO, London

Home Office (1994) *Probation Service Act 1993,* (Chapter 47), HMSO, London

Home Office (1995) *Hostels Handbook: Approved Probation and Bail Hostels,* Home Office and Probation Unit, London

Home Office (1998) *Delivering an Enhanced Level of Community Supervision: Report of a Thematic Inspection on the Work of Approved Probation and Bail Hostels,* HMSO, London

Home Office (2001) *Criminal Justice: The Way Forward,* Cmnd5074, Home Office, London

Hopwood C (1995) 'My Discourse/My Self: Therapy as Possibility (for Women Who Eat Compulsively) in *Feminist Review,* No 49, Spring, p66–82

Howard League for Penal Reform (1979) *Women and the Penal System: Memorandum from the Howard League to the House of Commons Expenditure Committee*, Howard League, London

Howe A (1990) 'Prologue to a History of Women's Imprisonment: In Search of a Feminist Perspective' *Social Justice*, Vol 17, No 2, pp5-22

Howe A (1994) *Punish and Critique: Towards a Feminist Analysis of Penality*, Routledge, London

Humphrey C (1978) 'Women, Taboo and the Supression of Attention' in Ardener S (ed) *Defining Females: The Nature of Women in Society*, Croom Helm, London

Hunt G, Mellor J and Turner J (1989) 'Wretched, Hatless and Miserably Clad: Women and the Inebriate Reformatories from 1900 - 1913', *British Journal of Sociology*, Vol 40, No 2, pp244-70

Hutter B and Williams G (eds) (1981) *Controlling Women: The Normal and the Deviant*, Croom Helm, London

Imray L and Middleton A (1983) 'Public and Private: Marking the Boundaries' in Gamarnikow *et al* (eds) *The Public and the Private*, Heinemann, London

Jarvis F V (1972) *Advise, Assist and Befriend: A History of the Probation and After-Care Service*, NAPO, London

Kelly L (1987) 'The Continuum of Sexual Violence' in Hanmer J and Maynard M (eds) *Women, Violence and Social Control*, Macmillan, London

Kennedy H (1992) *Eve Was Framed*, Chatto and Windus, London

Kidd, M (1999) 'The Bearded Lesbian' in Arthurs J and Grimshaw J (eds) *Women's Bodies: Discipline and Transgression*, Cassell, London

King J (ed) (1969) *The Probation and After-Care Service*, 3rd ed, Butterworths, London

Lacey N and Zedner L (1995) 'Discourses of Community in Criminal Justice' in *Journal of Law and Society*, Vol 22, No3, September, pp301-25

Leeson C (1914) *The Probation System*, PS King and Son, London

Lewis J (1992) 'Women and late-nineteenth-century social work' in Smart C (ed) *Regulating Womanhood: Historical Essays on Marriage, Motherhood And Sexuality*, Routledge, London

Liebling A (1992) *Suicides in Prison*, Routledge, London

Lindfield L (1992) *Locked Women: Disciplining the Experience of Venereal Disease in Nineteenth Century England*, unpublished Masters Degree Thesis, University of Lancaster

Loweson J and Myerscough J (1977) *Time to Spare in Victorian England*, Harvester Press, Brighton

MacKinnon C (1982) 'Feminism, Marxism, Method and the State', *Journal of Women in Culture and Society*, Vol 7 (3), pp515-44

Mahood L (1990) *The Magdelenes: Prostitution in the Nineteenth Century*, Routledge and Kegan Paul, London

Mandaraka-Sheppard A (1986) *The Dynamics of Aggression in Women's Prisons in England*, Gower Press, Aldershot

Marshment M (1993) 'The Picture is Political: Representation of Women in Contemporary Popular Culture' in Richardson D and Robinson V (eds) *'Introducing Women's Studies: Feminist Theory and Practice'*, Macmillan, London

May T (1991) *Probation: Politics, Policy and Practice*, Open University Press, Milton Keynes

McNay L (1992) *Foucault and Feminism: Power, Gender and the Self*, Polity Press, Cambridge

McWilliams W (1983) 'The Mission to the English Police Courts 1876 - 1936' *Howard Journal*, Vol 12, pp129-47

Monger M (1972) *Casework in Probation, 2nd Edition*, Butterworth, London

Morton F (1994) *Domestic Violence, Community Safety and Justice for Women*, London Action Trust, London

Naffine N (1987) *Female Crime: The Construction of Women in Criminology*, Unwin Hyman, London

Naffine N (1997) *Feminism and Criminology*, Polity Press, Cambridge

Oakley A (1980) *Women Confined: Towards a Sociology of Childbirth*, Martin Robertson, Oxford

Okley J (1978) 'Privileged, Schooled and Finished: Boarding Education for Girls' in Ardener S (ed) *Defining Females: The Nature of Women in Society*, Croom Helm, London

Otto S and Orford J (1978) *Not Quite Like Home: Small Hostels for Alcoholics and Others*, John Wiley and Sons, Chichester

Parsloe P (1972) 'Cross-Sex Supervision in the Probation and After-Care Service', *British Journal of Criminology*, Vol 12, No 3, pp269-79

Parsons T and Bales RF (1955) *Family Socialization and Interaction Process*, Free Press, Chicago

Player E (2000) 'Justice For Women' *Prison Service Journal*, November, No 132, pp17-21

Prison Reform Trust (2000) *Justice for Women: The Need for Reform. Report of the Committee on Women's Imprisonment*, Prison Reform Trust, London

Radford, L (1987) 'Legalising Woman Abuse' in Hanmer J and Maynard M (eds) *Women, Violence and Social Control*, Macmillan, London

Rafter N (1983) 'Chastizing the Unchaste: Social Control Functions of a Women's Reformatory, 1894 - 1931' in Cohen S and Scull A, (eds) *Social Control and the State*, Martin Robertson and Co., Oxford

Richardson D (1993), 'Sexuality and Male Dominance' in Richardson D and Robinson V *Introducing Women's Studies: Feminist Theory and Practice*, Macmillan, London

Richardson D (1993a) *Women, Motherhood and Childrearing*, Macmillan, London

Rimmer J (1986) *Yesterday's Naughty Children: A History of the Liverpool Reformatory Association*, Neil Richardson, Manchester

Sawicki J (1991) *Disciplining Foucault: Feminism, Power and the Body*, Routledge, London

Shaw M (1992) 'Issues of Power and Control: Women in Prison and their Defenders' *British Journal of Criminology*, Vol 32, No 4, pp438-52

Sheppard B (1979) 'A Survey of Residents of Hostels in the West Midlands' in Andrews J (1979; Appendix II) *Hostels for Offenders*, Home Office, London

Showalter E (1981) 'Victorian Women and Insanity' in Scull A (ed) *Madhouses, Mad-doctors and Madmen: The Social History of Psychiatry in the Victorian Era*, Athlone, London

Showalter E (1987) *The Female Malady*, Virago, London

Sim J (1990) *Medical Power in Prisons: The Prison Medical Service in England 1777 - 1989*, Open University Press, Milton Keynes

Simey M B (1951) *Charitable Effort in Liverpool in the Nineteenth Century*, Liverpool University Press, Liverpool

Sinclair I (1971) *Hostels for Probationers: A Study of the Aims, Working and Variations in Effectiveness of Male Probation Hostels with Special Reference to the Influence of the Environment on Delinquency*, HMSO, London

Sinclair I (1975) 'The Influence of Wardens and Matrons on Probation Hostels: A Study of a Quazi-family Institution' in Tizard J, Sinclair I and Clarke RVG (eds) *Varieties of Residential Experience*, Routledge and Kegan Paul, London

Smart C and Smart B, (eds) (1978) *Women, Sexuality and Social Control*, Routledge and Kegan Paul, London

Smart C (ed) (1992) *Regulating Womanhood: Historical Essays on Marriage, Motherhood and Sexuality*, Routledge, London

Smart C (1992a) 'Disruptive Bodies and Unruly Sex: The Regulation of Reproduction and Sexuality in the Nineteenth Century' in Smart C (ed) *Regulating Womanhood: Historical Essays on Marriage, Motherhood and Sexuality*, Routledge, London

Smith C (1996) *The Imprisoned Body: Women, Health and Imprisonment*, unpublished PhD thesis, University of Wales, Bangor

Smith H E (1878) *Smith of Doncaster and Connected Families*, unpublished report held at the Library of the Society of Friends, London

Spensky M (1992) 'Producers of Legitimacy: Homes for Unmarried Mothers in the 1950s' in Smart C (ed) *Regulating Womanhood: Historical Essays on Marriage, Motherhood and Sexuality*, Routledge, London

Timms N (1968) *Rootless in the City*, Bedford Square Press, London

Ussher J (1991) *Women's Madness: Misogyny or Mental Illness*, Harvester Wheatsheaf, Hertfordshire

Walkowitz J (1980) *Prostitution and Victorian Society*, Cambridge University Press, Cambridge

Walkowitz J (1982) 'Male Vice and Feminist Virtue', *History Workshop*, Vol 13, Spring, pp79-93

Weedon C (1987) *Feminist Practice and Post-Structuralist Theory*, Blackwell, Oxford

Weiner M J (1990) Reconstructing the Criminal: Culture, Law and Policy in England 1830 - 1914, Cambridge University Press, Cambridge

Wincup E (1996) 'Mixed Hostels: Staff and Residents Perspectives' *Probation Journal*, 43, 3, pp147 - 51

Worrall A (1990) *Offending Women: Female Lawbreakers and the Criminal Justice System*, Routledge, London

Worrall A (1997) *Punishment in the Community: The Future of Criminal Justice* Longman, Harlow

Young J (1981) 'Thinking Seriously about Crime: Some Models of Criminology' in Fitzgerald M, McLennan G and Pawson J (eds) *Crime and Society: Readings in History and Theory*, Routledge and Kegan Paul, London

Zedner L (1991) *Women Crime and Custody in Victorian England*, Clarendon Press, Oxford

Zedner L (1991a) 'Women, Crime and Penal Responses: A Historical Account' in Tonry M (ed) (1991) *Crime and Justice: A Review of Research*, University of Chicago Press, Chicago

Index